T0326447

Shaping Pay in Europe

A Stakeholder Approach

P.I.E. Peter Lang

Bruxelles · Bern · Berlin · Frankfurt am Main · New York · Oxford · Wien

A Joint Programme for Working Life Research in Europe

SALTSA is a programme for research on European working life run in close co-operation by the National Institute for Working Life in Sweden and the Swedish Confederation of Trade Unions (LO), the Swedish Confederation of Professional Employess (TCO) and the Swedish Confederation of Professional Associations (SACO).

The aim of SALTSA is to generate applicable research results of high academic standard and practical relevance. Research is carried out in areas like labour market and employment, labour law, work organisation and health and safety.

http://www.arbetslivsinstitutet.se/saltsa

JOINT PROGRAMME
FOR WORKING LIFE RESEARCH IN EUROPE
The National Institute for Working Life and The Swedish Trade Unions in Co-operation

Conny Herbert ANTONI, Xavier BAETEN,
Ben J.M. EMANS & Mari KIRA (eds.)

Shaping Pay in Europe

A Stakeholder Approach

"Work & Society"
No.53

© P.I.E. PETER LANG S.A.
Éditions scientifiques internationales
Brussels, 2007
1 avenue Maurice, 1050 Brussels, Belgium
info@peterlang.com; www.peterlang.com

ISSN 1376-0955
ISBN 13 978-90-5201-037-3
US ISBN 13 978-0-8204-6682-8
D/2007/5678/16

Printed in Germany

Bibliographic information published by "Die Deutsche Bibliothek"
"Die Deutsche Bibliothek" lists this publication in the "Deutsche Nationalbibliografie"; detailed bibliographic data is available on the Internet at <http://dnb.ddb.de>.
CIP available from the British Library, GB and the Library of Congress, USA.

Contents

Preface

We live in a society where most people have to enter into paid work to support themselves. Work and pay are the economic motors of our personal lives and of the whole society. Even though the ability and the opportunity to work have value in themselves for most people, also the importance of pay cannot be exaggerated neither at individual nor social level. But what is pay? What do the contemporary European pay systems look like? What meanings does pay have for different stakeholders? And how do different stakeholders shape pay? This book aims at answering questions like these.

The title of the book has two important connotations. Firstly, there is a proactive meaning in it: 'shaping pay'. We do not only describe, define, and illustrate European pay systems, but we also aim to provide a theoretical and practical leverage for shaping pay – for changing pay systems to correspond the needs, values, and hopes of different stakeholders. Secondly, we adopt 'a stakeholder approach'. In other words, rather than looking at pay systems from the point of view of the managers or employees, trade unions or employer associations, we step in all these shoes and experience pay from the point of view of all the parties. It is our hope that all the stakeholders will benefit from the book.

We would like to acknowledge the financial support from the SALTSA-research program. Especially we would like to thank Mats Essemyr from SALTSA's Work Organisation Program Committee for his help with many practical questions. We would also like to acknowledge the contribution from members of our group whose names do not appear in the authors' list: Per-Olov Bergström, Sweden; Fabio Bocchi, Italy; Niilo Hakonen, Finland; and Elisabeth Sundin, Sweden. Furthermore, part of our SALTSA-work has close connections to a collaborative research project with the European Foundation for the Improvement of Living and Working Conditions, and we gratefully acknowledge the Foundation's collaboration. Finally, we would like to thank our anonymous case companies for sharing their experiences on pay systems with us.

Conny H. Antoni, Xavier Baeten, Ben J.M. Emans, and Mari Kira

CHAPTER 1

Introduction: Shaping Pay

Mari KIRA[1] & Elizabeth NEU

Pay is an important topic for several stakeholders on the labour market. Individual employees and employers have an interest in pay issues as they are directly affected by pay levels and pay structures. If these actors are organised, their interests are advocated by trade union and employers' association representatives, respectively. But there are also other actors with interests in pay: for example, managers at different levels and human resource management specialists often handle pay matters in practice. Also national governments are important stakeholders as pay is strongly intertwined with *e.g.* taxation and social security issues. All these stakeholders are considering pay from different perspectives, and they also want to reach different goals with their engagement in pay issues.

The aim of this book is to discuss pay from various perspectives and to take different aspects into account. To achieve this, the book addresses pay systems and pay setting as work organisational issues thus illuminating their drivers and consequences, their structures and processes in the contemporary work organisations. Furthermore, the interplay between pay and organisational environments – national, cultural, ideological, and political environments – is addressed.

The book also aims at contributing to a better understanding on pay systems. If one wants to understand the various pay systems of a company, which pay elements and pay characteristics should one focus on? Which are the essential pay characteristics shaping an individual's pay and how could these characteristics be studied or audited? The book provides answers to both questions by presenting a practical yet sophisticated model on essential pay characteristics as a basis for an audit tool that can be used when assessing these characteristics.

[1] The research of Mari Kira has been supported by a Marie Curie Intra-European Fellowship within the 6th European Community Framework Programme.

A Multi-Stakeholder View on Pay: Conflicts and Opportunities

When it comes to pay setting within single organisations, the interests of different stakeholders tend to conflict. For an individual employee, pay often constitutes the main source of income and determines the standard of living. Naturally, there is an interest among employees to earn as much as possible, or at least to earn enough to experience the work done worthwhile. However, the amount of money earned also implies the value of a person on the labour market and to a company. Therefore, to an employee, it is not only important that pay is high enough, but pay also has to be reasonably fair and understandable; there has to be fairness and transparency in pay systems and pay setting procedures.

For the top management of a company, pay is a matter of providing employees with competitive compensation for their work; pay systems and levels affect the ability of a company to recruit and retain desirable competence. At the same time, pay is often one of the highest cost elements for a company, which means that the increases in pay have to be held under control. Pay levels and pay increases are thus issues of great interest to top management, as they affect the profitability and competitiveness of a company. Similarly, the shareholders, owners, or investors are interested in rewarding the 'right kind' of performance while holding the costs in control.

Pay setting is also one of the most important and most difficult responsibilities for first-line managers. Managers face high demands concerning fairness and objectivity; they have to be able to honestly assess the performance of their workers and to communicate the assessment outcomes in an appropriate manner. For managers, pay can function as a tool to reward excellent performance and also to motivate employees to perform well in the future. Accordingly, there are incentives for managers to give extraordinary employees significant pay raises. At the same time, however, pay levels should not be allowed to escalate beyond control.

Trade union representatives, in their turn, seek to look after employees' interests and make sure that nobody is discriminated against or treated unfairly. For human resource specialists, pay can include all the issues above together with such administrative questions as how do design and administer pay systems.

Put in this way, it becomes evident how complex an issue pay is. Different stakeholders have different demands and are guided by different norm sets. How should pay be approached in organisations? What roles can or should different stakeholders take when it comes to pay setting in organisations? This book is founded on the idea that it is fruitful to consider pay setting in organisations as a social process. We believe that issues like pay levels, pay differentiation, pay equity, and pay administration have to be discussed and solved through dialogue between different actors within an organisation. Different actors do not only have different interests in pay, they also have different sets of knowledge that can be valuable in handling the complex topic of pay. Furthermore, the different actors should be able to link their specific knowledge and interests regarding to pay with actual, concrete pay elements and processes in order to be able to influence the shaping of pay in a constructive manner.

Research and Development for Pay Systems and Pay Setting

When we bear in mind the various meanings of pay for different stakeholders, surprisingly little European academic research is carried out on pay setting and pay systems, especially at the level of operational employees. This may be explained by the fact that in Europe, the collective bargaining systems and legislation have taken pay issues out of the management's single-handed control sphere. Consequently, pay setting procedures and pay systems are often considered as externally given and, thus, unlikely sources for strategic advantage or any difference at all.

There are, however, scattered examples of private companies experimenting with what might be called innovative pay solutions: pay systems stemming from the unique aspirations of the company in question rather than from simply the general collective bargaining outcomes (*e.g.* Kira, 2000). In some countries, organisations within the public sector are also trying to follow suit by establishing result-oriented pay systems (*e.g.* Ylikorkala *et al.*, 2005). However, due to its contested nature and low perceived leverage, pay setting in Europe is quite conservative – the less it disturbs the life of an organisation, the better.

In the USA, pay systems – less regulated than in Europe – have gained more interest from the academic community. Similarly the executive pay, equally less regulated, has gained more attention than the pay of operational employees (this being the case on the both sides of the Atlantic). It seems that where pay is regulated weakly or not at all, it has been perceived as an operational part of organisational life and, thus, worth studying.

However, a pay system is not just a quantitative matter, but also a qualitative matter. It is not only a question of 'how much', but also simply 'how'. In Europe, collective bargaining sets some boundaries for pay systems, but they do not dictate pay systems in detail. Base pay levels may be given and even some regulations or guidelines may exist for pay system structures. Nevertheless, an organisation may influence the design and the function of the pay system. In some countries, like in Germany, collective labour agreements even contain 'opening clauses' stating that, as long as an organisation does not undermine the negotiated pay, it may design its own system. Therefore, even in Europe, and even when it comes to employees not exempt from collective bargaining, there are strategic advantages to be found in pay systems and in pay setting. Furthermore, the less pay systems are studied and the less there is interest in their development, the more likely it is that organisations (both private and public) end up implementing pay systems not suitable for their operations or objectives.

Therefore, this book aims at entering the seldom-sailed sea – to study the pay systems in the European Union. Giving a due attention to the institutional setting of the European pay systems – the prevailing legislation and collective bargaining systems – the book seeks to study, how European companies are approaching pay as an integral part of their operational framework, how alternative solutions and consequent strategic advantages can be found through pay systems, and how pay systems can be understood as relevant topics for research and development.

Pay: a Topical Issue

There are several reasons for why pay is a topical issue for research; the increasing integration of the world being one of them. The European Union, as a politic and economic force, has created new possibilities for the movement of labour, goods, and capital: a more thorough understanding of pay is needed in order to master it as a cross-national rather than as a national issue. But not only labour, goods, and capital move – ideas do as well. As noted above, when compared to Europe, pay issues have been less regulated in the USA and new types of pay systems and methods have been developed there. Alternative American approaches to pay have influenced the way pay is perceived also in Europe.

This development is strengthened by the fact that there are European companies keen to look for new approaches to pay as their environments and their operation principles have changed; the emergence of the post-bureaucratic era (*e.g.* Heckscher, 1994) has created a need to reconsider pay also in Europe. As a practical example, more elaborated pay-for-performance models replacing the traditional piece-rate pay have become a central topic both in the managerial and trade union discourses on pay as the performance criteria have transformed. New ways to reward performance are needed when organisational success is considered to stem from various and sometimes non-measurable sources. The awareness of European companies regarding the strategic meaning of pay is also promoted by recent national research efforts; for instance several authors of this book are carrying out sustained research on European pay systems within national research centres with close contacts to the corporate world.

Finally, studying pay makes also sense because there is a lack of common understanding on pay. Currently, there is a lack of knowledge derived from research on the elements of the European pay, the drivers and consequences of pay, as well as the spreading of different pay systems and methods used in Europe. Based on the experience of the authors of this book, within single companies the HR management and general management alike find it difficult to fully comprehend the pay systems they are applying; it is difficult to get a firm grip on all the various factors influencing pay and its numerous characteristics. Over the Atlantic, especially the multinational American companies similarly lack comprehensive knowledge on the European pay: how is it different from the American pay and where do the differences derive from? This book has been written to bring more clarity to the European pay, to offer practical tools in defining and auditing single pay systems, and also to present empirical data on European pay. The book, therefore, targets especially practitioners and practically oriented pay system researchers and developers: people wanting to understand European pay issues and systems better and wanting to learn to shape pay in a more professional manner.

The SALTSA-group: An International Collaboration on Pay System Studies

This book is the outcome from several years of collaboration in a group of European researchers interested in pay issues. The group was brought together and financially supported by the Swedish SALTSA research program. SALTSA stands for the joint program for working life research in Europe, and its partners are three Swedish trade unions – SACO, TCO, and LO[2] – and the National Institute for Working Life[3]. The program aims at bringing European researchers together to work on different contemporary working life issues – pay systems being one of

---

[2] SACO stands for "The Swedish Confederation of Professional Associations", TCO stands for "The Swedish Confederation of Professional Employees", and LO stands for "The Swedish Trade Union Confederation".

[3] For more information on the National Institute for Working Life, see www.arbetslivsinstitutet.se. For more information on the SALTSA program, see www.arbetslivsinstitutet.se/saltsa/default_en.asp

them[4]. The SALTSA program has thus enabled us to meet and to plan our exploration in the European pay systems. With the broad mandate to study European pay systems as a part of a work organisation's operation, SALTSA has given the direction to our work, but left the choice of the paths to cover open for us and the end point of our journey undetermined. Where we ended up going and how we got there is documented in this book.

The group members come from different European Union countries – Sweden, Finland, Germany, Italy, Belgium, The Netherlands, and The United Kingdom. The members also find their roots from different academic disciplines (business management, work psychology, sociology, etc.). What we share is the interest and active research work in the field of pay; for many of us SALTSA gave an opportunity to extend usually national research work to the international level. The diversity of the group has enabled us to approach pay issues from different perspectives (although finding the common tune has undeniably sometimes been quite hard).

From early on, to make our work manageable and to articulate the foundation of our shared effort, we set the following boundaries for our task. Firstly, as discussed above, the prevailing focus of the research on pay issues has been at the executive – at most managerial – level. We decided to concentrate on the pay systems of operational employees: white- and blue-collar employees working in a direct connection to the production or service processes of an organisation. Such focus would enable us to illuminate pay systems of a large portion of the labour force and study how legislative and collective bargaining regulations together with organisations' discretion shape pay systems. We also decided to focus on employees with long-term or permanent job contracts rather than to include different pay arrangements relating to short-term job contracts. Secondly, we decided to focus on pay systems – on base pay and variable pay elements. An alternative would have been to include other tangible pay elements such as benefits or even intangible rewards in our study. Focusing only on pay systems made the international comparison to some degree more straightforward. Thirdly, we have studied the pay systems of operational employees from the work organisational perspective or, in other words, from the perspective of business strategy and HR policy in particular. Pay setting is understood as a HR practice in the context of other HR practices, such as the design of the work organisation. Therefore, the question whether a pay system fits to an

---

[4] Interestingly, the trade unions (at least in Sweden) perceive pay systems as an important and interesting research topic, even though (as noted above) many researchers have failed to do so.

organisation's other practices or its strategies is an important question for us. Even though we are aware of the critique towards contingency approaches (see *e.g.* Drazin & Van de Ven, 1985), our studies led us to appreciate the importance of a pay system fitting to an organisation's overall practices. Finally, we focused on business enterprises – on the private sector – rather than included also the public sector to the study.

The Research Question and Methodological Approaches

The boundaries set for our study (outlined above) left us with the following research question:

What kind of pay systems are implemented in the European Union countries for operational employees with either permanent or long-term job contracts in the private sector?

Furthermore, the aims of this book (outlined in the previous sections) led us to elaborate this research question into six further questions: three are dealing with creating a better understanding on the European pay and three with the actual state of the contemporary European pay. The research questions relating to the better understanding on pay are:

1. *How can pay issues and pay elements be conceptualised?*
2. *What kinds of interests do various stakeholders have on pay issues? How do those interest shape pay systems?*
3. *How can existing pay systems be audited?*

To answer these questions, we first give an overview on the existing pay instruments and systems (chapter 2.1). We also developed a model on essential pay characteristics or pay characteristics that (based on the experience and expertise of the book's authors) are needed when trying to understand pay arrangements in a company (chapter 2.2). Furthermore, we devised a research tool for auditing pay systems. We also discuss the interests and approaches of different stakeholders regarding pay issues (chapter 3).

The three questions relating to the actual state of the European pay are:

4. *What are the general trends within the European pay?*
5. *How do national specific conditions influence pay systems in Europe?*
6. *How do national and multinational European companies deal with pay issues? What kind of pay systems do they use?*

To answer these questions, a sub-group of the SALTSA-group carried out an extensive study on European pay systems both by analysing already existing survey material at international and national levels as well as by carrying out case studies focusing on the retail banking companies in different European countries. This study was a collaborative effort with the European Foundation for the Improvement of Living and Working Conditions. Although the results from the European Foundation study have been reported elsewhere (Antoni *et al.*, 2005), they also contribute to this book (see chapters 4.1 and 4.2). In the retail banking case studies, the audit tool developed by the authors was applied. Furthermore, we used the audit tool to study the pay systems within a multinational European company. Audits were carried out in the Belgian, French, Dutch, and German subsidiaries of this company; different approaches towards pay present in these various countries were explored. Therefore, the case studies in the subsidiaries of the multinational company enable us to provide insights on how national conditions influence pay (when the company is the same in all cases) and the case studies in the retail banking companies in several European countries enable us to provide insights on how national and company specific conditions influence pay (when the sector is the same across the cases). All in all, the research methods applied have been both qualitative and quantitative, both academic writing-desk exercises and empirical field-work has been carried out for this book.

The Outline of the Book

The content of this book aims at reflecting the complexity of pay systems as a phenomenon. The diversity of our group has helped in achieving this aim by enabling us to cover the pay system topic from different national and disciplinary perspectives. Following this introductory chapter, the book is divided into four major chapters. In chapter 2, we start from the basics: define the usual instruments, systems and processes available for European companies when shaping pay. The concepts used in this book are clarified. The chapter also provides the reader with the latest evolutions in pay systems and their management. In chapter 2.1, an overview is presented about the existing pay instruments and the pay systems these instruments form. Chapter 2.2 explores essential pay characteristics, *i.e.* pay characteristics that need to be taken into account when shaping, reviewing or auditing a company's pay systems.

Chapter 3 draws attention to different stakeholders influencing pay, such as employers, employees, trade unions, and employer associations. All these various stakeholders have different interests in pay questions and can influence pay setting with their unique contributions. Chapter 3 thus reviews the points of view of different stakeholders on pay. It also fills an important gap by showing the different contextual factors that play a role in shaping pay systems and by explaining how those factors concretely influence pay strategy and design. Building further on these insights, a framework for strategic pay is developed.

Chapter 4 provides a more empirical approach to shaping pay in Europe: first, in chapter 4.1, the contemporary European pay systems and their consequences are described based on the available statistical material. Secondary analyses have been conducted to indicate, for instance, connections between pay systems, work organisational factors, quality of working life and organisational strategies (see Antoni *et al.*, 2005). In chapter 4.2, pay systems and pay outcomes in several European Union countries are reviewed. The aim of these country specific descriptions is to illuminate the contemporary issues in pay in these countries. In chapter 4.3, the focus is moved towards the single companies. The pay audit tool, mentioned in chapter 2, is first applied in retail banking companies in several European countries and then in European subsidiaries of a multi-national company. Through these national and cross-national case studies, contemporary pay practices in Europe are exemplified further. Simultaneously, the use of the pay audit tool developed by the authors is exemplified.

Finally, chapter 5 concludes the book with a discussion on the contemporary pay systems in Europe. The key issues from the book are summarised, and challenges for future pay setting and research are outlined.

References

Antoni, C.H., Baeten, X., Berger, A., Emans, B., Kessler, I., Hulkko, K., Neu, E., Vartiainen, M. & Verbruggen, A. (2005), *Wages and Working Conditions in the European Union*, Dublin: The European Foundation for the Improvement of Living and Working Conditions.

Drazin, R. & Van de Ven, A.H. (1985), "Alternative forms of fit in contingency theory", *Administrative Science Quarterly*, 30, p. 514-539.

Heckscher, C. (1994), "Defining the post-bureaucratic type", in C. Heckscher & A. Donnellon (eds.), *The Post-bureaucratic Organisation: New Perspectives on Organisational Change*, Thousand Oaks, California: SAGE Publications, p. 14-62.

Kira, M. (2000), *The Compensation Systems of Developing German Organisations*, Labor Policy Studies, Number 223, Helsinki: Ministry of Labor, Finland.

Ylikorkala, A., Hakonen, A. & Hulkko, K. (2005), *Tulospalkkauksesta Toivoa Toiminnan Kehittämiseen. Kokemuksia Tulospalkkauksesta ja Sen Kehittämisestä Terveydenhuollon Yksiköissä Vuosina 2000-2003* [Hope for Operational Development from Results Based Pay. Experience on Results Based Pay and its Development within the Health Care Provider Units in Years 2000-2003], Tykes raportteja 41, Helsinki: Tykes.

CHAPTER 2

Pay: What Is It about?

Ben J.M. EMANS

Nowadays, reward systems in companies are generally complicated and difficult-to-comprehend phenomena. They are unlikely to be otherwise, because in most of the organisations the human capital constitutes the major source of value creation, as well as the major source of operation costs. From both the perspective of creating competitive advantages and the perspective of cost control, perfecting the reward system is, as a result, a matter of organisational survival. The result often tends to look like a whole panoply of intertwined principles, tables full of data, tools, detailed algorithms and all kinds of procedures. In order to discuss properly reward systems, which is the purpose of this book, we need to put order in this panoply. Somehow, their components should come to stand out as well-defined entities. To that end, this chapter puts forward two approaches, both complementing each other. In section 2.1, the huge diversity of pay instruments and pay systems which can be found in modern organisations is displayed within a systematising frame. Next, in a more analytical and abstract way, section 2.2 presents an overview of so-called essential pay characteristics: starting with the premise that a pay system plays the role of optimising the employee-organisation-relationship, a model consisting of parameters which affect the way that role is played, is developed. Together, the two sections provide the conceptual framework which will be used in the subsequent chapters.

CHAPTER 2.1

Pay Instruments and Pay Systems

Xavier BAETEN & An VERBRUGGEN

Introduction

There seem to be a lot of misunderstandings about some pay concepts and their content. It turns to be obvious when we look at the usual mixture of terms used such as compensation, wage, pay, remuneration, rewards, incentives, etc. Moreover, in the 'real world', a clear distinction is not always made between financial and non-financial rewards. Promotion, for example, is a non-financial reward element. However, when promotion is not followed by financial rewards, it might loose any motivational power. Most of the time, non-financial rewards have an impact on financial rewards (Baeten, 2004).

Since an unambiguous approach is essential in dealing with this topic, we want to provide the reader with workable descriptions of the relevant notions concerning pay, pay structures, pay systems and pay processes.

In this chapter, we will first have a look at the terminology related to pay issues. Later on, we will discuss a non-exhaustive list of financial reward instruments, followed by a section on grade, pay structures and pay systems.

What Are We Talking about?

The terms 'reward', 'remuneration', 'pay', 'wage', 'salary' and 'compensation' are altogether linked to what employees receive in return for their contribution. Often, however, those terms refer to different ideas for different people. Some primarily view pay as a cost, while others link it with motivation, recognition or even to frustration and disappointment; others might see pay mainly as a sign of fairness; others, still, associate it with consumption opportunities, security, power… (Gerhart & Rynes, 2000), and "for some pay is vital for leisure time and recreation; many see the level of their pay as an expression of their success" (Kressler, 2003:113).

The most widely used term, both in business English and even in daily language, is *reward* (Kressler, 2003). The concept 'total rewards' is developed out of an idea that originated in the USA; it is steadily crossing over the ocean and gaining pace in Europe. "Total rewards" include *financial rewards* like base pay, contingent or variable pay, share ownership and employee benefits and *non-financial rewards*. Thus, financial rewards have to be viewed as only one element in the total compensation package an employee receives in return for his investment of time and energy. In addition to financial rewards, there are other benefits: a good working environment, recognition, quality of working life, the opportunity to learn and develop skills and competencies, a meaningful job content, work/life balance, etc.

After analysing many definitions and descriptions contained in various sources, we would propose the following definition for 'total rewards': *all types of direct and indirect, short and long term financial and non-financial returns employees receive as part of their employment relationship* (based on Baeten, 2004:216). This definition shows that reward should be viewed as the most momentous term, referring to both financial and non-financial earnings. In this chapter, and later on in this book, we will only deal with financial rewards.

Remuneration solely refers to the financial elements in the pay package, so we could argue that remuneration is *the total of direct and indirect, short and long term financial returns employees receive as part of their employment relationship*[1], *i.e.* cash, short and long term variables, benefits and perquisites[2].

Kressler states that, in American English, *compensation* has always been a popular term (Kressler, 2003), and it can, according to us, be used as a synonym of remuneration.

Total compensation/remuneration includes pay obtained directly like cash (base pay, merit increases, incentives, cost of living adjustments) or indirectly through benefits or services (pensions, health insurance, paid time off). It represents all the elements contained in rewards which can be valued in terms of money for an individual: it is the sum of base salary, variable pay and the value of employee benefits and pensions.

'Pay' and 'wage' can both be described as the pure financial return employees receive for their investment. A distinction is often made between *salary* and *wage*: salary refers to pay received by managers and

---

[1] Based on Milkovich, 2004.

[2] Perquisites ('perks') are benefits that address specific needs of all or some employees, and are most often tied to a specific job level. Examples are: transportation (company car), special discounts on company products, special risks and work assurance, use of company facilities, free meals, etc. (Kovac, 2003).

professionals. Their pay is most often calculated at an annual or monthly rate, rather than hourly, as is the case with wages (Milkovich & Newman, 1999).

Figure 2.1. Overview of the reward elements

			Some Examples
TOTAL REWARDS / TOTAL REMUNERATION / VARIABLE PAY / FIXED PAY: Base Pay	▸ Direct income		▪ Base Salary ▪ Hourly wage ▪ Add-ons
TOTAL REWARDS / TOTAL REMUNERATION / VARIABLE PAY: Short-term variable	▸ Direct income		▪ Cash bonuses ▪ Commission (Sales) ▪ Add-ons (e.g. shift work, overtime)
TOTAL REWARDS / TOTAL REMUNERATION / VARIABLE PAY: Long-term variable	▸ Deferred income		▪ Stock (ESOP, Restricted Stock, Performance Shares, Phantom Stock) ▪ Stock options ▪ Cash
TOTAL REWARDS / TOTAL REMUNERATION: Perquisites	▸ Income adding ▸ Services		▪ Company Car ▪ Discounts ▪ Meal Vouchers, company restaurant ▪ Gifts ▪ Sports facilities
TOTAL REWARDS / TOTAL REMUNERATION: Benefits	▸ Income security		▪ Medical and medical-related benefit payments (hospital, disability, accident) ▪ Life insurance ▪ Retirement plan

TOTAL REWARDS: Other non-cash rewards			▪ Time
			  ▪ Flexible working hours, compressed working week (year), additional time off, flexibility in granting time off, possibilities for part-time work
			▪ Place
			  ▪ Distance between workplace and home, telework, desk (ergonomics, space, comfort
			▪ Learning & development; talent management; coaching
			  ▪ Training budget, breadth of training entitlement, learning on the job, possibilities of job rotation/promotion
			▪ Psychic income
			  ▪ Recognition, accomplishment in the job, interesting work, trust, job title, image of the employer, working atmosphere
			▪ Company culture
			▪ Organisational participation
			  ▪ Being informed about the organisation, autonomy, responsibilities, being able to give input, participation in decision-making
			▪ Employment security
			  ▪ Job security, employment guarantees offered by the employer

(Based on Manas & Graham, 2002 and Baeten, 2004)

Figure 2.1 gives an overview of the different reward elements, together with their definition and some examples. Most of the elements will be explained in further details throughout the chapter.

Financial Reward Instruments

Financial reward elements can roughly be divided into base pay, variable pay and employee benefits (both financial and non-financial). These instruments are put together by means of different building blocks or tools, and result in a number of reward systems: short or long term instruments, related to active or non-active periods, linked with the job the individual is performing or with certain conditions (*e.g.* achievement or specific results); finally, they can be offered in direct monetary form or in kind (Baeten, 2004).

Base/Fixed Pay

Base pay is direct income and has to be viewed as one of the most important elements of the reward system, in terms of cost for the employer and in terms of recruitment and retention for the employee. Base pay is (for a certain period of time at least) a fixed wage component; an employer gives it at specific moments (monthly, weekly or daily) to an employee for the work performed. It constitutes the rate for the job performed and may vary according to the grade of the job or the level or skill required (Armstrong & Stephens, 2005).

Because of its fundamental importance, it is vital that a good structure for determining base pay is developed. A base pay structure "reflects the hierarchy of job grades and pay ranges established within an organisation" (Kovac, 2003:8). The grade of jobs is a specific area in a pay structure where all jobs with similar size and value are put together, usually on the basis of a (non-)analytical job evaluation. These grades can be linked to particular pay ranges that may be determined through the analysis of market rates and/or the reference to the company-specific concurrences and differentials. Each grade has a unique code, a minimum, maximum and midpoint[3]. Grades can either be narrow or broad, and thus more flexible. A pay or salary range specifies the range between the minimum and maximum rate that can be paid for a job in a specific grade. It then specifies the range through which job holders can make progress. A distinction is made between *grade* and *band* because a grade is, on average, narrower than a band. The amounts are not directly related to what an individual actually receives. They are rather used as

---

[3] A midpoint is the middle salary level in a salary range for a specific job grade or position. It is usually not far from the average of the minimum and maximum in a salary range.

reference points in making decisions among pay practices. In developing a structure, it is necessary to develop an internal hierarchy of jobs and determine compensable factors. Compensable factors are factors that determine what companies are willing to pay for (such as responsibility, the skills required, efforts, etc.) and can be defined as: "any characteristic used to provide a basis for comparing job content in a job-evaluation scheme" (Kovac, 2003:16). Grades and salary ranges have to be slotted in the market. Afterwards, individuals can be linked to their grades.

Periodic adjustments to base wages can be carried out on different bases and can, but do not have to, be part of collective bargaining:

- Seniority: this is called 'service-related pay'. It provides fixed increments which are usually paid each year on the basis of a continued service (Armstrong & Stephens, 2005).
- Age.
- The overall cost of living or inflation.
- Changes in what other employers are paying for the performance of the same work.
- Changes in performance and competencies of employees.

Employees can make progress within grades or ranges, or can be promoted to another grade or range. In order to make a decision about the variables for salary increases, it is necessary to weigh their importance as well, while taking into account the percentage of increase allowed. Merit pay is one method of linking salary raises to an assessment of the individual's merits.

Variable Pay

The concept variable pay is wide ranging. Basically, it refers to situations where pay is not guaranteed: it has to be re-earned, and is dependent on specific results like corporate performance, company performance (gainsharing, profit sharing), team performance (team-related pay) and individual performance. According to Rynes and Gerhart, many kinds of performance measures can be used as basis of a variable pay formula. They can be measured in terms of quantitative or qualitative criteria. The performance measures range from very concrete behavioural ones – *e.g.* accidents, absenteeism – to more aggregated measures of unit performance – *e.g.* productivity, cost, quality, customer satisfaction, delivery, cycle time. Measures of financial performance (*e.g.* return on sales/investment/equity, economic value added) (Rynes & Gerhart, 2000) can be found as well. Similarly, mere individual results can be measured and rewarded. Sales results are one example, but also other employees' performance can be measured in terms of communication, completion of projects, quality, timeliness, and so on. The assessment of these outputs can result in variable pay. As a result, these 'bonuses' are not consolidated in base pay and payments will usually be based on an assessment of performance or contribution (e-reward.co.uk, 17.12.2005). It is worth noting that variable pay can be determined by performance (output), but by input as well (competencies).

An *incentive* can be defined as "any form of variable payment tied to performance" (Kovac, 2003:46). The payment may be a monetary (like cash or equity) or non monetary award (like goods or travel). Some authors make the distinction between incentives and bonuses, by stating that performance goals for incentives are predetermined (Kovac, 2003).

In order to set up a variable pay plan, it is first necessary to decide on the employees who are eligible, and then determine the relative importance of variable pay compared to base pay and/or total rewards (Baeten, 2004). The organisation also has to decide on how the system will be funded, on the frequency of payout, and on what basis variable pay will be granted. Baeten states that the most important element is the link with the performance management process itself, namely goal setting, feedback, and performance review (Baeten, 2004). According to Brown and Turping, the proportion of variable pay, on average, in the European worker's pay package has increased by approximately 5% since 1995, and this trend is to spread at all levels (Brown & Turping, 1999). Today, the general rule seems to be the following: the higher the management position and the more highly qualified the task, the bigger the proportion of variable pay will be (Kressler, 2003). Incentives can be paid out under various forms like cash, pension plans, contributions, stock (options), shares, and so on. The size and the form of variable pay can be agreed on through collective bargaining, but this is by no means an obligation.

The size of cash bonuses and incentives is usually set in relation to base pay, as is the case for the level of pension contributions and some other benefits (www.e-reward.co.uk, 12.12.2005). This way, incentives establish a direct link between pay and performance that can be short or long term, tied to the performance of an individual, a team, a business unit, or a combination. Short term incentives (STI) use very specific performance standards, while long term incentives (LTI) focus efforts of employees on multiyears results (Armstrong & Murlis, 1998). A special form of bonus is the *labour market bonus*, which has been used to attract people on narrow labour markets. A deferred bonus plan is a system where part of the bonus is paid out later on. This kind of bonus is often used as a method for retaining or motivating employees: the part of the payment which has been postponed (deferred), can be raised by the employer on the basis of a long-term performance. Sometimes, employees are obliged to invest the delayed part in shares. Commonly

used LTIs are Employee Stock Ownership Plans (ESOP[4]) and performance plans (Armstrong & Murlis, 1998). A relatively new LTI are the
broad-based option plans (BBOP). When a company works with
BBOPs, it gives employees grants of options on company stock (Milkovich & Newman, 2004). Other widespread LTIs are stock option plans
and restricted stock.

Examples of short term incentives for individuals are *piece rate
plans* (the employee gets a set rate for each unit or service provided, or
for each item sold) and *standard hour plans* (pay is based on a faster
performance of the task than what is required by the standard time). As
far as groups are concerned, we can distinguish some team-based plans,
a.o. *gainsharing, Scanlon plans*[5], *Rucker plans*[6], *Improshare*[7] and
profitsharing.

According to a study executed in 1999 throughout Europe, 37% of
companies have set up team and collective bonus schemes together with
individual performance pay, in contrast with 2% of them which only
have team pay; the fastest-growing types of variable pay are combined,
multi-tiered bonus schemes measuring performance at company, team
and sometimes individual level (Brown & Turping, 1999).

Employee Benefits

Employee benefits are a kind of indirect pay, and are provided under
non-cash or non-direct cash form; they represent therefore indirect
economic compensation for a continued company membership (Bergmann & Scarpello, 2001). Employee benefits usually constitute more
than 20% of the total wage costs (Baeten, 2004).

---

[4] This plan makes it possible for employees to receive company shares that they
accumulate upon retirement or when leaving the organisation for other reasons.

[5] A Scanlon plan is named after its developer, Jospeh Scanlon. This is a gainsharing
plan designed to lower labour costs without lowering the level of a firm's activity.
Employees share in specific cost savings that come from employee effort. It *'involves
formal employee participation, a predetermined incentive formula and periodic
progress reporting'* (Kovac, 2003:91).

[6] A Rucker plan is similar to a Scanlon plan: *'a gainsharing cost reduction program
in which specific cost savings that result from an employee effort are shared with
employees'* (Kovac, 2003:89).

[7] Improshare (IMproved PROductivity through SHARing, developed by Mitchell Fein)
is easy to use and communicate (Milkovich & Newman, 1998). The difference with a
Scanlon/Rucker plan is that it measures work productivity of employees and ignores
aspects outside their control.

Table 2.1. Overview of employee benefits

Benefits	
Income security	• Pension and saving plans: *e.g.* defined contribution plans, defined benefit plans, etc. • Life insurance • Medical and medical-related benefit payments (for hospitalisation, disability, accident)
Perquisites	
Income adding	• Company Car • Meal vouchers • Meals in company restaurant • Payment for time not worked in addition to social security • Discounts • Gifts • Allowances
Services	• On-site services (laundry, ironing, shopping service) • Sports facilities • (Emergency) child care • Financial planning • Career advice • Medical check-up • On-site car parking • Tea, coffee, cold drinks

(Based on Baeten, 2004).

Little research has been carried out yet to examine the occurrence of employee benefits; however, plenty conversations with HR managers, have revealed that Table 2.1 gives an extensive overview of employee benefits. They can be subdivided into perquisites and benefits, and embrace three categories: those that provide income-security, those that add income and the so-called services.

Grade and Pay Structures

Grade and pay structures are key parts of reward systems. "A grade structure becomes a pay structure when pay ranges […] are attached to each grade, band or level" (Armstrong & Stephens, 2005:182). A pay structure is a logically designed framework in which different pay levels for jobs or groups of jobs can be defined on the basis of an assessment of their relative internal and external values (Armstrong & Murlis, 1998). This framework enables the organisations to implement their pay policies, makes it possible to define the span for pay progression and gives a basis upon which pay can be achieved and upon which monitoring and controlling the implementation of pay practices can take place. A grade or pay structure can also be seen as a medium through which the organisation communicates the career and pay opportunities (Armstrong & Stephens, 2005). Sometimes, the levels of pay in a structure have been negotiated for all the employee categories or for some of them, and are consequently part of a Collective Labour Agreement.

Figure 2.2. From job/role analysis to pay structures

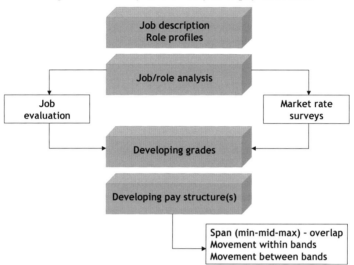

Figure 2.3. Pay structure

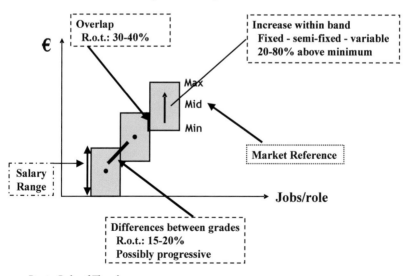

R.o.t.: Rule of Thumb
Min: Minimum; Mid: Midpoint; Max: Maximum.

A company's pay structure can be defined by the number of work levels, the pay differentials (the pay differences between levels) and the criteria used to determine those levels (Milkovich & Newman, 2004). These criteria are either *job-based* or *person-based*[8] (Milkovich & Newman, 2004). On the one hand, a job-based structure is based on the work content, *i.e.* tasks which are performed, behaviours and/or results which are expected. A person-based structure, on the other hand, focuses on the employee: the employee's skills or knowledge, whether they are used or not used in the job, or the competencies the employee is assumed to have (Milkovich & Newman, 2004). In a job-based structure, pay is immediately linked to the job, and personal characteristics do not matter that much. Employees receive instant pay rises when they move into a new job, even if they lack the capabilities. The pay system which is used is often a point-factor system that rates jobs by means of the compensable factors which are defined during the job evaluation process. Differentiating low and high performers is made impossible when using this structure.

Within an organisation, there may be one grade structure covering all the jobs, *i.e.* an integrated structure, or there may be more than one structure.

Armstrong and Stephens have identified the following pay structures: pay spines, narrow-graded structures, broad-graded structures, broad-banded structures, career family structures, job family structures, spot rate structures and pay curves (Armstrong & Stephens, 2005).

Pay Spines

A pay spine consists of a series of increasing pay points ranging from the lowest to the highest-paid jobs covered by the structure in which pay ranges for the jobs are established (Armstrong & Brown, 2001). In practice, pay spines are strongly related to seniority-based pay.

Table 2.2. Example of a pay spine

Spine Point	Amount
1	€ 1612.60
2	€ 1677.14
3	€ 1741.68
...	...
7	€ 2057.30
8	€ 2129.09

---

[8] The distinction between job-based and person-based pay structures reflects the distinction between algorithmic and experiential pay philosophies, as will be dealt with in chapter 3.2.

Pay spine increments between pay points vary between 2.5 and 3% from the top to the bottom of the spine, but may remain the same throughout the structure or can be widening when coming closer to the top. Job grades are aligned to the pay spine. Then, the pay ranges for the various job grades may be superimposed on the pay spine. Each spine has a maximum and a minimum. Progression is based on the length of service.

Nowadays, the trends we can highlight are the following: if performance-related pay is introduced, increments can be accelerated. Next to that, additional increments can be given above to those reaching the top of the scale. Pay spines are most often found in the public sector or in agencies and voluntary organisations which have adopted a public sector approach to reward management (Armstrong & Stephens, 2005). Pay spines are popular as well where operational employees are protected by collective agreements.

It seems that pay spines are managed by their own: the decisions have not to be made by line management or are made within an explicit framework. The need for managers to make possibly biased or inconsistent judgements on pay increases is severely limited. Therefore, pay spines appear to be fairer than structures where progression is governed by managerial decisions on performance or contribution. As a consequence, those systems are highly favoured by trade unions. However, downsides remain: people are being rewarded for their presence, and not for the value of their contribution. Moreover, pay spines appear to be very costly in organisations with low staff turnover, resulting in a drift to the top of the scale (based on the presentation of Xavier Baeten, 14.02.2006)

Narrow-graded Structures

A narrow-graded structure is a sequence of approximately 10 or more job grades into which jobs of equivalent value are placed. Grades are defined by a group of job evaluation points, so that any job for which the job evaluation score falls into a specific group, can be allocated to the grade linked to that group of points. Alternatively, grades can also be circumscribed by grade definitions that provide the information needed (*e.g.* description of possible job content) in order to match jobs set out under job demand factor headings (based on the presentation of Xavier Baeten, 14.02.2006).

Figure 2.4. Example of a narrow-graded structure

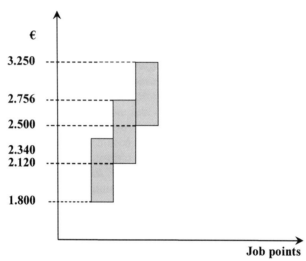

A pay range is attached to each grade and its scope ranges between 20 to 50% above the minimum. Progression can normally be achieved through performance, competence or contribution (a combination of both performance and competence). The overlap between ranges can be as high as 50%, and provides the possibility to differentiate between highly experienced employees at the top of a range and someone who is still learning at the bottom of the next range (Armstrong & Stephens, 2005).

Narrow-graded structures ensure that jobs of equal value are paid for equally. They are easy to be managed because of the large number of grades, through which subtle distinctions between various levels of responsibility can be made. A staff often prefers this structure, because it offers many opportunities for increasing pay by upgrading. We cannot ignore the downsides of such structures: there may be too many grades, causing a constant pressure for upgrading and thus grade drift (based on the presentation of Xavier Baeten, 14.02.2006)

The reward package for a typical employee who works for a representative European employer normally has a pay structure which consists of four or five grades for managers, and six or seven for non-managers; the median range widths from the top to the bottom are 25 to 50%, and traditional promotions up the grades are still the most commonly used tool to recognise and retain high-performing employees (Brown & Turping, 1999).

Broad-graded Structures

Broad-graded structures range from 6 to 9 grades, and can be managed in the same way as narrow-graded structures. The maximum of each pay range usually lies between 50 and 70% above the minimum. Organisations often introduce mechanisms to control progression within the grade and thus control costs (Armstrong & Stephens, 2005). These mechanisms limit the possibilities for the staff to reach the upper pay limit within the grade.

Broad-banded Structures

Originally, the number of bands in a broad-banded pay structure does not go beyond five, with a span ranging from 70 to 100% and relatively wide salary ranges, and typically with 100% or more difference between the minimum and the maximum. Thus, the range of pay in a band of a broad-banded structure is significantly higher than in a conventionally graded structure.

This kind of pay structure gives companies the advantage of having more flexibility in positioning people and in reaching delayering (a less hierarchical structure) in the organisation. A decrease in the number of grades also contributes to a reduction in the upgrading pressure, and diminishes the possibility of grade drift (Armstrong, 2005). Firms which are using broadbanding usually eliminate the traditional pay tools (*e.g.* point factor job evaluation, range controls) (Rynes, 2003).

In a broad-banded structure, the focus is mainly put on lateral career movement within the band and on the growth of competencies and ongoing development in the role.

However, nowadays, the original notion of broadbanding has shifted away: this is mainly due to problems raised by cost control and the lack of guidance and structure. Some organisations have had relatively bad experiences with broadbanding, owing to the massive flexibility. Due to the lack of good performance and assessments of competence, salaries tended to move upwards. That is the reason why some organisations developed midpoints within bands and subbands and shaped zones for individual jobs or groups of jobs. Job evaluation is used as a basis for deciding where reference points should be placed in relation with market pricing.

The width of bands depends upon the kinds of roles allocated to them and upon the opportunities for pay progression the organisation wants to provide for in a band. The boundaries of a band are mostly defined by job evaluation (Armstrong & Brown, 2001): jobs can be put into the bands by reference to market rates or by a combination of job evaluation and market rate analysis. Bands are regularly described in terms of generic roles relating to the band. The implementation of a broad-banded structure actually aims at fitting the pay structure in a delayered organisation, reflecting an emphasis on lateral progress, supporting flexibility and team working. Moreover, broad-banded structures support pay delivery approaches like competency-based pay, skill-based pay and career laddering, which better allows organisations to recognise and reward individuals and to make them moving up through the structure on the basis of their capabilities and contributions (Berger & Berger, 1999).

According to research carried out by Armstrong and Brown, in organisations with broad bands, 62% have band widths ranging from 50 to 75%, the rest of them have band widths ranging from 75 to 100% (Armstrong & Brown, 2001).

Career Family Structures

A career family structure consists of groups of jobs (families) with common characteristics, for example operations, finance, administration, marketing, IT. The level of responsibility, skill or competence required to perform the job can vary though, but the fundamental nature of the activities and the basic skills required are similar (Armstrong & Murlis, 1998). A career structure is "a single graded structure in which each grade has been divided into families" (Armstrong & Stephens, 2005:193).

A career family is normally built up by six to eight levels that are defined by the activities carried out and/or by the knowledge and skills or competencies needed to perform these activities. Some families may have more levels than others.

Job Family Structures

A job family structure strongly resembles a career family structure. An important difference between career and job families is that career family structures have a common grade and pay structure whereas in job family structures each job family has its own pay structure which takes into account different market rates between families. Moreover, the level/grade structures may differ in order to reflect the special characteristics of roles in the various families (Armstrong, 2005). Job family structures can result in unequal pay for work of equal value between job families (Armstrong & Stephens, 2005). Career families solve this problem by using market supplements which are easier to justify on an individual basis.

Job families are based on common processes: operations, administration, finance and IT, for example, can be put together in "business support" (Armstrong & Stephens, 2005).

Career and job family structures turn out to be very helpful in encouraging flexible working practices and multiskilling; furthermore, they encourage people to move from their jobs within the organisation (job rotation). Next to that, they flatten the organisational structure and offer the flexibility necessary to meet the occupational and labour market pressures (Armstrong, 2005).

Job family structures tend to be popular in organisations with a lot of experts and knowledge workers (Armstrong & Brown, 2001).

Spot Rate Structures

In some organisations, it has been decided not to use any graded structure at all for specific categories of employees (Armstrong & Stephens, 2005). This is, for instance, the case for categories such as senior management or for manual jobs where there is a skilled or semi-skilled market rate to be negotiated with the trade unions (rate for the job). It is easier then to implement a spot rate (or individual job grade) structure. This structure defines a distinct range for each job and is frequently used for jobs where differences between job sizes[9] are considerably huge. Sometimes, the spot rate is attached to a person rather than to a job. Individual pay rates for job holders whose rates have not been part of collective bargaining, can change. Job holders may be entitled to a bonus or other forms of incentive payment on top of the base rate (Armstrong & Murlis, 1998). Spot awards are awarded for exceptional performance (*e.g.* on special projects) or for performance which goes far beyond expectations, so that the employee ought to receive an add-on bonus (Milkovich & Newman, 2004).

Spot rates may be used where there is a very simple hierarchy of jobs (*e.g.* retail firms for customer service staff). They often exist in small or start-up organisations that do not want to be constrained by a formal grade structure and prefer to retain the maximum amount of flexibility (Armstrong & Brown, 2001). It may result, however, in serious unjustifiable inequities.

---

[9] An indication of the relative value of a job in terms of, for example, the level of responsibility as established by analytical job evaluation (e-reward.co.uk, 22.03.2006).

Pay Curves

Pay curves or maturity/progression curves represent a development of job family structures. Organisations tend to implement pay curves when they need to use different methods of handling pay determination and progression within job families. They provide different pay progression tracks through which people in a job family can move according to their competence and performance. Pay levels are determined by reference to market rates. This system does not provide a common level of movement for all the employees. Each set of job family pay curves will be adapted to reflect market rate movements (Armstrong & Murlis, 1998).

Pay Systems

Pay systems provide the employees with a financial recognition of their achievements, which can be about performance targets (on an individual, team or organisational level), competencies and skills (www.e-reward.co.uk, 10.12.2005). Moreover, they help to arouse motivation and commitment (Baeten, 2004). According to Tropman, a reward system should meet different goals dependent on the performance of the staff. It should encourage the retention of the best performing employees (top 20%) whose pay should be 20% or even more above the market. On the other hand, it has to balance the in- and outflow of the 60% regular do-the-job employees, who should be paid at the market level or slightly above the market. Finally, it should encourage departure of the bottom 20%. They should be paid 10 to 20% below the market (Tropman, 2003).

In the next part, we will successively discuss several forms of contingent pay, being "any potential pay or benefit that is dependent on employee behaviour or performance" (Kovac, 2003:19). Table 2.3 gives an overview of what companies can value and want to pay for.

Performance-related Pay

Performance-related-pay links pay (base and/or variable) to the individual (merit pay, individual performance-related pay), group (team-based pay) and/or organisational performance (profit sharing). It provides a contingent pay scheme which grants individuals financial rewards under the form of increases in base pay or cash bonuses, which are linked to an evaluation of performance mostly connected with agreed target objectives or outcomes (Armstrong & Stephens, 2005)

According to a research, 65% of companies have some kind of performance-related pay system (www.e-reward.co.uk, 2004)

Service-related Pay / Seniority-based Pay

Service- or seniority-based pay guarantees employees fixed pay increments, mostly paid out annually on the basis of continued service in a job or a company (Armstrong & Stephens, 2005).

Individual Performance-related Pay

A *merit pay* system is a specific pay-for-performance system; it establishes a link between increases in base pay and the outcome of the employees' performance evaluation (Milkovich & Newman, 2004).

Table 2.3 gives an overview of all the possible compensation methods based on objective measures, competences and results.

In most of the cases, merit pay is based on individual performance. However, it is theoretically possible to link it with team performance. This system is quite expensive for companies and it is often argued that it does not achieve the desired goal, which is the improvement of the employee and the corporate performance. Therefore, merit pay is often replaced by lump sum distribution. Lump sums only reward performance once, as opposed to merit pay which rewards performance 'for-ever'.

Performance related pay is associated with graded pay structures, individual job range structures and pay curves (Armstrong & Stephens, 2005).

Individual performance can also be reflected in variable pay, through bonuses or incentives which are linked to an assessment of the individual's performance.

Team-based Pay

According to Katzenbach and Smith, a team is a small group of employees who have complementary skills and are mutually accountable to each other in achieving common goals (Katzenbach & Smith, 1993).

Team pay is believed to enhance good teamwork, as opposed to the individual nature of individual performance-related pay. It is a method of rewarding groups of people who are working together in a formally established team on the basis of the results they achieve following their shared efforts (Armstrong & Stephens, 2005).

Table 2.3. Compensation matrix (Baeten, 2004)

Paid via / Criterion	Base pay entry	Base pay increases	Variable pay
Educational criteria			
Diploma	Education-related pay	Education-related increases	-
Time-related criteria			
Age	Age-related pay	Age-related increases	-
Length of service		Service-related increases	Seniority bonus
Job-related criteria			
Job	Pay the job	Promotion	-
Competencies			
Technical	Skill-based pay	Skill-based increases	Bonus based on technical competencies
Team-related	Competence-related pay	Competence-related increases	Competence-related bonus
Attitude-behaviour	Competence-related pay	Competence-related increases	Competence-related bonus
Results			
Individual	-	Merit pay	Bonus / Sales Commission
Team	-	Merit pay	Team bonus / gainsharing
Business unit	-	-	Team bonus / gainsharing
Corporate	-	-	Profit sharing / Stock-based remuneration
Group	-	-	Profit sharing / Stock-based remuneration

The payments are linked to short or long term team performance which is measured in relation to the performance objectives of the team itself or with another team's performance, *i.e.* the target team; those payments may be shared equally or proportionally among team members. Rewards for individuals may also be influenced by the assessment of their contribution to the team. There is no such thing as a typical team pay scheme; the implementation of team reward systems widely varies: the design is contingent on the requirements and the circumstances of the organisation, and these will always vary. Gomez-Meija and Balkin distinguished following monetary team rewards (Gomez-Meija & Balkin, 1992):

- Team Bonus – Bonus formulae relate the amount payable to individual team members to one or more measures of team performance or to the achievement of specifically agreed team performance (Armstrong & Stephens, 2005).
- Team Merit Pay – Cash adjustment to salary (recurrent) tied to achieving team behavioural and performance outcomes.
- Skill-based Pay – Adjustment to base pay rate of team members linked to team competence level.
- Spot Cash Rewards – Pay that is determined and distributed on a discretionary basis, taking into account team achievements.
- Gainsharing – Employees share the gains of the unit/department with interdependent teams. As such, gainsharing takes place at a more aggregated level. Gainsharing can also take place at a corporate level, and as such, it is an instrument of financial participation.

When companies decide to reward teams, they have to make sure the incentive is substantial. Some authors think that it should reach at least 8 to 10% of base salary, while others consider 5% as a minimum level. Furthermore, an equal amount has not to be received by everybody: it is possible to work with lump sums, with percentage of income or an assessment of individual members' contributions. Research has shown that 89% of companies using team rewards also offer rewards and incentives to individuals. 63% of them allocate rewards equally to each members of the team (McClurg, 2001). Research carried out by the Strategic Rewards Research Centre in 2005 shows that employees prefer to have a team bonus which is equally distributed.

Teams can also be rewarded in alternative ways. In some organisations, competence-related pay is viewed as the best method of varying the rewards of individual employees in line with their contribution to team results. In this case, competencies like team working and communication skills will play an important role. There are many other ways for rewarding teams: team goal-based incentive systems, team discretionary bonus systems, team skill incentive systems, team member goal-based incentive systems, non-financial rewards (positive feedback, praise, recognition) and organisation-based rewards (CIPD, 2003).

Table 2.4. Preferences for team bonus distribution

Criteria	% of respondents
Equal distribution between all the team members, irrespective of individual salaries	47%
The line manager decides on the distribution	19%
Distribution is based on the responsibilities within the team	17%
The team decides on the distribution	7%
Distribution in relation to the size of fixed pay	2%
Distribution is based on the age of the employee	1.5%
Distribution is based on seniority	1%

Source: PowerPoint presentation 22 November 2006 on the occasion of the Total Rewards Research of the Strategic Rewards Research Centre ©

Financial Participation

"Financial participation is a reward technique that links individual rewards with collective performance on the level of the firm (vs. team-based performance rewards)" (Gevers & Cludts, 2002:72).

Armstrong distinguishes three types of financial participation: profit sharing (payment in cash or shares related to the profit of the business), share ownership schemes (employees are given the opportunity to purchase shares in the company) and gainsharing (payment in cash related to the financial gains made by the company because of its improved performance) (Armstrong 2005). Financial participation can be subject to collective bargaining. This occurs in some countries where tax incentives are linked to specific plans of financial participation.

Financial participation schemes are set up to increase the employees' involvement in the business, while giving them a direct interest in the financial performance of the company in which they work. The underlying principle of financial participation is simple: a part of the employees' remuneration should be linked with the company's performance; the staff should have some financial stake in the profit or loss of the business in which they work. The schemes aim at aligning the interests of employees with those of shareholders. Most of the time, the employee is given a yearly premium on top of his base wage. This premium depends upon financial indicators, according to a predefined formula (Gevers & Cludts, 2002).

Financial participation can be linked to various indicators, but profit-based financial participation is the most common. We can make a distinction between cash-based profit sharing, share-based profit sharing and stock options (Gevers & Cludts, 2002; De Wortelaer, 2004). De Wortelaer goes further and also makes the distinction between performance participation, gainsharing and profit sharing. *Performance participation* refers to the actual production or productivity of the organisation, which constitutes the basis of the financial return received by the employer. *Gainsharing* refines performance participation by introducing some corrections through the input of company costs (labour cost, taxes, etc.). Gainsharing deals with terms like added and turnover value. It is worth noting that gainsharing can be part of team-based pay as well as financial participation, depending on the variables used. *Profit sharing* is based on more than the improved productivity of gainsharing (Armstrong & Murlis, 1998); it is a plan under which an employer pays special sums to eligible employees in cash or with shares belonging to the company and related to the bottom-line profits of the business:

- *Cash-based profit sharing schemes*: Profits may be directly distributed when a company gives its employees a percentage of its profits (or a percentage of the parent company's profits). Apart from their normal wages, employees then receive a variable bonus income, the amount of which is directly related to the general profit level of the organisation.

- *Stock/Share-based profit sharing schemes*: Financial participation may be indirect when the company distributes shares instead of cash. Those shares are usually frozen into a fund for a specific period before allowing employees to sell them (investment period).

- *Approved profit-sharing share schemes*: the company allocates a proportion of profit to a trust fund which acquires shares in the company on behalf of the employees (De Wortelaer, 2004).

Some countries have specific types of deferred income. France, for example, has its own systems of *mandatory and voluntary profit-sharing*. Mandatory profit-sharing (participation) is a statutory requirement in companies with a workforce of over 50 (lowered from 100 in 1990). Under this mechanism, introduced in 1987, companies set aside a statutorily defined percentage of their profits, or a higher proportion where special mandatory profit-sharing agreements exist, for delivering it to employees. Mandatory (for companies with more than 50 employees) deferred profit-sharing (*intéressement*), introduced in 1959 by President De Gaulle, links a percentage of workers' pay with the company performance in terms of profits or productivity, for example. This financial participation system has evolved into a system where employees' savings are invested in funds, which invest in turn in a diversified fund or in the employer's shares (Poutsma, 2005).

Stock options are the most common form of long-term incentives: "a company gives free of charge to all or some of its staff stock options that will enable them at some future date to purchase a certain number of shares in the employing company, for a price established at the moment when the options are allocated" (Gevers & Cludts, 2002:72). They offer potential and not guaranteed rewards. Any return is deferred and is often conditional. The emphasis rather lies on longer-term ownership than on definitive and immediately disposable cash values. They aim at aligning employees with the interests of stockholders (Longnecker, 2004). A *restricted share plan* is a plan in which employees are offered shares according to their performance. These shares are often blocked on a security account for a certain period, during which the shares may not be sold.

Gainsharing can be defined as a formula-based company – or factory – wide bonus plan which enables employees to share the financial gains made by a company as a result of the improvement in the organisational or team performance (Armstrong, 2005). Unlike profit sharing, it tends to be related to performance indicators on which employees can exert some influence, such as added value, quality and customer service. An agreed formula determines how productivity-generated savings are distributed. This is generally based on a performance indicator (added value or some other measures of productivity). Some schemes also incorporate performance measures relating to product quality, customer service, delivery or cost reduction. The three traditional gainsharing plans are *Improshare*, *Scanlon* and *Rucker* (see page 31 for details), but modern schemes tend to be based on special formulas, with key indicators moulded to meet organisational objectives.

Gainsharing aims at encouraging employees to focus their attention on the key areas of the business that generate improvements in organisational performance, while at the same time creating a motivated and committed workforce that wants to be part of a successful company.

Legislation and tax concessions probably have a powerful impact on the use of this kind of financial participation schemes: they are more usual when there is an extensive legislation and/or tax concessions. Research has also evidenced that financial participation has positive effects on employees' productivity (Pendleton & Poutsma, 2004).

Knowledge-based Pay

Knowledge-based pay is a system of pay differentiation based on education, experience or specialised training, that enables the employee to deal with a specific subject matter, or work in a specific field. The salary level may not depend on whether the individual uses this knowledge or not.

Competence-related Pay

A pay-for-competencies system seems to be quite simple: pay employees more when they become more competent, and pay the most to the most competent: this provides a "contingent pay scheme that rewards people wholly or partly by reference to the level of competence they demonstrate in carrying out their roles" (Armstrong & Murlis, 1998:299). People are paid for their ability to perform, while focussing on the attributes, personality traits and behaviours of an employee; at the same time, employees themselves are concentrated on developing breadth and depth of knowledge (Tropman, 2003).

Most of the HR professionals draw a distinction between competence and competency but this is by no means universal. Both terms are often used interchangeably. Competences refer to 'outcome', "the areas of work in which people capable of meeting the standards required because they have right levels of skill, knowledge and experience" (www.e-reward.co.uk, 10.12.2005). On the other hand, competencies, refer to input, "a behaviour, attribute or skill that is a predictor of personal success" (Kovac, 2003:17).

Some organisations opt for one pay-for-competence framework for all the employees across the organisation, which is often known as a *'core framework'*. This has the advantage of being simple and easy to communicate. However, as a set of generic competencies might not be generally applicable, some competencies might be irrelevant for some specific categories. As such, its generalisability might be limited.

Some organisations rather prefer to produce a core framework, but then complete it with *role specific competencies* in order to acknowledge the specific responsibilities and needs of managers together with other important groups. This approach enables to improve relatively easily the acceptability of a core framework to a diversified workforce.

Another option to consider is a *'menu' style approach*. This involves the production of a framework, from which employees with their manager selected a few competencies which are viewed as relevant for the role an individual performs. This approach improves the likelihood that competencies will be seen as realistic and relevant. Many organisations that use this approach provide guidelines to staff in order to help them to choose competencies, such as requiring that a certain number are selected.

The last option is to create a *different framework for different groups* within the organisation in order to take into account diverse needs. These types of frameworks can be more relevant and can be more easily customised or revised to take into account the changes in priorities and needs.

Competency-related pay has been quickly growing in the UK and the US, although it takes at least a year to be developed and implemented (Brown & Armstrong, 1999). The reasons for the popularity of competence-related pay, is the importance given to the employee's competence

47

as the basis for competitive success, organisational restructuring and the emphasis on individual and lateral growth and the solutions brought in order to address the failures of traditional merit pay schemes.

Competencies are generally linked to pay through a job-focused process that uses competencies as the criteria, wholly or partly, for assessing jobs; competencies can be linked to a more people-focused process as well that links pay levels and increases the level of competence reached by individuals. While sometimes pay is wholly determined on the basis of personal competence, it is often combined with traditional job- and results-focused systems, *i.e.* "pay for contribution" (Brown & Armstrong, 1999).

Research carried out in the UK has shown that 41% of companies using competence-related pay have incorporated it into performance related pay. 21% consolidates it into annual pay increases, and less then 15% either has a wholly competency-related pay scheme, or a competency-related bonus (Rankin, 2004/2005). A European survey, carried out in 1997 by Towers Perrin, showed that more than 20% were already linking skills and competencies with pay for part of their staff (Armstrong & Brown, 1999).

Nowadays however, competence-related pay seems to be getting less popular than it had been expected to be a couple of years ago. One important reason is that competence-related pay heavily relies on well-trained and committed line managers to measure and assess competence fairly and consistently. Line managers often complain about the difficulty and the amount of responsibilities they face (www.e-reward.data. co.uk, 12.12.2005).

Skill-based Pay

A skill-based pay plan provides a contingent pay scheme which rewards employees for the knowledge and skills they have acquired and used in practice. Skills typically refer to blue collar work, while competencies refer to white-collar work (Milkovich & Newman, 2004). Skill-based pay can help to achieve flexibility. It shows people that the organisation is interested in employees who 'grow, learn and develop'.

Rynes remarks that an increasingly important approach to skill-based pay uses bonuses instead of base wage increases to reward skill acquisition (Rynes, 2000). It is obviously a relevant approach when the knowledge base is quickly changing and/or is difficult to specify.

Contribution-related Pay

This is a relatively new concept, and is used for a process for making pay decisions based on assessments of the outcomes of the work carried out by individuals and the levels of skill and competence which have influenced these outcomes (Armstrong & Stephens, 2005). Pay increases or bonuses are both based on output (results) and input (competence) criteria: employees are rewarded for what they do and for the way they are doing it. Contribution-related pay takes into account those factors that contribute to the organisation's achievement of its long-term goals (Armstrong & Brown, 1999).

In practice, this system works within a broad-banded or job family pay structure.

Conclusion

Pay is one of the most complex areas to deal with. Furthermore, there are many possibilities available in order to set up real pay systems. However, most of the stakeholders who deal with and are interested in pay are not aware of the existing tools. This chapter aimed at filling this knowledge gap.

First of all, we started by defining some relevant concepts out of the current panoply of reward-related notions and the existing terminology. A complete overview of financial and non-financial rewards, like cash, bonuses, pension plans, company cars, training, holidays, just to name a few of them was given.

We then returned to the focus of this book, financial rewards, by looking more into detail to base and variable pay. The organisation has to select one or more pay structures, depending upon its organisational structure, flexibility and the number of hierarchical levels as well. Pay structures provide frameworks in which organisations can logically structure jobs or groups of jobs and link them to a specific pay level. Salary ranges within bands can vary between 20 and 100% and organisations have to decide on entry level, on factors that will determine salary increases, on band overlap, etc. Obviously, links will be established between the pay structure and the determinants of job value. But also pay systems should be developed, rewarding employees for their achievements, both at input and output level. Once again, there are many options, such as individual performance-based pay, team bonuses, profit sharing, competence-related pay, contribution-based pay, etc.

As such, this chapter has provided the reader with a thorough overview of what pay is exactly about, as well as with pay technicalities. Further on in this book, attention will be paid to which kind of pay system should be used under specific circumstances, as well as to the presence of pay systems throughout Europe.

References

Armstrong, M., Brown, D. (2001), *New Dimensions in Pay Management*, London: CIPD.

Armstrong, M., Murlis, H. (1998), *Reward Management*, London: Kogan Page.

Armstrong, M., Stephens, T. (2005), *Employee Reward Management and Practice*, London: Kogan Page.

Baeten, X. (2004), "Strategic Rewards and Reward Strategies" in K. Verweire, L. Van Den Berghe (eds.), *Integrated Performance Management*, London: Sage, p. 215-237.

Berger, L., Berger, D. (1999), *The Compensation Handbook*, New York: Mc Graw-Hill.

Bergmann, T., Scarpello, V. (2001), *Compensation Decision Making*, Orlando: Harcourt.

Brown, D. (1998), "The third way on pay", *People Management*, 5, p. 25.

Brown, D., Armstrong, M. (1999), *Paying for Contribution*, London: Kogan Page.

Brown, D., Turping, S. (1999), "European Reward Practices: Is 'Third Way' Pay the Future?", *Benefits & Compensation International*, 29, p. 15-20.

Chartered Institute of Personnel and Development (2004), *How to Develop a Reward Strategy*, London: CIPD.

De Wortelaer, J. (2004), *De Wet betreffende de werknemersparticipatie in het kapitaal en in de winst van vennootschappen*, Antwerpen: Intersentia.

e-research (2002), *Total Reward*, Cheshire: e-reward.co.uk Ltd.

e-research (2003), *Team Reward*, Cheshire: e-reward.co.uk Ltd.

e-research (2004), *Survey of Pay and Grade Structures*, Cheshire: e-reward.co.uk Ltd.

Gevers, A., Cludts, S. (2002), "Financial Participation: a complementary compensation instrument", *11th conference of the international association for the economics of participation (IAFEP)*, Brussels.

Gomez-Meija, L.R (1992), "Structure and process of diversification, compensation strategy, and firm performance", *Strategic Management Journal*, 13, p. 381-397.

Heneman, R.L. (2002), *Strategic Reward Management: Design, Implementation and Evaluation*, Greenwich: Information Age Publishing.

Katzenbach, J., Smith, D. (1993), *The Wisdom of Teams: creating the high-performance organisation*, Boston (Mass.): Harvard Business school press.

Kovac, J. (2003), *Glossary of Compensation & Benefits Terms*, Scottsdale: Worldatwork.

Kressler, H. (2003), *Motivate and Reward. Performance Appraisal and Incentive Systems for Business Success*, New York: Palgrave MacMillan.

Longnecker, B. (2004), *Rethinking Strategic Compensation*, Riverwoods: CCH Inc.

Manas, T. & Graham, M. (2003), *Creating a Total Rewards Strategy*, New York: Amacom.

McClurg, L.C. (2001), "Team rewards: how far have we come?", *Human Resource Management*, 40, p. 73-86.

Milkovich, G., Newman, J. (2004), *Compensation*, Singapore: McGraw-Hill.

Pendleton, A., Poutsma, E. (2004), *Financial Participation: The role of governments and social partners*, Luxembourg: Office for Official Publications of the European Communities.

Poutsma, E., Lighthart, E.M., Schouteten, R. (2005), "Employee Share Ownership Schemes in Europe. The influence of US Multinationals", *Management Revue*, 16, p. 99-122.

Rankin, N. (2004/2005), "The new prescription for performance: the eleventh competency benchmarking survey", *Competency & Emotional Intelligence Benchmarking Supplement*, London: IRS.

Rynes, S. Gerhart, B. (2000), *Compensation in Organisations: Current Research and Practice*, San Francisco: Jossey-Bass.

Tropman, J. (2001), *The Compensation Solution*, San Francisco: Jossey-Bass.

www.cipd.co.uk

www.e-reward.co.uk

www.worldatwork.org

CHAPTER 2.2

A Tree-like Representation
of Essential Pay Policy Characteristics

Ben J.M. EMANS

Introduction

A company's pay policy can be defined as the entirety of practices that determine how its employees are materially compensated for their employeeship. Many ways are found in the compensation literature to characterise these policies, for example in terms of the absence or presence of bonuses, the absence/presence of broad banding or the absence/presence of overtime pay. All these description methods make sense in their own way. Differences among and trends within organisations can be expressed in terms of the characteristics denoted, and pay policy outcomes, such as employees' pay satisfaction, can be empirically related to these characteristics. As is illustrated by the cited examples, however, these ways to describe pay realities are also subject to certain shortcomings. First, they only address one aspect of pay policies, whereas the meaning of pay policies cannot be understood unless all building blocks of employee compensation are taken into account. Second, the descriptive characteristics apply, to a higher or lower degree, to the outer surface of pay policies, that is, to the use of specific tools that have been adopted, rather than to the policies' inner substance, that is, the parameters that affect their functioning. Due to these shortcomings the resulting descriptions are not the best possible ones when the ambition is to meaningfully describe pay policy varieties or to investigate the pros and cons of these varieties. What is required is a kind of inventory of essential pay policy characteristics, made with the objective to list as exhaustively as is practically possible the factors that affect the performance of pay policies, without necessarily intending to picture the many different manifestations of these factors through their incorporation in concrete tools. Once these factors have been operationalised, such an inventory may help to design studies of pay policies and accumulate the outcomes of those studies.

Figure 2.5. Tree-like representation of pay characteristics

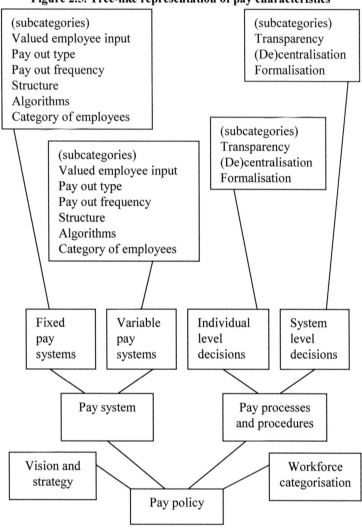

In this chapter an inventory is developed, intended to realise the above-mentioned objective. Starting from the premise that a pay policy serves as the material backbone of the prevailing EOR, the Employee-Organisation Relationship, we will unfold a number of categories and subcategories of pay policy characteristics. The combined contents of these categories are displayed in a tree-like representation (see Figure 2.5), with branches and side branches symbolising choices to be made by pay policy designers. As a whole, this tree, which will be expounded in the sections to follow, is thus designed in order to obtain an overview of the options one has when decisions have to be made about the set-up of pay policies in whatever organisation.

Pay Policies and Employee-Organisation Relations

An organisation's pay policy is one of the main components, if not the main component, of its prevailing Employee-Organisation-Relationship, in short its EOR, which constitutes the whole of exchanges of contributions that, as a rule, take place between an organisation and its workforce (Tsui, Pearce, Potter & Tripoli, 1997; Tsui, Pearce, Porter & Hite, 1995; Shore *et al.*, 2004). For employees the EOR, if satisfactorily modelled, serves the purpose of securing a sufficient level of experienced outcomes with respect to their work efforts, while for the organisation it serves to ensure that work is done in a way which is consistent with its strategic ambitions. Contributions made to the EOR by employees are, for instance, their time, skills, efforts and loyalty. The organisation's input, in turn, consists of attractive labour conditions, wages, learning opportunities and many other things. A pay policy, being the core part of an EOR, only covers a subset of those input/output exchanges. As far as employees' outputs are concerned, it merely includes their remunerations, while as far as their inputs are concerned it includes things they are required to accomplish in order to obtain those remunerations, or in short: the work they are required to do. Conversely, the organisation's output equals the employees' work accomplishments, while its input equals the remunerations provided.

The conceptualisation of a pay policy as the core part of an EOR is helpful when it comes to determine which issues are its essential characteristics, and which are not. Characteristics are essential as far as they affect the EOR quality, defined as the costs and/or benefits (inputs/outputs) associated with it as experienced by either the employees or the organisation. *Impact on experienced EOR profitability* can thus be viewed as the ultimate criterion for deciding whether pay policy characteristics should be considered essential.

Having conceptualised a pay policy in this way, we come to distinguish four main categories, split up in 20 subcategories (see Figure 2.5), of essential pay characteristics. The four main categories (see Table 2.5 for a first impression) are: 1) pay strategy and vision, 2) pay systems, 3) pay processes and procedures and 4) workforce categorisation. As will be explained below, it is the combination of these categories that results in experienced input/output balances associated with a particular pay policy and thus impacts on experienced EOR profitability.

Table 2.5. Four basic categories of pay policy characteristics

Category	Examples
1. *Pay vision and strategy*: The principles underlying the design of pay systems as well as pay processes and procedures.	* A firm intends to be an attractive employer, making use of relatively high pay levels. * A firm intends to promote team work and therefore favours incentives linked to team performances rather than individual performances.
2. *Pay systems*: The content part of pay policies (wage levels that are assigned to employees, degree of differentiation among employees, factors that determine levels and differentiation.	* On the average the maximum pay level associated with a specific job equals 160% of the corresponding minimum pay level. * For settling pay levels an employee's seniority is not taken into account.
3. *Pay processes and procedures*: The process part of pay policies (the way pay-related decisions are made).	* Unions are involved in pay system negotiations. * Individual pay raises are not negotiable.
4. *Workforce categorisation*: The distinctive treatment, in terms of pay system and pay procedures, of distinct groups of employees.	* Only white collars are eligible for pay system X (for example: a system with individual bonuses). * There is no grade system for the highest management positions.

The 'pay vision and strategy' category

The first category of pay characteristics, referred to as *pay vision and strategy*, is the most fundamental, and the least tangible one. The characteristics in it represent basic principles that underlie the pay policy, such as a firm's positioning relative to labour market conditions, or its tendency toward performance-based pay, rather than job-based pay (or the reverse). In a sense, the characteristics in this category do not add to the information derived from the other three categories (which are outlined below). The attributes in those, more tangible, categories can be said to be the translation, the manifestation of the strategy and vision characteristics. We included the vision and strategy category, though, for two reasons. First, there may be a discrepancy between the intended vision and strategy on the one hand, and the way things are operationalised on the other hand. In that case, the attributes of vision and strategy as such constitute a piece of reality. Second, the myriad of characteristics of the three tangible categories may obscure their underlying principles to the degree that an organisation is hardly aware of them. By including a separate vision and strategy category we force – so to speak – managers and other users of our model to become explicitly conscious of their own pay principles. In Table 2.6 we have listed, in a self-explanatory way, the most pressing choices an organisation is confronted with when considering its basic pay strategy.

**Table 2.6. Characteristics related to the 'vision and strategy'
and 'workforce categorisation' categories**

Strategy and vision	* Market positioning: overall pay level below, at or above labour market figures? * Degree of risk sharing by employees: to what degree are pay levels dependent on the firm's financial performances? * Differentiation: to what degree are pay differences among employees doing similar jobs desirable? * Focus on individual performances: to what degree are individual incentives desirable? * Focus on unit performance: to what degree are team or department incentives desirable?
Workforce categorisation	Distinguishing between and among: * Blue collars and clerical employees? * High, middle and low management? * Professional groups? * Core and flex personnel? * Part-time and full-time employees?

The 'pay systems' category

The second category, called the *pay system*, contains all characteristics that together determine the exchange of inputs and outputs, or to phrase it in a less abstract way: all characteristics that together determine what wages are paid for what kind of work, or conversely: which employee contributions are compensated by which levels of pay. Algorithms for linking performance levels to compensation levels, or for differentiating among jobs in terms of salaries associated with them, form part of this category. The characteristics in this category together affect the factual profitability of the EOR for the organisation as well as for the employees. This is why we can consider them as the main constituent of pay policies, assuming that factual profitability underlies *experienced* profitability (our ultimate criterion for essential pay characteristics, see the introduction).

Within the pay system category we distinguish two subcategories, related to systems of fixed (or job-related) and variable (or performance related) pay successively. This distinction is required, because the two system types can exist simultaneously within one organisation, being applicable to either the whole of the workforce or a part of it, while being entirely different from each other in terms of the input/output exchanges involved. For each separate system characteristics can be defined that determine its profitability for the employees and/or the organisation. More specifically, we have included characteristics (see Table 2.7) that define 1) the employee inputs that are valued (*e.g.* job attributes in the case of fixed pay, or someone's effort level, in the case of variable pay), 2) the type of pay-out used (*e.g.* cash salaries, or stock options), 3) the frequency of pay-out (*e.g.* monthly, or irregularly), 4) the so-called structure, the particular amount and nature of the wage-differentiation among employees (*e.g.* specificities of the grades system in use in the case of fixed pay, or the maximum size of a bonus in the case of variable pay), and 5) the pay-algorithms applied (*e.g.* the criteria for linking specific jobs to grades, or criteria for assigning bonuses)[1]. The characteristics contained in these boxes, which for obvious reasons are highly different in the two cases of fixed and variable pay, are listed in a self-explanatory way in Table 2.7.

The 'pay processes and procedures' category

Table 2.7. Characteristics related to the 'pay systems' category

Subcategory		Characteristics
Fixed pay	Valued employee input	* Job attributes, taken into account for settling levels of fixed pay. Possibly based on system of job evaluation and classification. * Job holder attributes that are taken into account, such as competence level, seniority and age.
	Pay out type	* Cash, or (also) other types such as stock, pension, add-ons.
	Pay frequency	* Weekly, monthly, etc.
	Structure of system	* Characteristics of the grade system in use, such as: number of grades/ number or steps within grades/ span of grades/ overlap between grades/ timing of progression within grades.
	Algorithms	* Criteria for grade assignment. * Criteria for employee's entry level in grade. * Criteria for progression within grade. * Criteria for moving to higher grade.
	Category of employees	* Category/categories of employees to whom fixed pay system is applicable.
Variable pay	Valued employee input	* Units (individuals, departments, plant, country) whose performances serve as the criteria for determining variable pay. * Performance aspects (quantitative features, qualitative features) that serve as criteria.
	Pay out type	* Cash, or (also) other types such as stock, pension, add-ons.
	Pay frequency	* Yearly, irregularly, otherwise.
	Structure of system	Calculation rules for determining variable pay: * Maximum value, relative to fixed pay. * Link with organisation performance (giving rise to a limited overall 'pool' for variable pay).
	Algorithms	* Weights of criteria (individual performance, unit performance; qualitative aspects, quantitative aspects) for assessing variable pay.
	Category of employees	* Category/categories of employees to whom the system is applicable ('eligible' employees).

---

[1] As is shown in Table 2.7 and in Figure 2.5, we have included a sixth subcategory of characteristics, labelled 'category of employees'. This subcategory will be treated in the section about workforce categorisation.

The third category of pay policy characteristics, called *pay processes and procedures*, refers to the decision-making processes that result in the settlement of the wages that are to be paid out. Examples are procedures for negotiating about pay system renewals, or procedures for deciding on individual salary raises. This category's characteristics thus specify *how* pay-related input/output exchanges between the organisation and its employees are settled (in contrast to the pay system category, outlined above, which refers to *what* is eventually exchanged).

The procedures contained in this category may more or less evoke feelings of fairness, or more or less inspire confidence and so on. Irrespective of their actual outcomes, they thus constitute a value for the organisation and for the employees, impacting among other things on the trust these two parties have in each other. They therefore can be said to co-determine the EOR-quality. They furthermore can be assumed to play a role in the step from factual to experienced EOR-profitability, as the more pay-related decision-making procedures are appreciated positively, the more the resulting decisions will be appreciated likewise (*cf.* Greenberg, 1987). It is for this very reason that the whole of these procedures has to be included as a (very broad) category of essential pay characteristics.

The characteristics contained in this category relate to qualities of two sets of decision-making processes, one dealing with decisions about the height of individual employees' wages and the other dealing with decisions about the design and maintenance of the pay system itself. Each organisation has its own system of procedures for dealing with these decisions. For both the organisation and the employees it is important to have insight into and control over these procedures. In order to characterise a pay system, we therefore need to define characteristics that reflect levels of insight and control. For that reason we have included characteristics related to the transparency, the (de)centralisation and the formalisation of procedures. (De)centralisation is included as it specifies who has the decision-making power, and thus the control over the outcomes of the decisions. Formalisation is included, as it is a way to ensure that decisions are made in a controllable manner.

There is a link between these categories of characteristics and the concept of procedural justice, as will be elaborated in section 3.2 of this book (which deals with the employee perspective on pay issues). Procedural justice is a perceptual phenomenon. It covers a number of elements of decision-making processes, which together add to the acceptability of decision outcomes in the eyes of people affected by those outcomes. The characteristics of the categories 'transparency', (de)centralisation and formalisation merely concretise the elements of procedural justice. In Table 2.8 the characteristics are listed in a self-explanatory way.

**Table 2.8. Characteristics related to
the 'pay processes and procedures' category**

Subcategory		Characteristics
System level	Transparency	* Communication tools used for explanation. * Clarity of the system as such. * Information disclosure.
	(De)centralisation	* Impact on decision-making of management/employees/unions/HR.
	Formalisation	* Structuredness of the procedures for the evaluation and renewal of the system.
Individual level	Transparency	* Explicitness of communication and explanation.
	(De)centralisation	* Negotiability of decisions. * Influence of supervisor on decisions. * Influence of HR on decisions.
	Formalisation	* Link to performance appraisal system. * Strictness of administration.

The 'workforce categorisation' category

The fourth and final category, called *workforce categorisation*, is a kind of preambulary one. A firm can have reasons for adopting distinct pay visions and strategies, pay systems and pay processes and procedures for different groups of employees, such as core employees as opposed to flex workers. One group may, for instance, be eligible for a certain bonus program while another is not. Or pay levels may be substantially different in two groups. Before discussing a firm's pay strategy, system and procedures, one therefore firstly has to spell out to what categories of employees the strategy, system and procedures apply, and in order to do so one has to know what categories of employees are distinguished, as far as pay issues are concerned. For each category, then, the strategy, system and procedures can be described in a meaningful way. For that practical reason we demarcated workforce categorisation as a separate category of essential pay policy characteristics. And for the same reason we have included in our tree-model 'categories of employees to whom a pay system is applicable' as an essential characteristic of pay systems (see Table 2.5). In Table 2.6, the categorisations applied by the organisations are listed.

The workforce categorisation adopted by an organisation is in line with its HRM-strategy, while indicating the way in which it discriminates between employees as regards the types of contributions they are expected to deliver and the types of rewards the system is willing to grant in return. It is therefore not only for practical reasons that it has to be included in the overview of essential pay characteristics. Just as is the case with the vision and strategy characteristics, we are dealing here with a basic approach to the way in which pay systems, processes and procedures are devised.

To conclude

In the preceding sections we outlined a model consisting of essential pay system characteristics, meant for meaningfully and unambiguously describing organisational realities as far as compensation issues are concerned. The next step is to develop an instrument for making these characteristics measurable. For the research presented in the Chapters 4.3.1 and 4.3.2 of this book, such an instrument has been developed[2]. It consists of boxes, corresponding to the categories of the tree-model, to be filled out in a kind of audit survey. As will be shown, the model as well as the instrument can be used for characterising both the existing situation as dealt with by an organisation and the ideal situation as envisaged by the different parties within this organisation, such as line management, HR management and employee representatives. The model can thus be used for numerous purposes, such as comparing an organisation's present state of affairs with an intended one, comparing views that exist within the organisation about the latter, describing trends within (categories of) organisations, comparing (categories of) organisations and, finally, investigating antecedents and consequences of pay systems that have actually been implemented. By using the model as a common vocabulary, the whole of discussions about this diversity of issues might become more focused.

References

Greenberg, J. (1987), "Reactions to procedural injustice in payment distributions: do the means justify the ends?", *Journal of Applied Psychology*, 72, p. 55-61

Shore, L.M., Tetrick, L.E., Taylor, M.S., Coyle Shapiro, J.A.M., Liden, R.C., McLean Parks, J., Morrison, E.W., Porter, L.W., Robinson, S.L., Roehling, M.V., Rousseau, D.M., Schalk, R., Tsui, A.S. & Van Dyne, L. (2004), "The employee-organisation relationship: a timely concept in a period of transition", *Research in Personnel and Human Resource Management*, 23, p. 291-370.

Tsui, A.S., Pearce, J.L., Porter, L.W. & Hite, J.P. (1995), "Choice of employee-organisation relationship: influence of external and internal organisational factors", *Research in Personnel and Human Resource Management*, 13, p. 117-151.

Tsui, A.S., Pearce, J.L., Porter, L.W. & Tripoli, A.M. (1995), "Alternative approaches to the employee-organisation relationship: does investment in employees pay of?", *Academy of Management Journal*, 40, p. 1089-1121.

---

[2]   Obtainable from the authors of this book.

CHAPTER 3

Stakeholder Perspectives on Pay

Xavier BAETEN

Stakeholders are individuals or entities which have a 'stake' in something or someone. This means too they have an interest in it. If we are applying it to the topic of this book, we can argue that the reward management textbooks' approach is mainly given from a one-dimensional perspective, *i.e.* from the employers' or industrial relations' points of view. We want to give, in this chapter, other fundamental insights in addition to the current knowledge, by adopting a stakeholder approach. More precisely, pay will be discussed from the points of view of the individual employer, the individual employee, as well as their organisations, *i.e.* unions and employers' associations. This approach already points out that unions' attitudes and visions do not always perfectly reflect their individual members' behaviours and aspirations. It happens within the employers' associations as well.

Chapter 3.1 starts with focusing on the employer because he is the stakeholder who has to pay out his employees and as such carries the costs. According to the employer, pay has to be managed and pay rises are strategically valuable. As a result, this chapter will provide the reader with a complete overview of the contextual factors that should be taken into account in order to shape pay systems. We will also examine the way these drivers play a role and are translated into pay systems.

We have evidenced that too many organisations do take into account the unions' perspective, but nearly ignore the individual employee's and their own workforce's in shaping pay systems. Therefore, chapter 3.2 will draw the attention onto the employee, whose interests are radically different. More specifically, the psychological 'black box' of pay, consisting of equity-related issues, justice and social categorisation, will be dealt with.

If we would have limited the debate around the individual employers and employees, we would simplify the business reality. As regards the operational employees specifically, joint regulation and collective bargaining are still playing a key role. Chapter 3.3 gives a thorough and intra-Europe overview on what happens with the joint regulation of pay. It focuses on the attitudes of the unions as well as the employers' associations' in various European countries. Once again, it will be crystal clear that there are specific country-related differences and trends, but some common views remain. Among others, we will refer to the increasing acceptance of performance-related pay.

CHAPTER 3.1

The Employer's Perspective on Pay: Strategic Pay

Xavier BAETEN

Introduction

Over the last decades, rewarding has evolved from a rather technical and administrative part of the HR-toolbox into a management discipline. Reward management is still embedded in the HR discipline, its biotope, but it is also narrowly linked with financial management, management accounting and control, corporate governance and last but not least strategic management. Employers become increasingly convinced about the strategic value of rewarding; they are trying to find out the way to develop reward strategies, systems and structures that provide them with competitive advantages. However, in practice, it is not as clear-cut as it sounds like in theory. We lack a conceptual framework and the reward systems are strongly driven by market practices. This leads to a competitive parity rather than a competitive advantage.

This chapter, which puts a stress on the employer's perspective regarding rewarding, aims at providing some original concepts and synthesis. First of all, we will analyse the role of rewarding within its broader strategic and HR-contexts. Afterwards, we will introduce the concept of strategic rewarding on the basis of a management framework by explaining the various dimensions of pay management. It is necessary to analyse, explain and mainly summarise the way and the degree to which different environmental factors might have an impact on pay systems; we will try to fill a deep gap in the research over compensation. The main challenge, indeed, from the employer's perspective is to manage to align pay systems with the contextual factors characterising the business environment. Last but not least, this chapter also provides the reader with a synthesis of the literature and research findings on strategic pay, a concept that originated in the late 1980s and is still very popular, both in academic and business environments.

Rewarding in Its (Strategic) HR-Context

Human Resource Management consists of a series of processes:

- Acquiring Human Resources: HR planning, recruitment and selection.
- Rewarding Human Resources: job analysis and design, compensation, benefits, performance evaluation.
- Developing Human Resources: training and development, career planning, competence management.
- Maintaining and protecting Human Resources: industrial relations and collective bargaining, health and safety, assessment (Ivancevich, 2003).

In turn, HR is not a stand-alone management discipline. Human Resource Strategies specify the use of HR practices in order to be aligned and consistent with the competitive strategy. Moreover, strategic management is about judgements and decisions which help companies in reaching their goals. These decisions are also called *strategic decisions*. Tactical decisions contribute to the competitive strategy as well. The development of pay programs, such as the setting up of grade structures, base pay levels, merit pay, competence-based pay programs, bonus schemes, are concrete examples of these *tactical* HR decisions (Martocchio, 2001). Until the late 1990s, pay was merely viewed as a part of these tactical issues. Since then, there is a clear trend within organisations to view pay, and probably its broader concept, rewarding, as a system existing within an organisation instead of a set of techniques. We will focus, now, on the integration of rewarding with other management processes and systems for the purpose of achieving organisational effectiveness (Heneman *et al.*, 2002).

The position and function of rewarding within its HR context has always raised debate as pay is considered to belong to the *hard* side of HR. the fundamental question that comes up in this respect is whether pay ought to lag or lead the design of other HR processes. Ledford and Heneman argue that pay should be a lag system because it needs other HR processes to be effective. Another argument which explains why pay cannot be used as a lead system in the HR toolbox, are the emotional responses to which changes in pay might lead. Pay is in fact, emotionally more loaded than other HR processes and systems. *External selection* is low in emotion because it only affects employees who do not belong to the organisation yet. The scores related to *training* remain relatively low because its payoffs are carried out in the longer term. *Career-related issues* present a medium emotionality because not everybody is interested in a career and because career aspects are more related to the longer term. Changes in *benefits* can have a direct impact (*e.g.* medical insurance), but in many cases such as pensions and life insurance, they only have a long term impact. Furthermore, employees do not seem to be well informed about the content of benefit packages and they hardly understand it because of the technicality of insurance-related benefits. Therefore, benefits have a medium emotional value as well. Performance management, and more specifically *performance appraisal*, tend to have more emotion related effects because most of the time, it affects pay. It can play a key role in determining pay increases (merit pay) or bonuses. Pay seems to have the most important emotional effect. Employees highly value their compensation because it enables them to meet their basic needs; moreover, it is a source of status and augurs success. Consequently, employees are extremely concerned about pay system changes (Ledford & Heneman, 2002). In brief, pay plays an eminent role within Human Resources Management. However, organisations should be very careful to use pay systems at the very beginning of series of organisational changes because they might negatively influence the level-playing field for related changes (Ledford & Heneman, 2002).

Strategic Rewarding

An Historical Perspective

The management of pay has been subject to important changes since the earliest 20th century. Before the Industrial Revolution, most of the active people were self-employed farmers or small business owners. The emergence of the manufacturing system led to the division of labour which depended on skills, efforts, working conditions, responsibilities, etc. To do so, personnel administration practices like hiring, training, settlement of wages, termination of employment, were developed. The responsibilities of the first personnel functions put the emphasis on the control over workers, which gave birth to scientific management practices. These practices had an impact on pay systems. As a matter of example, we have got the piece rate systems, rewarding individuals depending on the output they produced (Martocchio, 2001). The most scientific management models also gave birth to job analysis, a process used to define the relative value of jobs on the basis of factors such as the skills required, responsibilities, accountability, work environment, etc. (Armstrong & Stephens, 2005). From the 1980s onwards, personnel administration was transformed from a purely administrative function into a more strategic management discipline. Since then, pay practices as well were being designed for the purpose of contributing to the organisations' competitive advantage. The main reason which justifies this change lies in the technological evolution and the globalisation leading to an increased competition; since then, the employees are becoming key resources for the organisations' success. This technological evolution has modified the job requirements, and more specifically, has extended the range of tasks and responsibilities. Compensation systems, like skill- and competence-based pay systems, support these changes.

Another trend is the fact that increased competition has forced organisations to become more productive (Martocchio, 2001). Recent trends such as outsourcing invoicing and other back-office activities to lower-wage countries, as well as the development of HR Shared Services Centres, etc. are just a few examples.

A question still remains about the extent of importance of the human resources management in the current business environment, characterised by a huge influence of the financial markets and a significant pressure towards quarterly results, mainly in publicly listed organisations. As a consequence, the current main tasks and challenges of HR seem to be in lying off redundancies of people due to the above mentioned trends and pressures, while at the same time retaining and rewarding the best and key performers. To reach such a result, pay programs have to be more flexible and should increasingly focus on performance improvement (short term), whilst securing the competence development (long term performance) as well. Pay systems have to be aligned with the trend toward more flexible and less hierarchical organisations, which implies job rotation, career management, multi-skilling, etc., whose influence is significant on pay systems. This is an important shift in practices compared to the 1970s, which were characterised by fixed, negotiated general increases in base pay, supplemented by flat rate bonuses (Brown & Armstrong, 1999). This change is also significant as compared to the current prevalence of individual performance-related pay systems, which seem to be increasingly popular. However, problems remain within those systems: most of the time, they do not seem to have a positive impact on organisational performance and they damage teamwork and quality. Not surprisingly, it appears to Brown and Armstrong that those systems are "at the point of being intellectually and practically bankrupt" (Brown & Armstrong, 1999:11).

What Do Organisations Actually Pay for?

After drawing lessons from the past and following the identification of work-related roles by Welbourne, one of the major drawbacks of today's pay, and maybe even of HR systems, seems to be their unidimensionality. Table 3.1 gives an overview of the various work-related roles that should/could be supported by pay systems, what they stand for and what their indicators are.

Table 3.1. Work-related roles and their indicators

Work-Related Roles	Indicators
Job: basic tasks associated with the job	- Quantity of work output - Quality of work output - Accuracy - Customer service
Organisational member: activities linked with the business unit	- Helping others when it is not part of the job - Promoting the organisation - Transforming the organisation into a pleasant place to be
Entrepreneurial: suggestions resulting in cost reductions or innovation	- Launching new ideas - Implementing new ideas - Improvement of processes
Career: behaviours enhancing knowledge or skills	- Obtaining individual career goals - Developing skills needed for his/her career - Making progress in career - Seeking career opportunities
Team member: activities that help the team	- Seeking information for others in the team - Responding to the needs of others - Making sure the work group succeeds

(Based on Welbourne, 1997)

Each role can be stressed on by using specific pay systems. The job-holder role is emphasised by merit-based schemes, piece rate pay systems and sales commissions. The organisational member and entrepreneurial roles are underlined by gainsharing. The career role is supported at best by the use of skill- and competence-related pay schemes. And it will not be surprising that the team-member role goes together with team based pay. In her study, Welbourne found that in large firms, the job-holder role is by far the most important one in predicting performance appraisal scores (Welbourne, 1997). Job-role based pay systems are very popular since the late 1980s. From the beginning of the 21st century onwards, HR professionals are increasingly convinced that pay systems should be more balanced and should for example also pay attention to team performance, competencies, etc. However, this seems to be easier said than done. Many evidences show us that competence management as well as competence-based pay systems are loosing attractiveness because of the difficulties that seem to go hand in hand with their implementation and maintenance.

We believe that associating pay systems with the current business context is one of the most important challenges in nowadays' human resources management. The remainder of this chapter will specifically pay attention to this issue.

Strategic Rewarding Defined

A definition of strategic reward management, implying the employer's perspective, and based on both the academic literature and business practice, was developed.

Strategic reward management is about to develop, implement and adjust a reward mix which influences the employees' behaviour, skills and performance in order to facilitate the compliance with the organisation's objectives, in line with the organisation's culture and the employees' needs.[1]

Although this definition takes into account the employer's perspective, it already makes clear the employee is a very important stakeholder to be taken into account as well. Indeed, it is useless to develop reward systems and a reward mix that do not take into account the needs and preferences of employees. However, the most essential element in this definition is that, from the perspective of the employer, a pay system should make easier the compliance with the organisation's objectives. These objectives can vary a lot. For some organisations, financial profit-related measures are the most important goals. For others, like non-profit organisations, more social objectives prevail. In between both are measures such as customer satisfaction, revenues, employee satisfaction. These objectives should be translated into the pay systems that are used, one way or another.

It is worth noting that pay systems should not only be in line with the job's significance in terms of responsibilities, accountabilities, tasks, etc., but they should also influence both input (*i.e.* competencies, behaviours) and output (results).

During several brainstorming sessions, practitioners also stressed on the importance of aligning pay systems with the organisation's culture. According to them, it is a contextual factor which needs to be taken into account.

Approaches to Strategic Rewarding

The definition provided in the previous paragraphs, seems to be quite straightforward. However, discrepancies can be found in the literature, about the way to put this definition into practice. In the early 1980s, an increasing amount of writers advocated a more strategic approach to pay systems: an approach which is mainly based on linking pay to corporate and business unit strategies and missions. (Balkin & Gomez-Mejia, 1990). More than 20 years ago, Tichy *et al.* developed a framework with the aim of putting into practice strategic human resource management.

---

[1] This definition is based on brainstorming sessions held with the members of the Strategic Rewards Research Centre at Vlerick Leuven Gent Management School.

They aimed at linking strategies with HR management processes including selection, appraisal, rewards and development. At those times already, quite a lot of researchers found that many organisations' pay systems did not always lead to employee behaviour that was in line with the organisation's objectives. As a consequence, they considered the reward system as "one of the most underused and mishandled managerial tools for driving organisational performance" (Tichy *et al.*, 1982:54). They also raised the problem according to which pay systems too often encourage short-term results and behaviours at the expense of long-term goals (Tichy *et al.*, 1982).

There are many discussions and mixed research results with regard to the necessity of aligning HR systems, generally, and pay systems more specifically, to the external and internal context of the organisation: this is one of the important dimensions in the definition which was provided. There are three different approaches:

• Best practice: the aim is to identify the best HRM practices, whose adoption leads to better performance.

• Best fit: a link should be made between HRM in general and pay more specifically, together with the particular strategic and environmental context.

• A combination of best practice and best fit.

Best Practice

The concept of *High Performance Work Practices* perfectly illustrates the *best practice* approach. More concretely, it has been evidenced that the use of these practices, which include comprehensive recruitment and selection procedures, incentive compensation, performance management systems, employee's involvement, extensive training, have positively influenced the workforce motivation, retention, skills and knowledge, but also the organisation's financial performance. Huselid has found that a standard deviation increase in the use of High Performance Work Practices was associated with a 7 percent decrease in turnover and almost € 23,000 more in sales per employee. In this study, the use of incentive plans was measured by the proportion of employees who are eligible for company incentive plans, profit-sharing plans and/or gainsharing plans; the use of those plans has been also measured by the proportion of the workforce for whom the performance appraisals were used to determine their compensation. Importantly, the results suggested that the mere adoption of these practices was more important than the internal and external consistency (Huselid, 1995). Also Delaney & Huselid found very strong evidence that the so-called progressive HRM practices (selectivity in staffing, training and incentive compensation), are positively related to firm performance. Moreover, their impact was similar in for-profit and non-profit organisations. This study took into account perceptions of organisational performance. These results provide us with strong evidence that the way in which people are managed can influence its performance (Delaney & Huselid, 1996). Other authors have studied the performance outcomes of high-commitment work practices, characterised by employee participation (suggestion schemes, decision-making), freedom of expression, extensive teamwork, and reformulation of work to make the best use of his upgraded skills. In conclusion, the effectiveness of these practices consistently led to improvements in performance and was not contingent on a firm's strategy. In pay-related issues, the best practice approach still prevails as well. As a matter of concrete example, we put forward the importance of benchmarking and being informed on trends in the use of pay systems. Some people negatively describe these practices in particular and pay management more in general by calling it a 'copycat world'.

Best Fit

Best fit, which is also known as the *contingency* approach, stresses on the use of management techniques, such as pay management, differently carried out according to each circumstance (Buelens *et al.*, 2002). Strictly speaking, strategic rewarding in this context means that the effects of specific pay systems are different according to the business strategy, for example. In this respect, a distinction should be made between internal and external fit, on which we will more concretely focus later on in this chapter.

Gerhart & Rynes introduced another way of considering alignment, by distinguishing the horizontal, vertical and internal alignment. *Vertical alignment* refers to the fit between pay strategy and organisational strategy (Gerhart & Rynes, 2003). Under this approach, corporate and business unit strategies are said to predict significantly the pay system design (Boyd & Salamin, 2001). The link between organisational and pay strategies has raised interest among researchers and some of the findings will be reported later on in this chapter. *Horizontal alignment*, which is about the relationship between pay and other HR processes, such as staffing, development, performance management, lack research. At any rate, the modest research evidence suggests that there is less alignment than one might wish (Gerhart & Rynes, 2003).

A question that might come up is to know which one contains the most important dimension of alignment. In his study about High Performance Work Practices, Huselid has only found modest evidence for showing the effects of horizontal alignment on performance and little evidence for vertical fit. The results of his study did not support the assumption that horizontal or vertical alignment would have any additional value over the main performance effects of adopting High Performance Work Practices (Huselid, 1995). On the other hand, Gerhart & Rynes found it impossible to give further details on the topic of horizontal alignment due to the lack of empirical evidence on the way pay strategies work together with other HR practices. They even add a new dimension of alignment, called *internal alignment*, which is about the fit between various subdimensions of pay strategy. Once again, empirical evidence in this field is lacking. From a more conceptual point of view, one should take into account that internal alignment is important, especially from a total rewards perspective. For example, high levels of employees' participation in decision-making or information sharing should be aligned with the pay system. In this case, profit sharing or gainsharing, which are extrinsic rewards, will strengthen employees' participation, which is an intrinsic reward. In our opinion, it is necessary to provide empirical data in order to give further evidence to the hypotheses of alignment: there is a wide gap in this field of research.

In practice, however, fit does not seem to be easily reached. First of all, the formulation of the business strategy is a very complex process. Consequently, it is extremely difficult to bridge the gap between business strategy and HR strategy in general, and pay strategy more specifically. It should be taken into account, as well, that the process of strategic planning is sometimes irrational, which makes it even more difficult to reach alignment (Armstrong & Murlis, 2004).

Best Practice and Best Fit

Finally, the *mixed* approach combines best practice and best fit: best practices belong to the broader conceptual levels and best fit is placed at the firm level, concerning the design and implementation. Pay-for-performance might illustrate a best practice approach. However, the question of best fit comes up with regard to which concrete pay systems and structures should be used, which are both more operational issues. For example, one firm might use merit pay systems, whereas others might opt for stock-related compensation, team-based bonuses, etc.

The difference should be made, as well, between the amount to be paid out and the way to pay out (Gerhart & Rynes, 2003). While taking into account the trend towards more transparency as well as the importance of cost control, we can conclude that organisations do not have many spaces to make some distinctions among the pay levels. The main *strategic space* lies in the way of paying people. In their thorough overview on the alignment issue, Gerhart and Rynes put forward the *resource-based view* on compensation, which says that pay strategy and systems should help organisations to manage human resources in a way which is difficult to imitate. As a consequence, pay strategy becomes a source of competitive advantage. This view goes beyond the fact of assuming that organisations with the same business strategy will benefit from using similar pay strategies. It also directly challenges the common pay practice, which is strongly based on benchmarking with other organisations, which, in many cases, have the same size and come from the same sector. A concrete example of the way to translate the resource-based view into pay management is provided by Lincoln Electric (Gerhart & Rynes, 2003). This organisation was founded in 1895 and plays an active role in the design, development and manufacture of arc welding products, robotic welding systems, plasma and oxyfuel cutting equipment (www.lincolnelectric.com). Its strategy has always focused on quality, efficiency, and cost management. Scientific management principles, such as the so-called management of labour, were frequently used by the organisation. Following the above-mentioned best fit approach, one would expect the pay systems to be rather conservative in such an environment. However, the organisation took a unique path. It introduced an employee advisory board and job security in 1958. Some characteristics of its pay system include base salary and benefits below market levels, high bonus levels based on aggregate performance, very high bonus payout, transparency and employee's involvement. According to many authors and theories of alignment, there is a misfit, both with the strategy (vertical alignment) and between the HR and pay processes (horizontal and internal alignment). Apparently, this does not prevent the organisation from getting a competitive advantage by means of its pay system. To conclude, we could argue that companies should not strive for getting too much alignment because they will loose important opportunities to build a competitive advantage by using their pay system.

Strategic Rewards Framework

By taking into account both theoretical and practical insights, we have set up a framework in order to make the definition clearer, so that we can identify and structure the underlying dimensions of strategic rewarding.

Figure 3.1. Strategic rewards framework

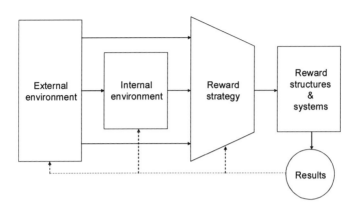

Each of the building blocks of this model and more specifically the links between the building blocks will be described in the following pages of this chapter[2].

The *pay strategy* is the most central element within this framework. It is influenced by both the *external and internal organisational environment*. There are many aspects that should be taken into account and that should play a role in developing a pay strategy. However, the importance of these factors might change over time and depend upon the organisation and its environment. Once the pay strategy has been determined, it should be translated into more concrete *pay systems* and *pay structures* and thereby put into effect. In turn, those should lead to *outcomes* and *effects*, like performance, motivation, etc. In the following paragraphs, we will more specifically deal with the way environmental factors might influence pay strategies and systems; we focus as well, on the thorough definition of a pay strategy. Although a lot of research has provided us with interesting results over the link between pay practices and their drivers, this research has always been rather one-dimensional and not sufficiently practice-oriented, *i.e.* the study of the influence of one environmental aspect on the pay system or specific elements of it. As far as we know, no research has brought the different pieces together nor has it studied the relative differences in terms of influence between these environmental factors. This chapter tries to provide a key added value while studying pay management from an employer's perspective.

---

2   As the focus of this book is on financial reward instruments, 'pay' will be used instead of 'reward'.

External Environment

An organisation does not stand on itself. It is active in and influenced by its (external) environment, both at the macro and the sectoral level. The *macro* level consists of:

- regulatory environment, *e.g.* tax legislation, labour legislation, social security legislation, statutory minimum wages,
- economic environment, *e.g.* inflation rate, interest levels, productivity,
- social environment, *e.g.* labour market, industrial relations, societal values and norms.

The *sectoral* level in turn, focuses on the industry in which the organisation actively works, on its direct competitors as well as collective bargaining at a sectoral level.

Regulatory Environment

There is a massive amount of legislation which directly influences pay systems. Tax legislation, social security legislation, labour law and company law play a role altogether in this field.

Tax legislation seems to influence strongly the prevalence of pay instruments and systems. Belgium, for example, introduced a specific fiscal treatment for stock options in 1999. As a consequence, a lot of organisations introduced these reward systems for their senior management, without, most often, establishing any link with the organisation's or with the employee's performance. In France, organisations employing more than 50 employees are legally obliged to practise profit sharing. There is also a specific tax treatment. As a consequence, profit sharing is much more important in France in comparison with other countries which lack a specific favourable treatment in terms of tax. More recently, more and more countries are considering or developing legal initiatives and/or corporate governance codes which deal with the disclosure of executive remuneration. This will force organisations and their Remuneration Committees to reconsider pay levels as well as pay instruments: this will probably have an effect on pay policies orientated towards operational employees, as well. Finally, legislation about minimum wage levels also plays a role and should be taken into account.

As tax legislation does, *social security legislation* importantly influences wage costs as well. This impact greatly varies, dependent on the level of social security provisions as well as their financing. For example, in France, Sweden and Belgium, the effect of social security contributions on the wage costs is important: it reaches 28.6% and 29.9% of labour costs. In Denmark however, they only represent 6.4% of labour costs because other ways of taxation finance the social security system.

The UK, where private funding is more important, stands between both extremes (12.6%) (Mermet, 2001).

Economic Environment

Inflation rates have an effect on wage levels. Although cost-of-living adjustments are not subject to regulation in most of the countries (except for Belgium and Luxemburg), they are taken into account either directly or indirectly in the setting up of wage. The economic climate also plays a role. Increases in wages tend to be higher in a favourable economic environment together with a positive economic outlook. In case of an unfavourable economic situation, the evolutions in wages are also affected. The recession of the early 1990s, for example, led to a stand-still in real wages (Mermet, 2001).

The unemployment rate is another factor that can play a key role. Phillips has investigated on the relationship between employment levels, inflation rates and the growth of nominal wages in the UK; he has found that the higher the unemployment is, the lower the wage increases are (Mermet, 2001).

Social Environment

First and foremost, *unions* as well as *collective bargaining* and its organisation, have an impact on both pay levels and pay instruments. Apparently, both extreme centralisation (at the national level) and decentralisation (at the company level) of collective bargaining are effective in controlling wage increases and improving employment levels. Intermediate arrangements seem to lead more to wage drift. Therefore, a coordination in decision-making seems to be extremely important regarding the control of wage costs. Generally, there are three categories of agreement:

- central: national or cross-sectoral agreements,
- sectoral: industry-wide agreements,
- decentralised: company agreements.

There are huge differences within Europe regarding the way collective bargaining is organised. There are neither main agreements nor recommendations in Austria, Denmark, France, Luxembourg, Spain and the UK. However, some common trends do exist. In most of the countries, the leading role is located at the sectoral level. Few countries are subject to a completely centralised system. The most centralised system can be found in Ireland. Belgium also has a centralised system, in which the social partners must set a maximum for wage increases every two years, which should then be applied at the sectoral and more decentralised levels. In Greece, the scope for central agreements is more limited because they only apply to sectors deprived of sectoral agreements. Portugal, The Netherlands and Sweden only make recommendations to the social partners, which provide them with a framework for collective bargaining. This tendency is also coming up in Germany. Mermet has noticed three key evolutions in collective bargaining. First, the decentralisation of wage bargaining. Secondly, collective bargaining is starting to cover a wider range which goes beyond the wages. Increasingly, bonuses, profit sharing and other forms of financial rewards are included. Therefore, the total rewards approach is getting prevalent. For example, some collective agreements deal with wages as well as working time reduction and join each other. The third evolution is about the institutionalisation of wage bargaining through the establishment of specific bodies which release reports and comments on wages evolutions (Mermet, 2001).

The *labour market* situation is the second dimension that should be taken into account when studying the external social environment. The balance between labour market supply and demand is a first subdimension to be taken into account. Pay levels and increases seem to be higher in the case of a tight labour market, which is nothing more than a supply-and-demand issue. For example, the demand has been high for skills and competencies related to electronic data processing over the past 30 years (Henderson, 2003). Generally, companies tend to become more creative in developing new forms of rewards when they face a tight labour market.

A second subdimension which is related to the labour market, and which seems to have an impact on pay, is *gender*. Many studies evidence differences in pay still exist between men and women. More specifically wages tend to be lower in industries and jobs where females dominate the workforce (Henderson, 2003). In general, the pay gap, on average hourly earnings, excluding overtime work and on a full-time basis, was not lower than 19.5% in 1993 in the UK (www.e-reward.co.uk). The pay gap appears to be smaller in Belgium, where women with the same job and seniority earn 4.7% less than their male counterparts. However, the difference seems to be higher for older workers (9.6%) in contrast with younger workers where the difference is nearly inexistent (0.5%) (Meijer, 2004). This might mean that more recent pay systems are less discriminatory. Another factor that might play a role in this field, are the (temporary) work interruptions which more frequently occur among female employees.

The third subdimension which is related to the labour market, are the *preferences* of present and future workforces. It is often said that the people entering the labour market are pretty much in favour of pay for individual performance as well as holidays, whereas the former generations were more focused on solidarity and approved of more seniority-based pay systems. This is due to changes in the employment deal. In former times, people were promised steady increases and a satisfying retirement income; nowadays, the concepts of employment security and lifetime employment within one organisation seem to belong to the past. HR departments should be fully aware of the complex mechanisms that play a role in this respect. This will be dealt with, in depth, in the chapter 3.2.

Another element that should be taken into account, and which also has something to do with the individuals' preferences, are the *national cultures* of the countries in which the organisation is located. Countries with a higher power distance – *e.g.* Mexico – will tend to adopt hierarchical pay structures, with multiple narrow salary bands, whereas countries with a lower power distance – *e.g.* Netherlands, Australia – will rather prefer egalitarian systems; it implies, for example, low pay dispersion between top earners and shop floor workers. Another cultural difference lies in the degree of individualisation. In individualistic nations (*e.g.* USA, UK, Canada), individual performance-related pay systems will be more popular, in contrast with more collectivist nations like Japan, where group-based pay approaches prevail more (Bloom & Milkovich, 1997). For example, stock options and employees' stock ownership are more appropriate in highly individualistic countries, with low uncertainty avoidance, and important power distance.

By trying to make the national cultural differences clearer, Yanadori & Milkovich have made some interesting differences in entry levels pays between Japanese and US firms, following the view that determinants of pay in the USA are not the same as in Japan. More concretely, US-based research has established a clear link between the size of the firm and pay levels. In Japan, on the other hand, entry levels were largely explained by the industry membership because of the prevalent practice of information sharing between Japanese firms. Industry membership explained more than 65% of the variance in entry-level base pay (Yanadori & Milkovich, 2003). This has a key impact on practitioners, because to a certain extent, they need to be aware of the rationales in the contexts of local employment.

While shedding light on this cultural issue into further details, a contentious point seems to appear between national cultures and organisational cultures. Some authors would call the above-mentioned national culturalist approach, which dictates that pay policies should be aligned with and strengthen national cultures (Bloom & Milkovich, 1998), *blatant stereotyping*. Many subcultures do not appear to be aligned with geographical boundaries (Bloom & Milkovich, 1997). Indeed, it may be misleading to have a look only at mean national levels without taking into account differences within cultures. It has already been found that many variations exist in individualism within one culture. This would mean that societal cultures only provide us with the very broad framework, and that we should pay at least as much attention to the organisational culture.

The Sector

As mentioned above, *collective bargaining* plays a key role at a sectoral level and it is an important factor in the external context which has an impact on the pay strategy and systems of the organisation. In many countries, including Austria, Belgium, Denmark, Finland, France, Germany, Italy, sector-level agreements define minimum wage levels (Mermet, 2001) which in turn have an impact on the company-level agreements.

Labour intensity is another contextual factor which plays a role, given that labour-intensive industries are characterised by lower pay levels. Capital-intensive industries have a huge need for highly skilled employees, who demand higher levels of pay. There is also a higher proportion of incentive rewards and there is more financial participation in capital intensive industries. Even more concretely, restaurants and retail businesses are known for paying lower wages whereas the financial services industry as well as the chemical industry pays higher wages.

Employment stability is another factor which is related to the sector in which the organisation is active. This factor plays a role because employees who are granted relatively high levels of employment security, are willing to accept lower levels of pay. As such, there seems to be a trade-off between pay and security (Henserson, 2003). The environmental (in)stability is in relation with this aspect: it refers to the volatility of the organisation's external environment. In unstable environments, competition is fierce and there are many competitive strategic decisions as well as complex problem-solving demands. There are forces that can adversely affect organisational success as well. Consequently, organisations in such an environment need a high-performing top management team. As far as pay is concerned, dispersed pay distributions best fit such an environment (Bloom & Michel, 2002).

In some cases, the *geographic location* of the organisation also plays a role. For example, wage levels tend to be lower in more rural areas. This evidences that the cost of living is taken into account.

Internal Environment

Pay strategies and systems should be fully aligned with the external environment in which the organisation is embedded. However, and that is a key point, the characteristics of the internal organisational environment also should influence pay policies. Compensation & Benefits professionals should at least be aware of the impressive number of aspects that could play a role in shaping the pay policies, such as:

- organisational culture
- strategy
- share ownership structure
- size
- profitability
- life cycle
- HR-environment and policies

Organisational Culture

Schein defines culture as "the set of shared, taken-for-granted implicit assumptions that a group holds and that determines how it views, thinks about, and reacts to its various environments" (Schein, 1996:236). He adds that norms are a manifestation of this, but that it is important to know that these norms go back to the underlying assumption most of the members with the same culture, for example employees within an organisation, never question (Schein, 1996). Buelens *et al.* make a link between organisational values, which underlie organisational cultures, and reward norms. Organisations that are characterised by collegial values like teamwork, participation, commitment, will have more egalitarian reward norms. Elitist values, which are mainly expressed by authority, are more linked with equitable reward norms, like pay the job and pay-for-performance (Buelens *et al.*, 2002). Kerr and Slocum even go further by assuming that cultures emerge from reward systems. Hierarchy-based pay systems, featured by formal salary structures, limited bonus amounts and important degrees of freedom for the line management, lead to clan cultures. The most important dimensions of these cultures are socialisation, relationships and collectivism. On the other hand, market based cultures are strongly based on purely contractual relationships, which makes relations more distant. These cultures originate from more quantitative, formula-based pay systems in which individual performance measures play a real key role.

Figure 3.2. Linking pay systems with corporate cultures

	Hierarchy-based	Performance-based
Reward System	• **Salary**: determined through a formal structure and plan • **Bonus**: relatively limited; based on corporate performance; rewards the team • **Performance management**: managers' jobs only broadly defined; performance defined quantitatively and qualitatively (e.g. interdivisional cooperation, long-term relations with customers, style) • **Leadership**: superiors are free to define the important aspects of the roles and play a critical role for the careers and success within the firm; frequent informal feedback	• **Salary**: promotion is directly related to specific performance criteria • **Bonus**: very significant part, based on individual performance • **Performance management**: managers' jobs specifically defined; accountability for results; evaluations are formula-based, few mechanisms for integration between divisions • **Leadership**: infrequent informal interactions, subordinate manager is not dependent on the supervisor for interpretation of results, autonomy

	Clan	Market
Culture	• Based on socialisation and internalised values and norms • Long and thorough socialisation process • Fraternal relationships • Collective rather than individual initiative • Older employees serve as mentors and role models • Considerable pressure to conform • Does not generate risk taking, innovation, feelings of personal ownership	• Contractual relationship • Increased performance levels exchanged for increased rewards as specified in a schedule • No common set of expectations regarding management style, members do not feel constrained by norms or values • Limited influence of superior on subordinate's rewards • Relations among peers are distant

(Based on Kerr & Slocum, 2005)

Strategy

The next element that should be taken into account when considering the internal environment and its effects on pay strategies, is the organisational strategy. We have noticed that many misunderstandings occur regarding what strategy exactly means. Therefore, we will start with an overview of the various underlying dimensions as well as the sequence, from *mission* to *actions*, over strategy.

- Mission: reason for the existence of the organisation; describes what the organisation does for whom.
- Vision: the overall direction the organisation has adopted; a feeling of movement towards a desired future.
- Strategy: choices that have been made concerning the way to achieve the organisation's vision.
- Goals: identification of the general ends within a time frame of 3 to 5 years.
- Objectives: short term targets for each goal.
- Actions: make objectives clearer by assigning responsibilities, time frames, etc. (Zuckerman, 1998).

For a proper understanding, it is also necessary to explain into further details what strategy is exactly about. Strategy has three underlying dimensions:

- Corporate strategy: answers the question *which business are we in?*
- Business unit strategy: *how will we compete?* For example, quality, efficiency, client relationships, development of new products.
- Functional strategy: whereas corporate and business unit strategy is mainly about strategy formulation, functional strategies are about the implementation of the above-mentioned strategies. Some examples include marketing strategy, human resources strategy and also reward strategy (Gerhart & Rynes, 2003).

There is quite a lot of research material that has studied the link between organisational strategies, pay strategies and systems. However, the current research is quite limited. First of all, the bulk of attention has been moved onto incentive schemes. Moreover, most of the studies have only taken into account the executive levels. As a consequence, it is difficult to generalise below these levels. The following paragraphs will summarise those findings about the alignment between pay strategies and corporate strategy on the one hand, and business unit strategy on the other hand.

Research has demonstrated that there are important distinctions in pay strategy according to the *corporate strategy*, being the degree of diversification. More concretely, corporate strategy was measured by the percentage of sales coming from the different product lines. The following categories were defined: single product, dominant product, related product and unrelated product. Unsurprisingly, organisations which are characterised by a high degree of diversification, need pay systems that communicate the *common good*. This is achieved through highly centralised systems in which external equity plays an important role. The figure below gives a synthesis of the findings, taking into account both strategy extremes.

Figure 3.3. Linking pay systems with corporate strategies

Low degree of diversification	High degree of diversification
• Relatively lower pay levels • More emphasis on incentives • Skill-based pay • Internal consistency - egalitarianism • Decentralisation of compensation decisions • Participation in the development of pay systems • Long-term orientation	• Higher pay levels • More emphasis on base pay and benefits • Job-based pay • External consistency • Centralisation • Higher degree of secrecy

(Based on Gerhart & Rynes, 2003)

Another finding is that pay should be more linked to the business unit results in highly diversified firms. In the case of less diversified firms, or when business units have to work closely together, pay should be linked with the overall corporate performance. As far as performance outcomes are concerned, the companies' growth is higher in terms of performance if those incentive systems exist (Gerhart & Rynes, 2003).

Boyd & Salamin were able to refine further the model thanks to their study within two financial institutions in Europe. They have found that bonuses should be considered as the favourite strategic weapon. They advise on relying on base pay to preserve consistency and on bonuses to promote flexibility (Boyd & Salamin, 2001).

Research has not only provided arguments for a fit between corporate strategy and pay policies, but also for a fit between *business unit strategy* and pay policies. More concretely, incentives seem to be more valuable in organisations that follow a prospector strategy. The underlying logic is the following: there is greater uncertainty because new markets and products are focused on. As such, the managerial discretion is higher, which requires the use of pay instruments in order to align interests with the promotion of risk-taking. Furthermore, it has been found that prospectors, who put a stress on stock-based remuneration, got a better financial performance. Also, a positive link was found between adopting a defender strategy and putting more emphasis on short-term incentives. The findings also suggest that some characteristics of administration go hand in hand, such as centralisation, secrecy and limited levels of employee involvement. Furthermore, broad-banded pay systems seem to fit better with innovation strategies (Gerhart & Rynes, 2003).

Figure 3.4 provides us with a synthesis.

Figure 3.4. Linking pay systems with business unit strategies

	Cost leadership-defender	Differentiator-prospector
Characteristics	• Searching for economies of scale • Routinisation • Efficiency • Procedures • Centralised decision-making • Limited and stable product-lines • High volume and market penetration	• Seeking to be the first of market • Product or service innovations • Flexibility • Rapid response to changing conditions • Decentralised decision-making • Broad, changing product lines
	⇩	⇩
Pay strategy & system	• Salary and benefits above the market • Emphasis on salary and benefits • Bases for pay: job, membership, individual performance, short-term, corporate performance, hierarchy • Administration: centralised, secrecy, management decides, bureaucratic	• Salary and benefits below the market, salary and incentives above the market • Emphasis on incentives • Bases for pay: skills, performance, aggregate performance, division performance, egalitarianism • Administration: decentralised, openess, employee participation, flexibility

(Based on Gerhart & Rynes, 2003)

There are two important additional insights that refine further the model of strategic alignment. First, it has been evidenced that pay strategies and systems in turn, have an impact on business unit strategy (Gerhart & Rynes, 2003): this means there is a two-way causal relationship. For example, stock ownership for senior managers implies greater spending on research and development. On the other hand, too much emphasis on short term performance for determining senior managers' pay, leads to less research-related spending. However, stock based compensation also has its limits. The research carried out on this topic has evidenced that stock ownership increased the risk taking by senior managers, which is not always in the interest of the company (Rynes & Gerhart, 2000). Secondly, it should be taken into account that the various environmental factors can influence each other; they might prevail much more in specific situations as well. For example, organisational goals, which belong to the internal environment, can overrule national cultural norms, which are part of the external environment. In this respect, Chen has studied many situations in which the priorities of organisational goal required pay strategies in contradiction with the broader normative beliefs and values of a nation. Due to the priorities of organisational goal, it was found that US employees preferred collective and individual equality as a basis for the allocation of rewards. Chinese employees on the other hand, preferred performance-and job-related needs and were in favour of differentiation. In other words, US respondents had a stronger humanistic orientation whereas Chinese people expressed stronger differential preferences, which contradicted the prevailing national norms and cultures (Chen, 1995)

Share Ownership Structure

Share ownership structures seem to play a key role in pay design, mainly at the senior management levels. For example, equity-based compensation prevails more in case of institutional ownership (Gomez-Mejia *et al.*, 2003).

In relation to share ownership, there is also the situation in which the organisation is a subsidiary whose shares lie in the hands of another organisation located abroad. The parent company can play an important role with respect to pay design in the subsidiary: different approaches seem to appear. *Exporters* strive for a strong alignment and unification of pay processes and procedures, leaving the subsidiaries with almost inexistent degrees of freedom. The main logic underlying this approach is that the use of the headquarters' pay systems will lead to efficiency and create a common mindset. At the opposite, *adapters* aim at creating compensation systems adapted to local contexts and cultures. They leave subsidiaries with important degrees of freedom. In between both, *globalisers* implement common pay systems across their subsidiaries, but they do not consider the home country as the archetype. Each approach seems to have its advantages and drawbacks. Moreover, a link can be made with the organisational strategy. Organisations with a differentiation strategy will be more in favour of an adapter approach, whereas single product strategies are more suitable with the exporter approaches (Bloom *et al.*, 2003).

Size

In many cases, the size of the company plays an important role in the field of pay levels. One might question the logic underlying this relationship at lower hierarchical levels. At managerial levels, there are some arguments which make a link between size and pay. First of all, large firms tend to have more hierarchical levels. As pay increases with promotion, companies with more hierarchical levels also tend to have higher pay levels. Secondly, managerial actions that increase efficiency per unit, will have a huge performance effect on larger firms. Thirdly, managerial jobs in larger firms can be described by larger responsibilities and more complexity. Finally, the supply of managerial talent for large firms is more restricted (Gomez-Mejia *et al.*, 1987).

Profitability

Higher profit margins and/or a higher degree of profitability will in most of the cases, have a positive influence on pay levels. This has to do with affordability. However, we should not overestimate the influence of profitability on the pay levels of executives. Many studies in this field have demonstrated that size is the main determinant and that performance of the firm has little or no effect on pay levels (Gomez-Mejia *et al.*, 1987).

Life Cycle

The life cycle concept can apply to the whole organisation as well as to its underlying business units. While some business units are active in a mature market, others might just enter new markets. This should also have an impact on the pay systems of the managers and, to a certain degree, of the employees belonging to these units. In the *start-up* phase, base pay levels as well as other incentives and benefits are very limited because the organisation has to re-invest the profit it gets. Long-term incentives play a key role and are an important instrument for aligning the interests of the employees with the interests of the organisation. The next phase, *growth*, is characterised by average levels of base pay, but as well by important long-term incentives. Short-term incentives become more popular as well as plans which associate pay with performance over three to five years. In the *maturity* phase, budgets and internal financial measures prevail. Consequently, short-term incentives are the most important pay element at this stage (Ellig, 2002). Performance measures which are used in pay systems will also differ according to the life cycle. During the growth phase, incentive systems should reward growth in revenues whereas bottom-line profit-related measures will mostly prevail during the maturity phase.

HR Environment and Policies

As mentioned above, first, there is a huge need for more and better horizontal alignment between pay strategies and systems, and secondly between rewarding and the other HR processes. First of all, the pay system should reflect the broader *HR strategy*. It should make clear what the critical roles and skills are, the working practices the organisation needs to support and whether team working is essential to achieve business goals.

The *organisation structure* is another element that should be taken into account. For example, research has evidenced that team-based pay is more efficient in organisations with stand-alone and sustainable teams with agreed standards and autonomy, whose members have got an interdependent work (Holbeche, 2001). Furthermore, broad-banded pay structures are more appropriate in flatter organisations. The same applies for organisations that want to stimulate horizontal job rotation. Narrow-graded structures can be a key obstacle if people want and have to move throughout the organisation. Organisations which also pay attention to career management should opt for career families because these will help the individual to learn which activities and competencies should be developed in order to gain pace through the career paths, which will also have an impact on pay levels.

Another important dimension of the HR dimension, are line management's *leadership* capabilities. Organisations in which line management is not very competent in evaluating and coaching people, could be better off using seniority-based pay systems in order to avoid counter-productive discussions and mistrust. On the other hand, if line management is well-trained in coaching, performance-related pay systems will help to strengthen the message they want to bring.

Finally, the *HR maturity level* of the organisation should be also taken into account. It does not make any sense to develop high-tech pay programs, associating pay with performance and competencies, in organisations lacking good underlying performance and competence management systems as well as line management capabilities.

Pay Strategy

After the scan of the external and internal environments, the necessary information has been gathered in order to develop a pay strategy, which can be viewed as the filter between the environment, and the more concrete and operational pay systems. This is a very difficult exercise in which important decisions on priorities have to be made. Furthermore, one should be able to describe thoroughly the relevant aspects of the environment as well as translating them into pay strategies.

According to our experience, many organisations have pay strategies that make no real choices and result more from a vague enumeration of common sense and market practices. In fact, a pay strategy should be a declaration of intent, providing direction and explaining which point the organisation wants to reach in the long-term with its pay policies. Therefore, it should be based on a gap analysis between what needs to be done and what is going on (Armstrong & Stephens, 2005). In addition to the long-term objectives, the pay strategy should also give clear and concise answers to the following questions:

- *How much to pay?* The pay strategy should make clear what the (intended) market position is, with regard to base pay, variable pay as well as total compensation.

- *How to pay?* An organisation should decide on the relative importance of the different pay instruments and the way to use them. Administrative and other supporting processes should also be part of the pay strategy.

- *What to pay for?* Organisations can pay for long-term performance, short-term performance, profitability, customer satisfaction, competence development, individual or more aggregated results, etc. Clear choices need to be made.

Pay strategies combine both the strategic level, linking pay management to the long-term business strategy and the managerial level, in which the horizon of 3 to 5 years is taken into account (Tichy, Fombrun, Devanna, 1982).

Pay Structures and Systems

Once the pay strategy has been determined and developed, the more operational-technical pay activities can start. Decisions should be made on the basis of determining job value; jobs and/or roles should be analysed and assessed, grade structures should be developed, bonus systems should be implemented, etc. this chapter does not aim at going into details on those technical matters. We advice the reader on looking at chapter 2.1 where we have given a thorough overview on pay structures and pay systems.

While pay strategies are related to the strategic and managerial levels, pay systems exist at the operational level (Tichy *et al.*, 1982).

Results

What are the results of pay systems? Broadly speaking, they should lead to satisfaction, motivation, financial performance, recruitment, retention and sustainability, among the most important of them.

Once the pay systems are in use, these outcomes should be frequently monitored in order to check whether they are still in line with culture, strategy, etc. and whether they lead to the desired behaviours. According to our experience, organisations do not sufficiently monitor the functioning and outcomes of their pay systems. The pay audit tool that was developed and which underlies the different case studies dealt with in this book can help organisations in this respect.

It should also be mentioned that the model in Figure 3.1 is a closed loop. We mean that once the pay systems have been developed and monitored, it might be needed to adapt elements of the internal environment, the pay strategy or even the pay systems themselves in order to ensure the realisation of the organisation's objectives.

Strategic Rewarding in Practice

In this chapter, a synthesis was made concerning the different factors that can have an influence on the design of pay systems as well as the way those influence the pay strategies and systems. As mentioned above, we do not know about any field research that has paid attention to the factors in the external and internal environment which play a role and to what degree they do so. In order to give a preliminary answer to this fundamental question, an investigation was organised by the Strategic Rewards Research Centre in which more than 30 organisations participated. First of all, we have found that none of the factors seem to play a key role. At the managerial level, in a decreasing order of importance, regulation, labour market, pay history, the strategy of the group the organisation is part of, the corporate strategy, pay practices of competitors, business unit strategy, profitability, economic situation, HR strategy, play a relatively important role. On the other hand, not one factor seems to be very important. We can conclude that a mix of internal and external drivers plays a role, at the level of managerial employees. Surprisingly enough, we also found that employees' opinions play a meaningless role. The same applies for societal values and norms.

When we focus on operational employees' pay systems, the main factors that play a role are linked to the external environment. More concretely, the most important factors are collective bargaining at sectoral level and national level, regulation, competitors, and the economic climate. The only internal element which plays a relatively important role is the organisation's pay history. In the case of operational employees, the employees' opinion is even the least important element. Elements that could be considered to be relatively strategic, like the organisation's people management capabilities, the phase in the life cycle and the business unit's profitability, are part of the least important factors (Baeten, 2005). This also makes clear that organisations should strive to free up some strategic space in order to obtain a better alignment between the internal environment and the operational employees' pay systems. It seems to prove also that collective bargaining at sectoral level dramatically limits the strategic space. Another conclusion that could be drawn from the results, is that the current situation might differ from the ideal situation, in which much clearer choices are made and in which the internal (strategic) environment plays a much more important role.

Conclusion

This chapter has focused on the employer's perspective on pay systems and has provided the reader with a framework for strategic pay, clarifying the process step-by-step. First of all, it was argued that the role of pay systems has evolved from a more administrative tool in former times, into a strategic one nowadays. Increasingly, pay is viewed as a management system rather than being only a set of techniques. As such, and also because of its role in the strategy implementation, pay actually plays a more eminent role within HR Management. We could even speak of a new management discipline. This strategic role is stressed further by the fact that job design is more flexible and that organisations have less hierarchical levels. In this context, pay systems need to be more flexible and have to be able to translate the organisation's characteristics and objectives into pay systems. This is exactly what strategic pay is about.

However, in practice, it is much more complicated. Defining strategic pay as a way of linking pay systems with strategy, is too narrow. First, a much broader set of contextual factors should be taken into account and which can play a more or less important role dependent on the situation. Among them, here are some examples: organisational and national cultures, phase in the life cycle, shareholder structure, structure of collective bargaining, labour market characteristics, sector and even gender. Secondly, a very important challenge consists in going beyond best fit and developing a pay system which is not only in line with strategy, but also with the other HR processes. Maybe even more important, the reward systems, which consist of financial as well as non-financial instruments, should also be internally aligned and should try to be *unique*, even if this might not seem to be always in line with the organisation's strategy.

Strategic pay management is about having a feeling with and a clear view on the contextual factors, being able to make priorities and clear choices leading to pay strategies. Technical insights and competencies will then enable the pay/reward manager to translate these strategies into concrete pay systems. To conclude, the combination of strategic insights with detailed technical knowledge on pay systems and the association of creativity with these technical tools is a huge challenge for organisation's HR and Reward Management departments.

References

Armstrong, M. & Murlis, H. (2004), *Reward Management*, London: Kogan Page.

Armstrong, M. & Stephens, T. (2005), *Employee Reward Management and Practice*, London: Kogan Page.

Baeten, X. (2005), *Determinants of Remuneration Design*, PowerPoint presentation on the occasion of the meeting "Does Performance Pay?", Strategic Rewards Research Centre, Vlerick Leuven Gent Management School.

Balkin, D.B. & Gomez-Mejia, L.R. (1990), "Matching Compensation and Organisational Strategies", *Strategic Management Journal*, 11, p. 153-169.

Bloom, M. & Michel, J.G. (2002), "The Relationships among Organisational Context, Pay Dispersion, and Managerial Turnover", *Adacemy of Management Journal*, 1, p. 33-42.

Bloom, M.C. & Milkovich, G.T. (1997), "Rethinking International Compensation: From Expatriate and National Cultures to Strategic Flexibility", Working Paper 97-24, Centre for Advanced Human Resource Studies, Cornell University.

Bloom, M.C. & Milkovich, G.T. (1998), "A SHRM Perspective on International Compensation and Reward Systems", Working Paper 98-11, Centre for Advanced Human Resource Studies, Cornell University.

Bloom, M.C., Milkovich, G.T. & Mitra, A. (2003), "International compensation: learning from how managers respond to variations in local host contexts", *International Journal of Human Resource Management*, 14:8, p. 1350-1367.

Boyd, B.K. & Salamin, A. (2001), "Strategic Reward Systems: A Contingency Model of Pay System Design", *Strategic Management Journal*, 8, p. 777-792.

Brown, D. & Armstrong, M. (1999), *Paying for contribution. Real performance-related pay strategies*, London: Kogan Page.

Buelens, M., Kreitner, R. & Kinicki, A. (2002), *Organisational Behaviour*, New York: McGraw Hill.

Chen, C.C. (1995), "New Trends in Rewards Allocation Preferences: A Sino-U.S. Comparison", *Academy of Management Journal*, 38, 2, p. 408-428.

Delaney, J.T. & Huselid, M.A. (1996), "The Impact of Human Resource Management Practices on Perceptions of Organisational Performance", *Academy of Management Journal*, 39, 4, p. 949-969.

Ellig, B.R. (2002), *The Complete Guide to Executive Compensation*, New York: McGraw-Hill.

Gerhart, B.A. & Rynes, S.L. (2003), *Compensation: Theory, evidence, and strategic implications*, London: Sage Publications.

Gomez-Mejia, L.R., Larraza-Kintana, M. & Makri, M. (2003), "The Determinants of Executive Compensation in Family-Controlled Public Corporations", *Academy of Management Journal*, 46, 2, p. 226-237.

Gomez-Mejia, L.R., Tosi, H.L. & Hinkin, T. (1987), "Managerial Control, Performance, and Executive Compensation", *Academy of Management Journal*, 30, p. 51-70.

Heneman, R.L., Fay, C.H. & Wang, Z.-M. (2002), "Compensation Systems in the Global Context", in R.L. Heneman (ed.), *Strategic reward management: design, implementation and evaluation*, Connecticut: Information Age Publishing, p. 5-34.

Henderson, R.I. (2003), *Compensation Management in a Knowledge-Based World*, New Jersey: Prentice-Hall.

Holbeche, L. (2001), *Aligning Human Resources and Business Strategy*, Oxford: Elsevier.

Huselid, M.A. (1995), "The Impact of Human Resource Management Practices on Turnover, Productivity, and Corporate Financial Performance", *Academy of Management Journal*, 38, 3, p. 635-672.

Ivancevich, J.M. (2003), *Human Resource Management*, New York: McGraw-Hill.

Kerr, J. & Slocum, J.W. (2005), "Managing corporate culture through reward systems", Academy of Management Executive, 19, 4, p. 130-138.

Ledford, G.E. & Heneman, R.L. (2002), "Compensation: A Troublesome Lead System in Organisational Change", in R.L. Heneman (ed.), *Strategic Reward Management: Design, Implementation and Evaluation*, Connecticut: Information Age Publishing, p. 259-272.

Martocchio, J.J. (2001), *Strategic compensation: a human resource management approach*, New Jersey: Prentice-Hall.

Meijer, J. (2004), "Vrouw verdient gemiddeld 5% minder dan man", *De Morgen*, 17.11.2004.

Mermet, E. (2001), *Wage formation in Europe*, European Trade Union Institute, Brussels: ETUI.

Rynes, S.L. & Gerhart, B.A. (2000), *Compensation in Organisations: Current Research and Practice*, San Francisco: Jossey-Bass.

Schein, E.H. (1996), "Culture: The Missing Concept in Organisation Studies", *Administrative Science Quarterly*, 41, p. 229-240.

Tichy, N.M., Fombrun, C.J. & Devanna, M.A. (1982), "Strategic Human Resource Management", *Sloan Management Review*, 23, p. 47-61.

Welbource, T.M. (1997), "Pay for What Performance? Lessons From Firms Using the Role-Based Performance Scale", Working Paper 97-26, Centre for Advanced Human Resource Studies, Cornell University.

www.e-reward.co.uk, 27 October 2004.

www.lincolnelectric.com, 27 February 2006.

Yanadori, Y. & Milkovich, G.T. (2003), "Minimising Competition? Entry-level Compensation in Japanese Firms", Working Paper 03-20, Centre for Advanced Human Resource Studies, Cornell University.

Zuckerman, A.M. (1998), *Healthcare Strategic Planning*, 37, Chicago: Health Administration Press.

The Employee's Perspective on Pay: Equity, Need, Justice, Culture and Categorisation

Ben J.M. EMANS

Introduction

The money earned by an employee represents a value encompassing his/her spending possibilities as well as other important outcomes, such as the status associated with it (Lawler, 1971; Thierry, 1992, 1998). Earnings thus form one of the entities that make one's work worthwhile. They add to the positive side of the balance of benefits and costs of an employment and accordingly influence the employees' willingness to enter, to stay, and to play their role within the organisation. This is, in a nutshell, the employee perspective on pay system design. In order to fit that perspective, a company's pay system has to yield sound cost-benefit balances for all the employees. Viewed from the employee perspective, pay system design thus hinges on the relationship between the money an employee earns on the one hand and his/her willingness to work on the other hand.

This relationship has been the subject of theoretical controversies (see Thierry, 1998, for an overview), with standpoints ranging from the view that monetary rewards can never serve as motivators (the well-known theory of Herzberg, cf. Herzberg, 1968) and may rather undermine the intrinsic motivation of employees (cf. Deci, 1975), to the perspective of man as a *homo economicus*, subjected to the straightforward rule of "the more you are earning, the more you get motivated" (cf. Lazear, 2000). Today's consensus seems to be heading toward the economic position (see discussions by Wruck, 2000 and Ledford & Heneman, 2000). That is not to say, however, that the relationship between pay and work motivation is an uncomplicated one. Far from being a linear issue, it encompasses a number of different psychological factors. Below, we will discuss five of these factors, referred to as equity, need, culture & power, procedural justice and social categorisation respectively. Simultaneously, we will show how these factors tend to be incorporated in negotiated pay systems.

Equity

A basic concept, as far as the relationship between pay and willingness to work is concerned, is equity (Adams, 1965), or perceived input/output balance. It is an abstract concept, which refers to the balance as experienced by the employees between their 'input' and 'output', that is, between the things they offer the organisation (input) and the things they take from it (output). An employee's input can be equated to the the the entirety of the work he or she accomplishes for the organisation, whereas pay and the values associated with it typically form part of his/her output (together with other valuable entities, such as personal development and social contacts). The equity principle constitutes a basic condition for people's pay satisfaction and willingness to work. Inequity exists when earnings and other outputs are perceived to be either less ore more valuable than the whole of inputs. As far as one's earnings are concerned, this circumstance corresponds to a situation of experienced under- or over-payment. Both situations tend to be disliked by the average employee, who is consequently inclined to redress the balance of equity by adjusting either the input or the output side of the equation. So the motivational force of pay systems results from people's tendency to create, maintain or restore equity. More specifically, it is rooted in the tendency to adjust one's (work)input to the way one's output has been determined by the pay system. Among other things, the art of designing pay systems therefore consists of fixing, for each employee, the output value at a level that matches the required input. This is echoed in the generic term '*compensation*', as used for wages, which are supposed to compensate for delivered work. In short, output has to compensate input[1].

Abstractly worded as it is here, the equity requirement seems to constitute a rather straightforward problem, consisting of a simple input-output equation to be solved. The problem, however, is actually nearly impossible to solve, because the parameters of the input side of the equation (the parameters representing the value of the whole of the

---

[1]   In compensation literature the twin concepts of internal and external equity are used. These concepts are akin to, but different from equity as it is conceptualised here. The common element in the concepts is that each of them refers to input/output ratios. The internal/external equity concept relates to the comparison of an employee's own ratio with corresponding ratios of colleagues inside (internal equity) or outside (external equity) the organisation. These comparisons contribute to the assessment of an individual employee's output/input ratio as being positive or negative. The more basic equity concept, as it is used here, just refers to the outcome of this assessment, encompassing all facts and considerations (such as internal and external comparisons) that contribute to it. Social comparison, as a basis for pay appreciation, is discussed below in the section about social categorisation.

employee's work efforts) are hard to assess, for employees no less than for employers.

To put it in a simple way, the value of an employee's (work) input can be said to equal his/her contribution to the organisation's value creation. As such, it may vary from low, or even negative, to high, being the outcome of a diversity of commodities put into the organisation, such as time, effort, performances, initiatives, courage, expertness, experience, talents, stress endurance, undergoing hardships, running safety risks, educational background and resources of any kind. In most instances, though, this contribution is hard to identify and to assess. This has mainly to do with the task-interdependencies that exist among employees, as a result of which the whole of their contributions can never be fully disentangled as pockets of individual contributions. The input side of the equity equation can therefore only be a matter of esti-mation. In fact, it can only be tentatively inferred from the invested time, expertise and other commodities. This gives rise to a number of ques-tions which need to be answered in order to solve the input/output equation, without the availability, however, of objective answers.

Qualitative problem: equity parameters

First, there is a qualitative question to be posed about the selection of commodity parameters in the input side of the equation: which underly-ing commodities have, or do not have, to be considered? For instance, the main difference between so-called 'algorithmic' and 'experiential' pay philosophies (Gomez-Mejia, 1992), has bearing on the commodities that are, or are not valued, with the experiential philosophy stressing commodities such as individual performances, team performances, and the performance of the organisation as a whole, and the algorithmic philosophy emphasising commodities such as job type, seniority and educational level of individual employees. Gomez-Mejia & Balkin (1992) describe these philosophies as two opposite endpoints of a continuum, the last one (experiential), in contrast to the first one (algo-rithmic), representing a flexible approach of compensation, meant to contribute to the organisation's adaptability to external developments. What is illustrated here, is that the selection of commodity parameters is a matter of managerial choice, rather than an objectively given matter of fact.

Quantitative problem: equity paradigms

Second, there is a quantitative question to be posed about the algo-rithms applied to the parameters selected: how to translate the defined inter-employee input differences into inter-employee pay differences, that is, how to weigh the different commodity-parameters that have been selected? In the most extreme case, all the parameters are given the weight zero. In that case, the equity formula degenerates into an equality formula. No input-related pay differences then result. All the other solutions imply some degree of non-equality, that is, of pay differentiation. Depending on the solution chosen, the resulting non-equality may be large or small and more or less related to each of the selected input commodities.

Solving the qualitative and the quantitative problems

Decisive guidelines for answering both questions, the qualitative and the quantitative one, are hardly available, as can be demonstrated by the many different answers given to them in different cultures. This does not, however, release the designers of pay systems from the task of justifying the given answers objectively. In order to solve the resulting paradox, they are left no choice but to refer to all imaginable kinds of reasons, facts and evidences, by making use, for instance, of systems designed for job analysis, which are supposed to determine in a calculation-like way, applying quantitative formulas, the value of different job types. Due to their sheer existence, systems such as these, especially when they acquire a bench-mark status and are shared by multiple companies, serve as a tool for justifying systems of pay differentiation. For employees they consequently serve as a tool to derive their pay satisfaction level.

When being asked about the amount of money they earn, people often do not exactly know what to answer. Thierry (2005), for instance, refers to research outcomes which show that only 60% of the people employed have some idea about their net income. This curious fact seems to contradict the claim that equity is a basic condition for pay satisfaction: how can employees assess whether there is equity, that is, whether they are under- or overpaid, if they have no idea of their actual salaries? The answer is that equity is a perceptual phenomenon. As is the case with perceptions in general, they result from multiple, more or less sharp and more or less blurred cues. The feelings one has about the genuine value of one's own job and of one's own performance, are most often blurred, and may therefore play only a secondary role in the coming about of equity, regardless of how relevant they are in themselves. In contrast, the reassuring knowledge that these values are assessed in accordance with some benchmark, stands out as a sharp cue, and can consequently generate equity feelings.

Need

The justification for pay differentiation becomes more complicated when next to the equity principle a second principle, namely need, is taken into account. Earnings are not only a matter of input compensation. In addition to an employee's input, his or her need for money may also be viewed as a justification for his/her pay level. This is reflected in the terms '*livelihood*' or '*living*' as used for the income one earns. This term reflects the fact that wages are being paid simply in order to enable employees to live: as a counterpart of the input-output match, a match between the employees' necessities of life on the one hand, and their spending capacities on the other hand, has to be achieved. This is the need principle. Just as is the case with the equity principle, it gives rise to both a qualitative and a quantitative question.

The qualitative question now is the following: which attributes of an employee's life have to be taken into account when assessing his/her need-for-living? Features such as age, number of children and home-work distance are among those that may therefore be included as parameters in a pay system. The subsequent quantitative question then regards the way in which these parameters are handled, and the weight they are given. The definition of some bottom line is at stake here: disregarding whatever specificities, what is the pay level needed by every employee? Specific need parameters may be introduced thereafter to calculate additional need levels.

In sum, pay system design, viewed from the employee's perspective, first implies deciding on the selection of input and need parameters, and second, determining the algorithms for dealing with these parameters. Entirely rational rules do not exist for making these decisions. The paradox is that the conclusions resulting from them need nonetheless to be appreciated as being reasonable by the employees involved.

Designing pay systems is therefore to a high degree an exercise of justification aimed at giving the people involved the confidence that equity is realised and needs are respected. From a motivational point of view pay systems have to be designed in such a way that they do instil that confidence. The psychology underlying the design of pay systems thus does not so much deal with equity and need fulfilment as objective states of affairs, but more with perceptual dynamics. A pressing question therefore is: how do perceptions of equity and need fulfilment come about? In the following sections, three psychological entities that shape these perceptions will be dealt with in depth.

Culture and Power

Perceptions of equity and need, malleable as they are, are culturally embedded. In a sense, they reflect the views about what is valuable and required held by people who share some national or organisational culture. In order to understand pay systems from an employee's point of view, one therefore has to take into account the way in which the surrounding culture is experienced by the employees. Furthermore, related to the impact of culture, there is the impact of existing power relationships between interest groups involved (unions, professional associations and others) who may, or may not, set their stamp on the culture. A pay system simply has to be adapted to its surrounding culture in order to produce adequate levels of equity and need-satisfaction as experienced by employees. This forms part of what in post-institutional economics is called the working of 'institutional forces' (for applications to pay issues see Gerhart & Rynes, 2003:16-17, 88-89). Due to these forces, for instance, a substantial pay differentiation between high and normal performers is more easily negotiable in the UK than it is in continental Europe, whereas in Germany, more than elsewhere, sticking to bureaucratic grade systems based on job-related pay seems to be an unquestioned basic principle in pay negotiations. On the other hand, in France, Italy and Spain employees' competencies may play a relatively important role in establishing pay levels (Brown, 2000). Referring to these institutional forces is the most straightforward way of justification that system designers have at their disposal. Therefore, on behalf of their own distinctive cultures, countries and companies can largely diverge as regards the shape and importance of both equity and need formulas that are being applied.

Cultures and customs, however, are not unequivocal and fixed entities. To some extent they are being moulded and interpreted in a never ending process. Part of designing pay systems consequently consists of shaping culture to such a degree that these systems' parameters and algorithms come to be judged as acceptable, if not self-evident, by the parties involved. Two behavioural theories, to be dealt with below, can be applied to elucidate this process. Their focal points are procedural justice and social categorisation respectively, two entities that, viewed from the employee perspective, stand out by themselves as building blocks of pay systems.

Procedural Justice

When actors agree on procedures to be followed in a decision-making process, and when these rules are strictly followed, the outcomes of that process tend to acquire a status of justification, no matter how justifiable they may be in fact (Folger & Cropanzano, 1998: chapter 5). This is the essence of procedural justice. When applied to payment systems it has been demonstrated to add to employees' pay satisfaction (McFarlin & Sweeney, 1992; Folger & Konovsky, 1989; Greenberg, 1987).

Folger and Greenberg (1985), who introduced the concept of procedural justice into the HRM field, identified four dimensions applicable to compensation-systems. Two of them represent opportunities for 'voice', a term coined by Hirschman (1970) to denote attempts to influence decisions that affect one's own situation. Voice-opportunity dimensions are related to two steps in the pay-decision-making process. One applies to the input phase of that process, when decisions are made with regard to the specific commodities that are evaluated and the way in which these commodities are valued. Employees may, to a higher or lower degree, be involved in these decisions. This is called the *participation* dimension. High participation reflects a high level of procedural justice. The second voice-opportunity dimension applies to the last phase of decision-making, when the individual payment decision is finally made. Employees may, to a higher or lower degree, be entitled to raise their voice against that decision. This is called the *recourse* dimension. Recourse, just like participation, lies at the core of procedural justice.

In addition to the voice dimensions Folger and Greenberg have identified *accuracy of information* (in full: accuracy of the information that underlies the pay decisions) as a third dimension of procedural justice. The information used by the decision makers may be more or less verifiable, more or less complete and more or less reliable. The more this kind of accuracy is guaranteed, the more the employees involved will have a sense of procedural justice. It is important to note that it is not the relevance of the information that is at stake here. Relevance is not measurable. Without the availability of decisive guidelines it is always open to discussion (see the above-mentioned about equity and need parameters). Its elusiveness can be said to be compensated by the objectivity of the accuracy parameter.

Finally, as a fourth dimension of procedural justice, Folger and Greenberg have identified *transparency*. Transparency, as applied to reward systems, means that it is made clear to the employee which aspects of his/her work, experience and other types of input are taken into account in the decision-making process and in what way they are processed. Having the opportunity to monitor the decision-making processes as a result of a fair amount of transparency, employees may feel confident that the procedures will be applied properly, resulting in consistent and fair decisions.

Pay systems tend to be rather bureaucratised phenomena. This is the direct result of the need to create procedural justice. Rules with respect to the involvement of employees in the decision-making processes, the publication of the outcomes of these processes, the assessment of performances and the analysis of jobs are just examples of tools for bringing about the required participation, recourse, information accuracy and transparency (see the elaborated example in Van Tuyll, Kleingeld, & Rutten, 2002). From the employees' point of view, the resulting bureaucracy, notwithstanding its drawbacks, is thus a necessary condition for pay satisfaction and motivation.

Social Categorisation

A truly fundamental condition for perceived equity and need with respect to payment decisions is the conception of the employees according to which people similar to them are paid equally. Generally speaking, people tend to compare themselves with similar other people in order to assess their own situation (Festinger, 1954). This raises the important question: who is considered to be (dis)similar to whom? Are blue collars comparable to white collars? Seniors to juniors? Full-timers to part-timers? Middle managers to top-managers? There is not any objective answer to this kind of questions (apart from those derivable from some general equal opportunities legislation). They have to be answered in detail, though, when pay differences among categories of jobs or among categories of employees have to be explained. What is required therefore is a vocabulary, shared by all members of the organisation, with labels indicating the homogeneous categories of employees that (are said to) exist within the company as well as across the company's borders.

**Figure 3.5. Relevant factors of pay system design,
viewed from the employee perspective**

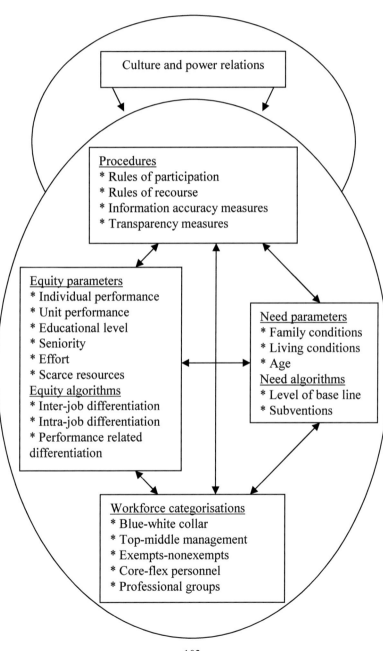

This is reflected in a number of aspects of pay systems as they are found in companies. First, it is reflected in the existence of two, three or even more separate pay systems for different employee categories, with the distinction between exempts and non-exempts being the most eye-catching one. Differences between these pay systems tend to be related to pay levels, the degree of pay-differentiation, and bases for pay-differentiation. The taken-for-grantedness of the distinction between exempts and non-exempts, or between other employee categories, is an essential condition for justifying each of these differences. Second, within each separate pay system a number of categories of functions are usually defined, with each of them having its own wage-limits. Grades, with their bottom and top values, are then linked to each category. Third, across the company borders, categories of employees are defined, such as specific professional groups that are viewed and treated as special species of employees. In terms of social comparison theory, these three work force categorisation systems together define which other people serve as 'comparison others' to each individual employee. As such, they help to simplify the equity and need assessment questions. These linguistically embedded categorisations therefore form part of a company's pay strategy, just as the rules of procedural justice do.

Conclusion

In sum, we come to the conclusion that a pay system, in order to fit the employees' perspective, that is, to induce the employees' pay satis-faction and job motivation, has to consist of an appropriate amalgam of a well-chosen selection of equity and need parameters, together with carefully elaborated algorithms for dealing with these parameters, and supplemented with properly designed procedures as well as widely accepted workforce categorisations. 'Appropriate' does not only mean that the parameters, algorithms, procedures and categorisations them-selves are positively appreciated by the employees, but also that they fit in with each other as well as with the existing culture and power rela-tions. In Figure 3.5 the resulting decision space of system designers who want to take the employee perspective into account is presented, includ-ing the most common options that exist for each of its components. The 'tree-like' representation of pay systems, as unfolded in chapter 2, can be easily recognised. It shows that, rather than the separate components, it is the Gestalt of those components together that shapes the nature of a company's pay system, and consequently determines the way in which it fits in with the perspective of the employees.

Two final remarks need to be made. First, the way in which the em-ployees' perspective is conceptualised here is different from the way in which employees themselves, or their representatives, tend to word it.

Unions, for instance, when negotiating pay systems, tend to bargain about pay levels and – in doing so – put forward need and equity arguments for defining the appropriateness of the pay levels. Their arguments are presented as being self-evident. In that respect, they are not any different from those of the employers, who, in order to define the appropriateness of the pay levels, also put forward their own self-evident arguments (related to the firm's profitability, or its strategy, for instance). Far from representing an objective state of affairs, however, this self-evidence, as far as it exists, is linked to the taken-for-grantedness of cultural norms, procedures and categorisations. Culture, procedures and categorisations thus also have to be taken into account, if we want to understand the employee perspective, no matter how un-mentioned these entities tend to be when employee representatives give their views.

Second, the way the employees' perspective is conceptualised here is also slightly different from the way issues, such as work motivation and pay satisfaction, are explained in psychological and economic theories. Excellent overviews of these theories are given elsewhere (*cf.* Gerhard & Rynes, 2003:48-151; Thierry, 1998, 2002). Most of them (*e.g.* agency theory, expectancy theory, equity theory, goal setting theory) relate pay levels to levels of work motivation, work performance and pay satisfaction. From this basis onwards they all fit in with the formula of input/output balance, inherent in the equity concept. In addition, and similar to what is mentioned above, the concept of procedural justice tends to be included in the theory overviews. This chapter was not intended to redo these overviews. Instead, an attempt was made to picture the employee's perspective on pay systems by including factors that can be derived from familiar theories, and complementing the resulting scheme with other factors that impact on the employees' appreciation of pay systems. As such, this chapter offers a more inclusive overview of factors to be considered by pay system designers when taking the employee perspective into account. In the pay system audit model that is mentioned elsewhere in this book (see chapters 2.2 and 4.3.2) all of these factors are incorporated.

References

Adams (1965), "Inequity in social exchange", in L. Berkowitz (ed.), *Advances in experimental social psychology*, Vol. 2, New York: Academic Press, p. 267-300.

Brown, D. (2000), "The third way; the future of pay and rewards strategies in Europe", *Worldatwork Journal*, 9(7), p. 15-24.

Deci, E.L. (1975), *Intrinsic Motivation*. New York: Plenum.

Festinger (1954), "A theory of social comparison processes", *Human Relations*, 7, p. 117-140.

Folger, R. & Cropanzano, R. (1998), *Organisational justice and human resource management*, Thousand Oaks: Sage Publications.

Folger, R. & Greenberg, J. (1985), "Procedural justice: an interpretive analysis of personnel systems", *Personnel and Human Resources Management*, 3, p. 141-183.

Folger R. & Konovsky, M.A. (1989), "Effects of procedural and distributive justice on reactions to pay raise decisions", *Academy of Management Journal*, 32, p. 115-130.

Gerhart, B. & Rynes, S.L. (2003), *Compensation; Theory, Evidence and Strategic Implications*, London: SAGE publications.

Gomez-Mejia, L.R. (1992), "Structure and Process of diversification, compensation strategy and firm performance", *Strategic Management Journal*, 13, p. 381-397.

Gomez-Mejia, L.R. & Balkin, D.B. (1992), *Compensation, Organisational Strategy and Firm Performance*, Cincinnati, OH: South-Western Publishing Company.

Greenberg, J. (1987), "Reactions to Procedural Injustice in Payment Distributions: Do the Means Justify the Ends?", *Journal of Applied Psychology*, 72 (1), p. 55-61.

Heneman, H.G. (1985), "Pay satisfaction", *Research in Personnel and Human Resources Management*, 3, p. 115-139.

Herzberg, F. (1968), "One more time: how do you motivate employees?", *Harvard Business Review*, 46 (1), p. 53-62.

Hirschman, A.O. (1970), *Exit, Voice and Loyalties: Responses to Declines in Firms, Organisations and States*, Cambridge, MA: Harvard University Press.

Lawler, E.E. III (1971), *Pay and Organisational Effectiveness: a Psychological View*, New York: McGraw-Hill.

Lazear, E.P. (2000), "Performance pay and productivity", *American Economic Review*, 90, p. 1346-1361.

Ledford, G.E. & Heneman, H.G. (2000), "Compensation, a troublesome lead system in organisational change", in: M. Beer & N. Nohria (eds.), *Breaking the Code of Change*, Boston: Harvard Business School Press, p. 307-322.

McFarlin, D.B. & Sweeney, P.D. (1992), "Distributive and procedural justice as predictors of satisfaction with personal and organisational outcomes", *The Academy of Management Journal*, 35, p. 626-637.

Van Tuyll, H.F.J.M., Kleingeld, A., Algera, J.A. & Rutten, M.L. (2002), "Performance measurement and pay for performance", in S. Sonnentag (ed.), *Psychological Management of Individual Performance*, New York: John Wiley & Sons, p. 349-370.

Thierry, H. (1992), "Payment: which meanings are rewarding?", *American Behavioral Scientist*, 35, p. 694-707.

Thierry, H. (1998), "Compensating Work", in P.J.D. Drenth, H. Thierry, & Ch. J. de Wolff (eds.), *Handbook of Work and Organisational Psychology*, East Sussex, UK: Psychology Press, Vol. 4, p. 291-319.

Thierry, H. (2002), "Enhancing Performance through Pay and Reward Systems", in S. Sonnentag (ed.), *Psychological Management of Individual Performance*, New York: John Wiley & Sons, p. 325-347.

Thierry, H. (2005), "Bijgeluiden van Belonen" [Pay Noise], *Tijdschrift voor HRM*, 8, p. 61-71.

Wruck, K.H. (2000), "Compensation, incentives and organisational change", in M. Beer & N. Nohria (eds.), *Breaking the Code of Change*, Boston: Harvard Business School Press, p. 296-305.

CHAPTER 3.3

Unions, Employers' Associations and Collective Bargaining over Pay

Guy VERNON, Renée ANDERSON,
Xavier BAETEN & Elizabeth NEU

Introduction

Pay arrangements are not merely subject to the attitudes of individual employers and employees, but are subject to social regulation by social actors beyond these categories. This is most particularly the case for non-managerial employees; the bulk of the workforce in all countries.

Within Europe, the governments of nation states typically have some direct role in shaping pay arrangements. A number of the nations of Europe feature statutory pay minima, with those of The Netherlands and France the greatest by any gauge (OECD, 1998, Table 2.3). Yet whilst these particular national minima are in excess of the Federal Minimum in the US, even they are set at levels too low to be of direct significance to the pay arrangements of most larger, or multi-national, employers (Vernon, 2005a). Similarly, whilst in France profit sharing is now mandatory in private sector organisations with a workforce over 50 (Van het Kaar & Grunell, 2001), specific legislative encouragement of pay arrangements is more generally of little import. It is collective bargaining, not statutory regulation, which is of general significance. Employers' associations and unions are the central social actors in shaping pay arrangements. In practice, if not always in principle, works councillors are usually closely associated with unions, and so can reasonably be subsumed with them.

In this context, this chapter first surveys the attitudes of unions and employers' associations to pay and pay structures. Recognising that there is limited use in viewing the attitudes of these interest organisations as free-floating, or in considering attitudes without reference to the formal institutions prevailing, the chapter then turns to examine the manner in which collective bargaining typically confines and shapes pay arrangements in the nations of Europe.

Union perspectives on pay arrangements

Unions have a central place in the shaping of pay arrangements and systems in Europe, and hold more subtle and indeed varying views than is sometimes recognised. In a very general sense, unions do of course simply desire that pay always be higher. However, whilst pay is a central area of union consideration, pay is not unions' only priority. Unions have interests extending well beyond the terrain of pay, to non-pay benefits, work organisation, working conditions, the broader work environment and employment levels. Moreover, they have typically internalised the trade-offs which they face to some extent in the conduct of negotiations, so that for example it is widely understood in union circles that pay should not be pursued without regard to employment consequences (*e.g.* Swenson, 1989).

Given the bluntness of a crude posturing for more pay across the workforce they represent, discussions within unions centre on matters of pay structure and systems. Generally, and a little loosely speaking, unions have tended historically to favour pay structures in which pay depends predominantly on the job role, qualifications, certificated competences, seniority/age or documented experience. Moreover, they have generally sought to contain pay differentials within their bargaining arena. This still tends to be the case, though unions have developed a variety of responses to the discussion burgeoning since the 1980s around variable pay, bonuses and, at its most general, pay-for-performance (PfP). Since pay-for-performance has become such a focus for debate and activity in the field of reward, and since there has been such cross-national and to an extent cross-sectoral variation in union response, it is union attitudes to pay-for-performance specifically which are the focus here.

In many nations, particularly within Europe, employers must typically take some account of the stance of unions towards PfP. Even where this is not necessitated by national or local conditions the views of union representatives can be a useful guide to managers. This is perhaps particularly the case with regard to PfP, as individual employees often conceive such contingent pay in terms of some abstract idealised principle in ignorance of its practical implications.

Unions at different levels in different nations, informed by their various traditions, strategies and purchase, vary in their approach to pay systems. In particular, it is impossible to do justice to the variation in attitudes from the views of the leadership which is present at workplace level within nations. This is of most importance in systems where, as in the UK, there is no great coherence or articulation amongst leadership, full-time officials and local activists. However, meaningful generalisation about the attitudes typical in the unions of the nations of Europe is possible. The importance of the union movement in *Sweden* is in little doubt, despite its traumas in the early 1990s. Its centrality to the employment relationship in Sweden makes the stance of the movement of particular interest in discussion of the attitude of unions to PfP. Swedish industrial unions (*i.e.* sector-wide organisations) and local unions (so-called 'workplace clubs') are generally well articulated and in a position to exert influence on developments. Generally, Swedish unions accept the elimination of the distinction between manual and non-manual employees, increasing differentials, and the individualisation of pay. However, they stress that individualised pay is to be determined by principles negotiated at the level of industry, and applied through local negotiations at the level of the company and workplace (Martin, 1995). Unions are content that job ladders based on competence should determine pay, as long as training is a universal right. Individualisation can then proceed in the sense that individuals can climb at different speeds, but the role of management in determining whether individuals have acquired necessary competence is controlled (Martin, 1995).

Swedish unions are generally rather less keen on PfP, whether it is individualised or based on group or company performance. Outside of the construction industry, Sweden's industrial unions achieved their objective of the replacement of piece rates with time-based pay, including monthly salaries, by the close of the 1980s (Berg, 2000). As piece pay waned, discussion amongst Swedish employers of PfP in other forms spread (Martin, 1995). Swedish unions and their confederations, including LO, the manual employees' confederation, accept PfP in principle although seeking to limit it to 10% of salary and stressing the importance of collective bargaining at all levels (Berg, 2000). They seek 'objective' pay systems in which bonuses are based on clear task-oriented criteria as opposed to subjective management assessments of cooperation or performance. They see this not only as ensuring justice in pay, but as vital if PfP is to encourage the competence development which they see as so important (Kjellberg, 1998).

The approach of unions in the other Nordic nations has been similar in many respects. *Norwegian* unions accept PfP in principle, though seeking to limit its extent and preferring it to be based on group or company performance and insisting on collective bargaining (Van het Kaar & Grunell, 2001). *Danish* unions are rather more receptive to the individualisation of bonuses, but stress the importance of objective measures of performance to avoid discrimination and favouritism (Scheuer, 1998), and take a similar stance in other respects (Van het Kaar & Grunell, 2001). Within *Finnish* unions there is ongoing debate around PfP and reticence on the part of SAK, the manual employees' confederation (SAK, 2000). Yet generally Finnish unions seem the most content within the Nordic block with PfP, if very much favouring group or most particularly company bases such as profit sharing schemes. These give companies the flexibility through the economic cycle which Finnish unions see as the principal contribution of PfP (Van het Kaar & Grunell, 2001). Again, Finnish unions insist on collective bargaining over PfP.

What of *Germany*, often thought the home of a particularly significant union movement? The compression of pay differentials in general has not been a particular priority in comparative context (Jacobi *et al.*, 1998; Swenson, 1989). Yet Germany's industrial unions have been keen that employees are paid for their time, rather than their effort or productivity; this has been seen as the responsibility of management. Whilst there is a long German tradition of pay-for-performance, the unions have historically sought to limit its traditional form, employing the slogan 'Piecework means murder'. Schulten (2000) notes that more recent PfP initiatives have generally been introduced outside existing agreements, such that unions fear greater decentralisation and the weakening of industrial bargaining. There is a dispute within the German union movement about more modern forms of pay-for-performance, particularly around financial participation – share ownership or profit-related pay.

Increasingly though, there is acceptance of PfP within the German union movement, with the focus shifting to how unions may shape what is seen as an inevitability (Schulten, 2000). IG Metall, the engineering union, has sought clear criteria on how to establish company performance for performance-related payments. Moreover, they have sought to ensure that local unions or more commonly the works councils who operate in their stead have a right to negotiate the actual criteria. They maintain that the PfP component should not only be on top of the collectively agreed fixed pay, and indeed constitute a small portion of it (*e.g.* 10%). IG Metall has resisted the attempts of Gesamtmetall to use the Christmas bonus as a fund for a company performance-related-pay component. Beyond engineering, IG Bergbau, in construction, IG Chemie in the chemical industry, and IG Energy in the energy sector have pursued clauses in industrial agreements on performance-related-payments as a main priority. The principal concern of German unions is that there should be negotiation, preferably at industry level, over the nature of pay-for-performance, and that it should be in addition to basic pay.

The largest *Dutch* union federations prioritise job preservation and the containment of unemployment rather than wage levels or equalisation (Visser, 1998). However, there was union resistance leading to strike action over the introduction of pay-for-performance initiatives at Philips, at Akzo and at ING in 2000 (Van het Kaar & Grunell, 2001). In *Austria*, unions have generally rejected recent employer demands that the increases in basic rates specified in industrial agreements be divided into fixed and flexible components. However, the unions do not seek to inhibit employee representatives on works councils, who are usually union members, engaging in informal negotiations on pay-for-performance beyond the minimum rates the industrial agreements lay down (Traxler, 1998).

In *Italy*, unions have been concerned about increasing management attention afforded the appropriate reward of the more skilled. However, unions are influenced by the notion that they must be prepared to allow greater differentiation to represent an increasingly heterogeneous workforce and so to preserve the institutionalisation of the employment relationship. Moreover, they see PfP as a means for members to gain from firm level productivity advances (Regalia & Regini, 1995). The second largest confederation, CISL, is particularly keen that local negotiations allowed by sectoral agreements should be of substance, and indeed content that they should centre on PfP, particularly around company performance (Van het Kaar & Grunell, 2001). Despite historical trajectories similar in many respects (*e.g.* Hyman, 2001), *French* union confederations' attitude to PfP is very different. French confederations see PfP as the unacceptable shifting of risk to employees (Van het Kaar & Grunell, 2001). Yet the very limited significance of collective bargaining in France (Vernon, 2006) implies that French unions may posture for political effect with very little regard to the implications for actual pay arrangements.

The approach of *Belgian* unions to pay arrangements is intriguing. Union attitudes are typical in many respects, responding to mounting pressure for a move away from a significant age-based component with pay proposals for an experience-based component. Yet Belgian union leaderships are exceptionally determined in their defence of income security, displaying for example an absolute commitment to the specification of an automatic cost-of-living adjustment to pay. The attitude of Belgian unions to pay-for-performance is still more striking – all the more so as their contemporary relevance in collective bargaining implies that they cannot as do French unions posture without regard to their practical impact. Belgian unions took stands of principle against pay-for-performance at IBM and the GIB retail group around the turn of the millennium, resulting in strike action (Van het Kaar & Grunell, 2001) The largest confederations denounce financial participation such as profit sharing. However, these confederations have also commented on the process of implementation, insisting on strict conditions and procedures to be jointly regulated (Van het Kaar & Grunell, 2001). This is indicative of their acceptance of PfP, if only as an unpleasant inevitability. Moreover, the articulation of Belgian unionism is weak (*e.g.* Vilrokx & Van Leemput, 1998), presenting the distinct possibility that local negotiators, at the level of company or workplace, take a softer line on the principle of PfP, if not on the necessity for collective bargaining in its implementation.

Unions in the *UK* fear that profit-related or individualised pay may be deliberately intended to erode or marginalise unions (Kessler and Purcell, 1995). Unions predominantly oppose individual performance-related-pay (PRP). This though is the principal form of PfP in the UK; an indication of unions' declining relevance. The sole confederation, the TUC, has announced support for wider share ownership (Gilman, 2000), perhaps principally as it sees this as marginally preferable to PRP. Where they can, unions seek to regulate performance appraisal, securing and assessing procedures, and to limit the extent of exposure of employees to risk (Gilman, 2000). Broadly though, unions have so little opportunity to shape pay-for-performance, and so little expectation that rhetorical denunciations of it might promote membership or militancy, that they do not trouble to forge a coherent approach.

Ultimately, then, whilst there are marked cross-national variations in the conversations occurring in unions and union movements, there are nonetheless common features. Instinctively, it seems that unions have generally regarded pay-for-performance with suspicion. The concept is quite at odds not only with the predominant solidaristic slant of unionism but with the notion that it should be employers that bear risk. Moreover, it can seem to threaten the institutionalisation of the employment relationship and thus the very existence of unionism itself. However, when pressed by employers or indeed by employees, unions which sense some opportunity to shape developments generally accept the principle of PfP. This is not to say that there may not sometimes be some gap between the stance of leaderships and workplace representatives.

Generally, though, unions now regard the devil as in the detail. Usually, whilst unions are often keen that no groups should be excluded from PfP where it is introduced, they are also keen to see the performance related element of the pay package confined to a modest proportion of total remuneration; rarely more than 10%. They are often keen also to compress the variation of bonus payments in practice, such that employees have only a few percent of their total pay truly at risk. It is in these respects that union concerns with the sheer extent of the exposure of employees to risk survive.

Beyond this containment of the practical effect of PfP though, unions typically have procedural concerns. Firstly, they generally regard it as vital that PfP be subject to collective bargaining, such that it does not immediately threaten the institutionalisation of the employment relationship. Generally, unions prefer that this collective bargaining of PfP should be at multiple bargaining levels, as with other elements of pay. Beyond the limitation of the exposure of their members to risk, their concern in such negotiations is that PfP arrangements should be transparent, and that there should be an ex ante specification of objective criteria for the achievement of bonuses. Unions are uneasy not only that a vague promise may not be fulfilled but that, where PfP is at least partly dependent on individual or group performance, there may be victimisation or favouritism of individuals or small groups by line managers. The tendency of unions to favour PfP which is not significantly based on assessments of individual performance, but on that of a group, department or firm, despite the issue of 'line of sight', seems to an extent related, although this is also indicative of their concerns that PfP can be de-motivating. In many respects, the evolving response of unions to the PfP agenda is indicative of the responsiveness of collective bargaining to the concerns of employers and employees.

The perspectives of Employers' Associations

Generally speaking, cross-national commonalities in the approach of employers' associations to pay arrangements are still more obvious. Quite generally, they seek a containment of pay costs via organised industrial relations. Their emphasis on the general containment of costs, may at times even bring them into conflict with their members, who are sometimes more sensitive to the local implications, as in Germany in 1995 (Thelen, 2000). However, under pressure from members, they have quite generally favoured a decentralisation of pay determination, towards company where possible. They favour in particular a shift away from fixed bases to pay towards a focus on pay-for-performance. Employers' associations quite generally promote variable pay, regarding it as allowing greater company level flexibility, competitiveness and robustness in the face of the business cycle, sharing corporate risk and motivating employees (Van het Kaar & Grunell, 2001). A brief discussion of the flavour of attitudes in nations with more significant employers' associations underlines the generality of employers' associations approach.

In *Belgium*, discussions around pay in employers' associations focus quite heavily on the automatic cost of living-adjustment of pay and on the implications for wage costs. Although the Belgian wage norm implies that pay increases cannot exceed those in neighbouring countries, employers' associations are not in favour of the generally prevailing system by which increases in the cost of living are automatically translated into pay increases, in a manner similar to the Scala Mobile abandoned in Italy in the 1990s, and consider that pay increases should be lower in sectors and companies operating in highly competitive and global markets (Langerock, 2005). As they see it, the prevailing system unreasonably limits their bargaining space, and results in a wage price spiral which increases labour costs and decreases competitiveness (Mouton, 2002). Beginning in the food and wood sectors, and supported by the Belgian government, employers' associations have successfully pursued agreements which allow lower real wage increases at higher inflation rates.

The Belgian situation is unusual. In *Sweden*, through the 1980s employers' associations put more emphasis on changing pay differentials than on overall labour costs (Hammarström *et al.*, 2004). The principle private sector association, SAF, and its still more encompassing successor, SN, began to favour pay determined at company level to suit the conditions of the employer, and in particular to render pay more sensitive to deteriorations in profitability (de Geer, 1992). It also pursued an individualisation of pay arrangements to suit the shift it detected in the character of work, and to motivate and develop employees (Andersson, 1993). The Swedish employers' associations have stressed though that differences should be systematic and legitimate, and thus promoted the training of the managers responsible locally for pay arrangements.

Public sector employers' associations have pursued decentralised pay setting in Sweden (Bender & Elliott, 2003) inter alia. The Swedish national agreement for central government employees of 2005 reflected concerns of employers' associations, stressing that 'pay should stimulate improvements of effectiveness, efficiency and quality... pay should be individualised and differentiated and reflect attained goals and results for each employee.' The Swedish Association of Local Authorities has taken a much more detailed interest in the actual design and operation of pay systems, articulating the same principles.

There has been much interest in and discussion of the possible implications of the erosion of the content of multi-employer agreements in *Germany*, and indeed also of their complete abolition (*e.g.* Jacobi *et al.*, 1998). Employers' associations in Germany have successfully pursued hardship clauses on pay levels, allowing firms in specific conditions to pay rates below those agreed for general application at industry level, but these have been rather little used (Schulten, 2000). They have more recently sought a change in the Collective Agreement Act which would make possible deviations for poorly performing companies from the terms of prevailing industrial agreements themselves. German employers' associations are enthusiastic about PfP of all forms, and seek to advance its general role whilst leaving the detailed arrangements to company bargaining. More specifically, concerned at the possibility that PfP might be paid in addition to existing rates, with a resulting increase in overall labour costs, they have sought to shift the balance between the fixed and variable components of pay. They have pursued the deployment of the conventional German Christmas bonus as a PfP fund. In *Austria*, the peak employers' organisation, the WKÖ, seeks company level flexibility in the extent and form of PfP (Van het Kaar & Grunell, 2001). Employers' associations in *The Netherlands* seek more 'individual variation' in pay (Visser, 1998:300).

Employers' associations are generally keen that the processes of decentralisation and a greater local flexibility in pay are organised by a framework of multi-employer negotiations. This can be interpreted not only as a matter of the instinct of employers' associations for self-preservation but as an acknowledgement of the dangers to individual employers of unorganised decentralisation (see *e.g.* Thelen, 2000). With regard to PfP specifically the stance of employers' associations may also express concerns that without multi-employer negotiation such systems may otherwise spread only in addition to the complex array of payments to which employers are already committed.

Employers and Employees United: Pay Formation

The Strategic Space for Reward

What then of the 'strategic space' for reward (Vernon, 2005a) – of the form of the collective bargaining over pay arrangements to which individual employers are subject? Consistent with notions of globalisation, there prevails a popular view that pay arrangements are similar across the advanced industrialised world. In stark contrast, a common presumption within the social science and employment relations literatures is that pay inequality and more specifically pay-for-performance is a creature of the Anglo-Saxon nations, and most particularly the US and now the UK, where collective bargaining is weak. Each view may be found amongst managers, and each contains a grain of truth and at the same time is quite misleading.

The Coverage of Collective Bargaining

Across the European nations of the OECD, typically the bulk of a nation's employees are touched by the provisions of collective agreements. Even in the nations newly acceding to the European union this is generally the case, although collective bargaining coverage is apparently under 5% of the national workforce in the largest of them: Poland (Behrens & Traxler, 2003, Table 1). Moreover, rates of collective bargaining coverage for national workforces as a whole tend to express the cross-national comparative situation with regard to both manual and non-manual employees. Nations with high coverage amongst manual employees also tend to feature high coverage amongst non-manual employees (Traxler and Behrens, 2003, Table 2). The very wide disparity between coverage amongst manual and non-manual employees in Spain is exceptional, and in large part due to the limits of the rights to collective bargaining for state employees, who are predominantly non-manual. In principle, then, collective bargaining appears of relevance in driving pay developments within Europe.

The extent of collective bargaining coverage in European nations hinges critically on multi-employer agreements (Traxler *et al.*, 2001). Moreover, multi-employer agreements confront managements as something external and are thus external drivers of pay systems, to the extent that they impact. In contrast, local agreements, at the level of the company or establishment are subject to the cultures and strategies of the management of the firm, even if they are also framed by a larger industrial agreement. Whilst it often seems that managers do not see it in this way, local agreements thus reflect in part management's own positions and priorities. Of course, management's local bargaining partners sometimes appear very much to them as an external force, even if they appreciate the extent to which their agenda is informed by the prevailing industrial agreements. Yet whilst managements find it difficult in practice, they may align their collective bargaining agenda with their HR and broader strategic priorities, and indeed seek to engage unions in discussion of possible futures. Such drivers are thus to a great extent not only company-related but in the remit of management.

Of multi-employer agreements, industry-level agreements are particularly important as they tend to embody implications of multi-industry agreements if any, as well as featuring their own content. Such agreements are secured by negotiations between unions and employers' associations in which larger firms are generally particularly influential (*e.g.* Traxler *et al.*, 2001). In principle, as where there is a regional industrial agreement in a region where there is only one large employer in the region concerned, industry agreements might effectively represent single employer agreements from the point of view of the large firm, though certainly not from smaller. In practice though, in nations where regional industrial agreements are the norm there tend to be strong similarities between the agreements reached in one region and those in others, as for example in Germany. Thus, industrial agreements confront companies both small and large as external influences on their pay arrangements.

In national industries, such as German engineering, where industrial bargaining predominates, the terms of such bargains are of some relevance even for firms that step outside industrial negotiations to secure company-level agreements. The terms of the industrial agreement necessarily cast a shadow on local negotiations, and most often provide some minimum standards, effective defaults, which company level agreements can rarely in practice transgress, whether legally, with regard to the default available to employees, or merely with regard to the expectations of their employees. As Arrowsmith *et al.* (2003) note with regard to Belgian engineering, employers' associations often stress that employers stepping outside the industrial agreement would face the same issues in local bargaining with local unions.

Many of the differences in collective bargaining arrangements continue to be centred on nation rather than industry. Data on the coverage amongst that part of the workforce legally entitled to collectively bargain, excluding for example the Beamte in Germany (hence 'adjusted' coverage), are shown in Table 3.2. below. Generally speaking, such adjusted coverage rates for a particular nation tend to be very similar overall and within manufacturing specifically. The rates tend to be a little lower, but the ranking of nations very similar in financial services and indeed in construction. In other industries, the cross-national situation is not nearly so neat (Traxler and Behrens, 2003, Tables 1 and 4). Nonetheless, overall adjusted coverage is a pretty good indicator of the sheer extent of the reach of collective bargaining across the workforce in a wide range of industries, including some at the core of multi-national activity.

Table 3.2. Adjusted coverage of collective bargaining, European nations, 2001

Nation	Adjusted coverage rate
Austria	98%
Belgium	>90%
Denmark	83%
France	90-95%
Germany	63%
Hungary	34%
Netherlands	88%
Norway	70-77%
Poland	1%
Slovakia	48%
Slovenia	100%
Spain	81%
Sweden	>90%
Great Britain	36%

(Derived from Traxler & Behrens, 2003)

The substance of multi-employer bargaining

Much of the variation in the agendas of multi-employer bargaining and content of multi-employer agreements is also cross-national rather than inter-industry. In part this is related to the differing national traditions of unionism and employer organisation. In part it is due to cross-national differences in the sheer weight of multi-employer bargaining, which in turn hinges on the support afforded it by local unions, individual employers and the state. Vernon (2006) shows that generally a nation's multi-employer agreements are more constraining of local agreements about basic or fixed pay, which remains the vast bulk of total pay for the vast bulk of employees, the greater is the aggregate density of union membership. Thus, in the Nordic nations multi-employer agreements are comparatively restrictive of local pay agreements whilst in France they are mostly inconsequential. Moreover, Vernon (2006) also shows that in nations of greater union density, local union organisations tend to be better developed. Greater union density is associated with more stringent collective bargaining at multiple levels.

Comparative case studies of organisations in particular industries bring out the limitations of such aggregate analysis. Recent case study research has compared the role of industry bargaining in pay determination in engineering and financial services, in Belgium, Germany, Italy and the UK (*e.g.* Marginson *et al.*, 2003; Arrowsmith *et al.*, 2003). This shows that there is dramatic variation in collective bargaining coverage between these four nations, and little difference between these industries. Yet there is variation between industries around the regulatory effect of multi-employer agreements, with multi-employer agreements having more content and being a more important reference point for company-level negotiations in engineering. Moreover, works councils and local unions are of much greater significance in engineering.

Collective Bargaining and Pay Outcomes

What then of the relationship between collective bargaining and pay arrangements on the ground? There is no evidence that nations in which collective bargaining is more widespread and substantial feature higher (or lower) average pay levels, whether in US$ or purchasing power parities (PPP). Several of the high pay nations are nations with limited collective bargaining, and several of those with significant collective bargaining, with the lower average pay group similarly mixed (see Freeman, 1994). Cross-national comparative variation in average pay hinges on other political and economic features.

However, there is evidence that within the borders of nations more significant company or establishment level collective bargaining is often associated with companies or establishments having higher average pay levels. The 'union pay premiums' estimated have tended to be greater where there is little or no multi-employer bargaining, as has long been the case in the US and Canada and has increasingly been the case in the UK from the early 1980s (Blanchflower & Freeman, 1992). The bulk of Europe features much greater emphasis on multi-employer bargaining, which the available evidence suggests results in smaller union pay premiums. Moreover, the 1990s saw an erosion of union pay premiums, apparently related to intensified product market competition (Heery, 2000). Even in the UK, it seems that by 2000 union pay premiums may have disappeared entirely for men generally, though remaining at 10% for women (Machin, 2001). Blanchflower & Bryson's (2003, Table 7) results suggest that the latter finding may be largely attributable to a substantial union pay premium for part-time employees.

The effect of collective bargaining on the pay structure is much more profound than that on average pay levels. Within the UK, pay inequality amongst unionised employees is very much lower than that amongst those who are non-unionised, even taking account of compositional differences in these groups. Despite the dramatic erosion of unionism of collective bargaining in the UK, these are such as to have substantial implications for the overall pay distribution within the UK (Metcalf *et al.*, 2001). Moreover, there is a very strong cross-national, and indeed historical, relationship between union density and the compression of pay differentials of all sorts (Vernon, 2005b; Rueda & Pontusson, 2000). Given the status of density as a gauge of the cross-national comparative weight of collective bargaining (Vernon, 2006), the significance of collective bargaining for the pay distribution is clear; more exacting frameworks of collective bargaining compress the pay structure. Sweden is much more equal than the UK or France.

With regard to the implications of the collective bargaining of the precise form of pay arrangements; pay systems, the situation is still more complex. Generally speaking, multi-employer agreements tend not to be directly restrictive of pay systems or of PfP specifically. Yet their specification of minimum pay rates or increases has implications which cannot be transgressed by attempts to relate pay to performance or indeed other criteria. This implies that payment for performance must be made on top of such agreed pay. By implication this allows much room for maneuver to more successful companies capable of affording larger pay bills per employee, but is of course restrictive for less successful operations. Generally, though, there is a good deal of scope for local bargaining in the shaping of pay systems, as the following brief discussion of nations where collective bargaining is usually considered of particular relevance indicates.

The continued strength of *Swedish* unions, and multi-employer bargaining, makes the Swedish situation of particular interest. In construction, the industry agreement makes special provision for very substantial PfP, whether piece based or bonuses contingent on targets, such that 20% of all hours worked are rewarded according to results. This though is unusual – more generally industrial agreements are marked not by restriction but more by silence on these issues. Martin (1995) argues that Swedish engineering employers did not pursue the negotiations at local level on pay-for-performance allowed by the prevailing higher level agreements, preferring to complain about their restrictiveness. More recent developments have a similar flavour. Towards the millennium, despite the continuing importance of industrial agreements and prevalence of local collective bargaining in Sweden, there seemed more space for pay-for-performance, including individual PRP, than ever (Hayden & Edwards, 2001). Despite this, pay-for-performance had not spread to some sectors even of relatively weak local union organisation, and indeed had shown a general decline as a proportion of total pay (Kjellberg, 1998). It is difficult to imagine that managers have been precluded by collective bargaining from a pursuit of PfP. Similarly in *Finland*, PfP is regulated by some sectoral agreements, in e.g metalworking and paper, but even in these industries there is much room for local negotiation in implementation (Van het Kaar & Grunell, 2001.)

In *Germany*, often regarded as subject to particularly stringent collective bargaining, the situation appears similar. Typically, much is left by confederal or industrial agreements to be determined at the level of the establishment or enterprise. Thelen (*e.g.* 2000) stresses the flexibility involved in German collective bargaining. Certainly, industry agreements have long regulated piece work. Yet, despite their concern, unions have struggled to deal with the newer pay-for-performance agenda in industrial agreements (Kurdelbusch, 2002). Even within engineering, where industrial bargaining is thought of particular importance, the 1990s have seen opening clauses allowing PfP to be agreed locally, at the company or establishment, in conjunction with works councils. A senior official of IG Metall commented that company-level negotiations are now 'creative', and that 'there's more space for variation.' (Marginson *et al.*, 2003:171). Arrowsmith *et al.* (2003) note that the general bargaining attitudes of works councils and local union representatives vary dramatically, even within the engineering sector.

Collective bargaining of pay systems is principally through the works agreements established under the codetermination and negotiation rights afforded works councils. Bargaining over rewards for the meeting of targets and over financial participation occurs principally at the company or establishment. This occurs either formally in company-level agreements for those companies outside their relevant employers' association, or informally through works councils for the majority of companies remaining party to multi-employer bargaining. Moreover, in some companies there is no collective bargaining over pay systems of any sort, and pay-for-performance has been introduced solely by management initiative (Schulten, 2000).

Within large engineering firms, where pay systems are regulated by the industrial agreement, individual performance-related-pay is prevalent, but tightly circumscribed; "downgrading hardly exists and bonuses are often consolidated" (Kurdelbusch, 2002:331). Moreover, there is much contention in engineering industry negotiations over the replacement of previously fixed payments with profit-related pay. It is probably in this sector that PfP has been most restricted by collective bargaining in practice. However, the agreements in engineering have been unusually restrictive of local arrangements.

Generally there has been a strong growth in the use of PfP since the mid-late 1990s (Kurdelbusch, 2002). A good deal of flexibility from managements' viewpoint is evident more generally. A substantial minority of the largest 114 German companies analysed by Kurdelbusch (2002) appear to have substantially changed their payment systems in the period 1994-2000. Where entirely new PfP schemes have been introduced, these have been financed mostly from what were previously fixed payments, without eating into the fixed payments which are required by relevant industrial agreements. As Kurdelbusch (2002) suggests the very variety of PfP arrangements apparent in Germany implies that collective bargaining is not much of an obstacle to PfP itself. However, it is clear that where works councils exist, as they typically do, they usually insist on their right to negotiate. They prioritise the transparency of arrangements and the preservation of the existing fixed payments. If the latter is threatened they seek to dilute the implications of PfP in practice (Kurdelbusch, 2002).

The *Belgian* inter-sectoral agreement of 2000 on financial participation is an attempt to frame local practice nationally, but still acknowledges the latter's role (Marginson *et al.*, 2003). There is much negotiation at company level around both pay and payment systems. A senior official in one of Belgium's engineering unions commented that "anything is possible, as long as it's negotiated" (Marginson *et al.*, 2003:171). Within ICT, although Belgian employees are, unusually, covered by a multi-employer agreement, this is a default agreement of very limited content (Margionson *et al.*, 2003). In Italy, the sectoral agreement for engineering, the most heavily joint regulated industry, allows PfP, but there has been much company-level controversy about the appropriate criteria for gauging performance (Marginson *et al.*, 2003). Within banking, negotiations about PfP occur at company level (Marginson *et al.*, 2003).

Conclusion

In Europe, the actors and institutions of collective bargaining are typically of much import in the forging of pay arrangements for non-managerial employees. Nor is this generally a matter of hollow procedure. Whilst there is no relationship between the coverage, structure or weight of collective bargaining and average levels of compensation, collective bargaining is very strongly linked to pay differentials or pay inequality. Where collective bargaining is not only formally extensive but of substance, and most of all where it occurs at multiple levels, pay structures are generally very much more compressed. Nonetheless, there is much flexibility in pay arrangements even where systems of collective bargaining are stronger. Of particular note, it is not the case that collective bargaining precludes the application of the principle of PfP, even where collective bargaining is significant at multiple levels. Multi-employer bargaining rarely precludes PfP, and local employee representatives of whatever form rarely refuse it in principle.

However, where there is established local union representation and/or a works council with statutory rights to negotiation, or indeed co-determination, over pay systems, local employee representatives will expect to bargain over the design and operation of all forms of reward, including pay-for-performance. This usually means the containment of the extent of compensation constituted, for the average employee, by pay-for-performance. Representatives also typically devote close attention to the criteria and procedures involved in the application of the scheme. They may also strongly favour particular classes of pay-for-performance; group-based over individually-based for example.

It warrants stressing that the perspectives of union representatives are a distillation, if a particular distillation, of the views and attitudes of members past and present. Generally, employers seeking to pursue even a PfP agenda in a thorough and professional manner will most likely find much room for discussion left by multi-employer agreements and local employee representatives.

References

Alsterdal, L. (2005), Vad är ett bra arbetsresultat? Individuell lön och verksamhetsutveckling i kommuner och landsting, Sveriges Kommuner och Landsting, Stockholm.

Andersson, E.R. & Harriman, A. (1999), *Rätt lön på rätt sätt*, Arbetslivsinstitutet, Solna.

Andersson, M. *et. al.* (1993), Bra lönebildning - företagets och medarbetarnas bästa affär, SAF, Stockholm.

Arbetsgivarverket (1996), Konsten att sätta lön. En fråga om förnuft eller känslor?, Fritzes, Stockholm.

Arrowsmith, James, Paul Marginson and Keith Sisson (2003), "Externalisation and internalisation in Europe: variation in the role of large companies", *Industrielle Beziehungen*, 10, 3, p. 363-392.

Behrens, M. & Traxler, F. (2003), "Collective bargaining coverage and extended procedures", EIRObservatory 02, p.i-viii.

Bender, K.A., Elliott, R.F. (2003), *Decentralised Pay Setting. A study of the Outcomes of Collective Bargaining Reform in the Civil Service in Australia, Sweden and the UK*, Ashgate Publishing Limited, England.

Blanchflower, D.G., Freeman, R.B. (1992), "Unionism in the United States and other advanced OECD countries", *Industrial Relations*, 31, p. 56-80

Blanchflower, David and Alex Bryson (2003), "Changes over time in union relative wage effects in the UK and US revisited", in John T. Addison and C. Schnabel (eds.), *International Handbook of Trade Unions*, Cheltenham, Edward Elgar.

Carlsson, P. (2003), *Lönesättning*, Björn Lundén Information AB, Näsviken.

De Geer, H. (1992), *Arbetsgivarna - SAF i tio decennier*, SAFs förlagsservice, Stockholm.

Emans, B. *et al.* (2003), "Pay for performance in Europe: prevalence and national differences", Paper presented at European Congress on Work and Organisational Psychology, Lisbon, May 2003.

Ferner, Anthony and Richard Hyman (eds.) (1992), *Industrial Relations in the New Europe*, Oxford, Basil Blackwell.

Ferner, Anthony and Richard Hyman (eds.) (1998), *Changing Industrial Relations in Europe*, Oxford, Basil Blackwell.

Freeman, Richard. (1994), "How labor fares in advanced economies", in Freeman R. (ed.) *Working under Different Rules*, London, Sage.

Gilman, Mark (2000), "Variable pay: the case of the UK", Mimeo prepared for the European Industrial Relations Observatory.

Goetschy, Janine. (1998), "France: the limits of reform", in Ferner, A. & R. Hyman (eds.), *Changing Industrial Relations in Europe*, Oxford, Basil Blackwell.

Hayden, A. & T. Edwards (2001), "The erosion of the country of origin effect: a case study of a Swedish multi-national company", *Relations Industrielles*, 56, 1, p. 116-140.

Heery, E. (2000), "Trade unions and the management of reward", in G. White and J. Druker (eds.), *Reward Management. A critical text*, London, Routledge, p. 54-83.

Hyman, Richard. (2001), *Understanding European Trade Unionism: Between Market, Class and Society.* London, Sage.

Jacobi *et al.* (1998), "Germany", in Ferner, A. & R. Hyman (eds.), *Changing Industrial Relations in Europe*, Oxford, Basil Blackwell.

Kessler, I. and Purcell, J. (1995), "Individualism and collectivism in theory and practice: management style and the design of pay systems", in P. Edwards (ed.), *Industrial Relations: Theory and Practice*, Oxford, Blackwell, p. 337-368.

Kjellberg, A. (1998), "Sweden: restoring the model?", in Ferner, A. and R. Hyman (eds.), *Changing Industrial Relations in Europe*, Oxford, Blackwell.

Kurdelbusch, A. (2002), "Multinationals and the Rise of Variable Pay in Germany", *European Journal of Industrial Relations*, Vol. 8, No. 3, p. 325-349.

Langenberg, S., "Er heerst nog steeds apartheid op de werkvloer", in *Knack*, 01.12.2004.

Langerock, J. (2005), "Na moeizame besprekingen in de raad van bestuur zegt het VBO ja aan IPA", Persbericht, VBO.

Lilja, Kari (1998), "Finland: Continuity and Modest Moves towards Company-Level Corporatism", in Ferner, A. & R. Hyman (eds.), *Changing Industrial Relations in Europe*, Oxford, Basil Blackwell.

Machin, Steve (2001), "Does It Still Pay to Be in or to Join a Union?", Mimeo, CEPR, LSE.

Marginson, P., J. Arrowsmith & K. Sisson (2003), "Tipping the balance? The changing relationship between sector and company level bargaining", Paper for the IIRA World Congress, Berlin, September 2003.

Marginson, P., K. Sisson & J. Arrowsmith (2003b), "Between Decentralisation and Europeanisation: Sectoral Bargaining in Four Countries and Two Sectors"; *European Journal of Industrial Relations*, 9, 2, p. 163-187.

Martin, A. (1995), "The Swedish model: demise or reconfiguration?", in R. Locke, T. Kochan & R. Piore (eds.), *Employment Relations in a Changing World Economy*, Cambridge, MA, MIT Press, p. 263-296.

Metcalf, David, K Hansen and Andy Charlwood (2001), "Unions and the sword of justice: unions and pay systems, pay inequality, pay discrimination and low pay", *National Institute of Economic and Social Research Review*, 176, April, p. 61-75.

Mouton, A., "Strijd om heilige koe", *Trends*, 07.02.2002.

Norén, K.-H. (1998), Individuell lönesättning för alla. En handbok för små och stora företag, Sveriges verkstadsindustrier, Stockholm.

OECD (1998), "Making the Most of the Minimum: Statutory Minimum Wages, Employment and Poverty", *Employment Outlook*, Paris, OECD.

OECD (2003), *Wage Dispersion Database*, Paris, OECD.

Palm, A. (2000), Affärsstödjande lönebildning. Individuell lönesättning i praktiken, Ekerlids förlag, Stockholm.

Regalia, Ida & Marino Regini (1995), "Italy", in Locke *et al.* (eds.).

Regalia, Ida & Marino Regini (1998), "Italy: the Dual Character of Industrial Relations", in Ferner, A. and R. Hyman (eds.), *Changing Industrial Relations in Europe*, Oxford, Blackwell.

Rossens, E. (2003), "Regionale problematiek", Document, VBO.

Rueda, David & Jonas Pontusson (2000), "Wage inequality and varieties of capitalism", *World Politics*, 52, April, p. 350-83.

SAK (2000), Report.

Scheuer, M. (1998), "The Service Sector in the Federal Republic of Germany", in Austrian Federal Ministry for Economic Affairs, Department Industry (ed.), Business Services and Employment, Annex: Contributions of five UE-member States on their Situation of Business Services. Vienna, p. 2-17.

Schulten, Thorsten (2000), "Variable pay in Germany", Mimeo prepared for the European Industrial Relations Observatory.

Swenson, Peter (1989), *Fair Shares: Unions, Pay and Politics in Sweden and Germany*, London, Adamantine.

The European Foundation for the Improvement of Living and Working Conditions (2005), *European Industrial Relations Dictionary*, www.eurofound.eu. int/areas/industrialrelations/dictionary/index.htm.

Thelen, K. (2000), "Why German Employers Cannot Bring Themselves to Dismantle the German Model", in T. Iversen, J. Pontusson & D. Soskice (eds.), *Unions, Employers and Central Banks*, Cambridge, CUP.

Traxler, F. (1998), "Austria: Still the Country of Corporatism", in Ferner, A. & R. Hyman (eds.), *Changing Industrial Relations in Europe*, Oxford, Basil Blackwell.

Traxler, Franz, Sabine Blaschke and Bernhard Kittel (2001), *National Labour Relations in Internationalised Markets*, Oxford, OUP.

Van het Kaar, Robbert & Marianne Grunell (2001), *Variable pay in Europe*, European Industrial Relations Observatory, 2001/4.

Vernon, Guy (2005a), "International Pay and Reward", in Edwards and Rees (eds.), *International Human Resource Management*, London, FT/Prentice Hall.

Vernon, Guy (2005b), "Labour Market Organisation and Pay Inequality", Paper given at SASE Budapest, July 2005.

Vernon, Guy (2006), "Does Density Matter? The Significance of Comparative Historical Variation in Unionisation", *European Journal of Industrial Relations*, 12, p. 189-209.

Visser, Jelle (1998), "The Netherlands: the Return of Responsive Corporatism", in Ferner, A. and R. Hyman (eds.), *Changing Industrial Relations in Europe*, Oxford, Blackwell.

X. (2005), "De waarheid achter het generatiepact', VBO.

CHAPTER 4

Pay Systems, Strategic Alignment, and Outcomes: European Data and National Differences

Conny H. ANTONI

While chapter 2 has made a contribution to our basic understanding of pay systems by clarifying concepts, and chapter 3 has provided the idea of the stakeholder approach, chapter 4 adopts a more empirical approach to shaping pay in Europe: First, chapter 4.1 offers a description of the contemporary European pay systems and the connections between pay systems, work organisational factors, quality of working life, and organisational strategies. In chapter 4.2, pay systems and pay outcomes within six European Union countries (Belgium, Finland, Germany, The Netherlands, Sweden, and United Kingdom) are reviewed. The specific descriptions of these countries aim at clarifying the contemporary issues raised by pay in these countries. These countries were chosen for representing both small and large countries, as well as founding members and comparatively newly acceding countries in the EU. In chapter 4.3, the focus has moved onto single companies. In the retail banking case studies, the audit tool developed by the authors, was applied in three different banks in Belgium, Finland, and Germany. This enables us to give insights on the way national and company's specific conditions influence pay (the sector being kept constant). Furthermore, we have used the audit tool to study the pay systems in a European multinational company. Audits were carried out in the Belgian, French, Dutch, and German subsidiaries of this company; various influences and approaches to pay which exist in these countries were explored. Therefore, these case studies enable us to get glimpses of the way national conditions influence pay (the company being constant).

CHAPTER 4.1

Pay Systems, Strategic Alignment, and Pay Outcomes: Results of Europe-wide Research

Conny H. ANTONI & Ansgar BERGER[1]

To gain a better understanding of the way pay is shaped in Europe, we need empirical data to deepen our knowledge about the use of pay systems, their incidence, and possible consequences for employees and organisations. When pay systems are designed and set into function, it is not enough to expect positive outcomes. By means of empirical data, we can learn about the possible negative and positive outcomes which are linked with particular pay systems and their driving factors. In this chapter, on the basis of European surveys and case studies (see Antoni *et al.*, 2005), goes a description of what is known as:

- Prevalence of pay systems in Europe
- Relationships between pay systems and environmental factors (personnel, organisational, and institutional factors and employment conditions)
- Relationships between work organisation and pay systems
- Relationships between managerial strategy and pay systems
- Relationships between quality of working life and pay systems
- Relationships between organizational performance and pay systems
- Relationships between performance, work organisation, strategy, and pay systems

This analysis is based on the theoretical assumptions of the strategic management approach developed by Tichy, Fombrun, and Devanna (1982). They put forward that company's effectiveness requires the alignment of strategy, organisation structure, and human resource management. Consequently, reward systems should be in line with the corporate and business unit strategies in order to have an influence on the organisational performance (Gomez-Mejia, 1992; Lawler, 1990,

[1] The authors would like to thank Jessica Jockers and Felicia Werk for their assistance in data analysis and literature research.

1995). If managerial strategy, work organisation, and pay systems are not aligned, this might put into conflict goals and steer mechanisms with potentially detrimental effects both on performance and quality of working life. The ambiguity and conflict regarding goals are mainly responsible of the stress and impair the employees' well-being and performance.

Concerning these issues, two types of survey data about salaries in Europe are available: one focuses on representative samples of individual employees, the other on representative samples of workplaces or companies. In many European countries, different institutions periodically carry out surveys with representative samples of individual employees; additionally, the European Foundation makes such surveys at a cross-national level (Almovadar *et al.*, 2005). They ask about many different aspects of working conditions, but only consider the following three aspects of salaries: the gross or net income, the elements included in that income and the employees' assessment of the salary received. Questions making distinction between base or fixed pay and variable or performance based pay (pay-for-performance) are usually not included. Data are only available on the balance between fixed and variable pay in Spain and in the UK. Furthermore, the design of this kind of survey does not provide information on managerial strategies or organisational performance.

Several national and cross-national surveys concerned with workplaces or companies, include questions regarding compensation as well. At a cross-national level, the EPOC survey (EPOC Research Group, 1997; Sisson, 2002) on direct participation enables us to analyse the prevalence of various remuneration systems dependent on the type of participation and other variables of that study. The Cranet survey on international human resource management analyses the incidence of financial participation, *i.e.* share ownership and profit sharing, based on organisational characteristics and human resource management instruments (Pendleton, Poutsma, Brewster & van Ommeren, 2001). However, both provide little information about working conditions and focus on different aspects of the remuneration systems.

National surveys on pay apply different definitions and sampling methods, hence their results are difficult to compare and to interpret (Emans *et al.*, 2003). Furthermore, they usually cover none or only a few aspects of working conditions. For this reason, we focus on two Pan European surveys carried out by the European Foundation: the European Survey on Working Conditions (ESWC) 2000 (Paoli & Merllié, 2001) and the Employee direct Participation in Organisational Change (EPOC) survey (EPOC Research Group, 1997). The ESWC survey is based on representative samples of individual employees and aims at giving an overview of the state of working conditions in the European Union, as well as indicating the nature and content of changes affecting the workforce and the quality of work. In the third ESWC (Paoli & Merllié, 2001), questions regarding modern forms of variable pay (team bonus; profit sharing; income from shares) were added for the first time. The EPOC survey (EPOC Research Group, 1997; Sisson, 2002) focuses on the nature and the extent of direct employee participation in European enterprises, but also includes questions about pay systems to analyse relationships between remuneration systems and direct participation.

The main indicators of pay and pay systems in these studies are the income level and the presence or not of different types of pay systems, such as fixed salary, piece rate, and productivity payment, payments which are based on the overall performance of the company (profit-sharing scheme) or on the overall performance of a group or income from shares. An aggregate indicator "Modern forms of variable pay" is defined to make the distinction between the traditional piece rate systems and forms of variable pay: on the one hand, the traditional piece rate systems follow the tradition of only rewarding workers for fast work and high quantities; on the other hand, the forms of variable pay have a broader focus on the overall performance and reward in addition to the effects of working smarter. The aggregate indicator "Modern forms of variable pay" refers to companies which have team bonus and/or profit sharing and/or income from shares. The advantage of this aggregate measure is that more cases are included, which allows more detailed analyses. Furthermore, aggregation seems to be justified given that the included indicators show similar result patterns for most of the variables.

Many studies have used different forms of participation, task variety, and task autonomy, as well as the presence or not of teamwork or job rotation as indicators of work organisation. The common practice to aggregate these aspects into one single High Performance Work Organisation (HPWO) variable can be questioned, because this leads to a comparison between apples and oranges (*e.g.* the effects of job rotation depend on the heterogeneity of the respective tasks). Therefore, we have given a definition of HPWO in our analysis of the ESWC 2000 survey, which is based on the following task characteristics: time and task autonomy, task variety, responsibility, and participation. As only aspects of direct participation were measured in the EPOC survey, we analysed the intensity of group delegation, which is a key aspect of HPWO, team autonomy alike.

Managerial strategy is not referred to, in the ESWC 2000 nor explicitly in the EPOC study. In the analysis of the EPOC data we used the question concerning management initiatives regarding product innovation as an indicator of an innovation strategy, to be able to measure this variable at all.

Although both surveys are data sources which are the latest provided by the European Foundation, it is necessary to bear in mind that the data have been gathered in 2000 – in the ESWC 2000 – and in 1996 for the EPOC survey. Concerning the descriptive data about the prevalence of pay systems or other variables, information is not recent and might be outdated. Nevertheless, the information concerning relationships between pay systems and other variables is still valuable when we want to understand better the functioning of pay systems. There are some evidences which reveal the consequences and outcomes of some pay systems: those evidences help to make informed choices and shape pay systems. In the following parts of chapter 4, findings we carried out at the European level are described and compared with analyses we made at national level in six countries (Belgium, Finland, Germany, The Netherlands, Sweden, United Kingdom), which we had chosen for national comparisons. They are described in more depth and compared with other national studies in the next chapter.

Prevalence of Pay Systems in Europe

Basic or fixed pay without variable pay is by far the most dominant pay system reported in the ESWC 2000 survey; the modern forms of variable pay remain exceptional, as only six out of one hundred of employees receive it. In contrast, every third workplace in the EPOC study, approximately, reports the use of modern forms of variable pay for the largest occupational group. Considerable differences between countries exist, which might be due, in part, to supportive government legislation (Poutsma, 2001). Nevertheless, the incidence of variable pay, particularly the use of share and share option schemes is increasing throughout the EU and the more traditional forms, like piecework particularly, are decreasing (Van het Kaar & Grünell, 2001).

Figure 4.1 gives the comparative breakdown of the occurrence of different types of pay systems among the included countries based on ESWC 2000 and the EPOC data. Obviously, there are differences between countries in terms of prevalence of pay components, especially with regard to variable pay elements. The striking percentages for countries in Figure 4.1 reach more than 100% because people were likely to answer positively for more than one pay component in the ESWC 2000 interview. For instance, people surveyed can report that they receive base or fixed pay together with an additional income from shares. From the overall picture in Figure 4.1, we can conclude that base or fixed pay is the most dominant pay component reported in the ESWC in 2000. High rates for modern forms of variable pay are found in Finland (10%)

and Sweden (10%); the lowest rates are related to Belgium (4%) and Germany (5%). The highest rates concerning piece rate or productivity payment are found in Finland (16%) and Germany (7%). An above average rate for all the forms of variable pay (piece rate, additional payment, pay based on the performance of a group/team or company or income from shares) is reported in Finland (23%). High rates for base or fixed pay and a small amount of other variable pay components are reported in Belgium.

Figure 4.1. Percentages of a) types of pay systems and percentages of b) modern variable pay by country

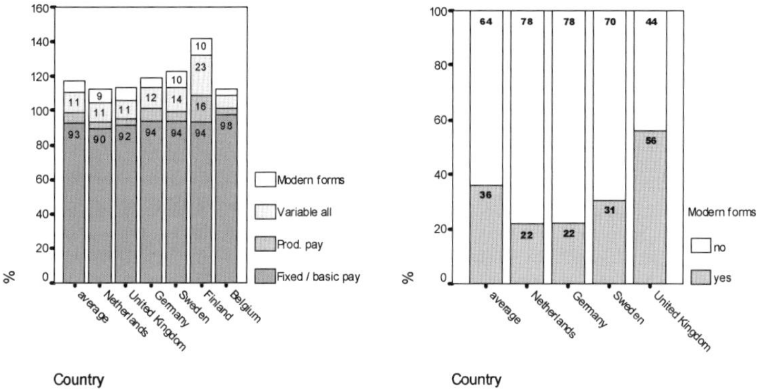

The adoption of a management perspective as illustrated by the EPOC survey, contributes to the report of much higher rates. More than half of all the people surveyed in the UK (56%) estimate that modern forms of variable pay prevail in their company. This is almost twice the proportion in comparison to the other countries. Higher rates for the EPOC data could result from sample differences or different knowledge and frames of reference, when answering pay-related questions. The samples of both studies are difficult to compare, because the ESWC is based on random sampling ensuring representativeness, whereas representativeness of the EPOC could be questioned because of the sampling method, the low response rates and the questions which focus on the largest occupational group of the respective company. Furthermore, employees might not be able to tell their pay components as accurately as management does (some might not even know their pay components, according to what we experience in our own empirical studies). Another aspect of this problem might be raised because employees focus on pay practice, whereas the answers of management are given according to pay systems: *i.e.* employees might get stable income ("fixed" pay); however, pay systems have components, which could vary in principle, but do not so in practice. The time gap of four years for the obtention of data between the surveys (EPOC 1996; ESWC 2000) could also explain the differences within countries, but other studies show that variable income has generally increased over time.

Relationships between Pay Systems and Environmental Factors

In this section, we analyse the relationships between pay systems and environmental factors (*cf.* Figure 4.2 encompasses personnel (gender and age) and organisational factors (sector and size), working conditions (contract type and flexible working times), and institutional factors (union density and employees' representatives)).

Figure 4.2. Pay system and environmental factors

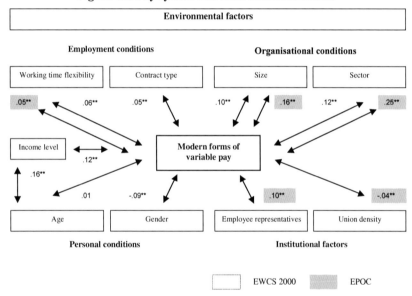

Personnel Factors and Pay Systems – Gender and Age

ESWC 2000 analysis shows that the proportion of men receiving piece rate or productivity pay, additional payments, and modern forms of variable pay is higher for each of these categories in comparison with women. We find similar results in analysis carried out at national level such as The Netherlands which shows the biggest difference between men and women within this sample whereas the UK shows the smallest one – it is almost non-existent. Women also tend to receive a lower income. According to our analysis of the data, this could not be explained by a higher proportion of females working on temporary or fixed term contracts or different types of jobs. We should consider job discrimination as the main reason for justifying this finding.

There is not any link between the types of pay systems and age, because distinct pay systems are found within age groups. Modern forms of variable pay and age are not significantly linked, neither in analysis carried out at cross-national level nor at national level.

Organisational Factors and Pay Systems – Sector and Size

The analysis of the ESWC 2000 data shows that modern forms of variable pay are significantly more often found in the private (8%) than in the public sector (2%). Establishments in the public sector seem to rely on traditional compensation strategies and forms of remuneration, which include to a higher degree, base or fixed pay. The findings of the EPOC survey show similar results. Performance-based pay at the team or company level and income from shares are more commonly used within private sector companies. 42% of managers working in privately owned establishments responded that their company introduced modern variable pay schemes. In comparison with the proportion of 9% in public companies, this result illustrates the imbalance in the prevalence of modern variable pay components between sectors. Differences in the spread of pay systems between ESWC and EPOC results could be explained by the probable better overview and level of knowledge managers have about the pay system used by the company they are working for. The positive relation between modern variable pay and private sector companies that has been found for the overall samples of both surveys could be replicated for all the countries, among others Sweden shows the strongest relationship in both surveys.

The bigger the company, the more it is using different pay systems as part of its total remuneration. Companies with a great number of employees seem to be more open minded and more capable to use performance-based pay at the team and company level or income from shares as a part of their compensation strategy. Data from both ESWC 2000 and EPOC surveys support the assumption that modern forms of variable pay are more frequently found in bigger companies. At national level, the strongest relationship has been found in Finland, which means that there is a stronger link between modern forms of variable pay and larger companies in Finland than in other countries covered by this secondary analysis. There are not any significant relationships which have been found in the case of Belgium (ESWC 2000) and Sweden (EPOC). First, we can interpret this positive relation between modern forms of variable pay and size as following: larger scale companies might have to be more flexible to keep their head up on the competitive job market and therefore are maybe more likely to adopt innovative compensation systems. Second, what can justify the observed national differences are specific statutory factors, legislation, and national tax policies that further or hinder the use and spread of modern variable pay.

Working Conditions and Pay Systems – Contract Type and Flexible Working Times

An investigation carried out on the relationships between pay systems and employment conditions (contract type, working time flexibility) reveals that the proportion of employees who receive modern forms of variable pay is higher when they are working on an unlimited contract (ESWC 2000). Long term or permanent contracts seem to be positively related to group/team or company performance-based pay or income from shares. At the national level, these findings could not be replicated for the six countries which have been selected: Finland and Sweden show significant negative relations, which means that people working on unlimited contracts are less likely to receive modern forms of variable pay than people working on fixed-term or temporary contracts, whereas in Belgium, Germany, The Netherlands, and UK are deprived of significant relationships. These rather unusual results might be due to country-specific laws and regulations. Especially in the Scandinavian countries, modern forms of variable pay seem to be more common with temporary contracts.

In accordance with ESWC 2000 findings, the EPOC data show that there is a weak, but significant association between the employees working in workplaces with working time flexibility and modern forms of variable pay. At the national level, in the context of the ESWC 2000, these findings could not be replicated for the selected countries. In each of the six countries, negative relationships between modern forms of variable pay and working time flexibility have been found, although these relations are only significant in Germany and in the UK. That means that at the level of these selected countries, organisations with variable pay are less likely to adopt flexible working time schemes. The analysis of EPOC national sub-samples puts forward an inconsistent pattern of results: Whereas Germany, Sweden, and UK support the cross-national results, there is not any relationship between working time flexibility and modern forms of variable pay in The Netherlands.

Institutional Factors and Pay Systems – Union Density and Employee Representatives

Institutional factors play a key role when it comes to the implementation of pay systems. The EPOC survey provides data on which the influence of indicators representing institutional factors can be exam-

ined. Indicators have been formed from questions in the EPOC questionnaire that ask whether employee representatives (of trade unions,
workers councils, and/or advisory committees) are recognised for the
purposes of consultation/negotiation and joint decision-making together
with the density or degree of union membership, *i.e.* the proportion of
union members within the workforce of a company. It seems that a
higher degree of employee representation is associated with a higher
incidence of modern forms of variable pay. Subsequent analysis shows
that this relationship exists regardless of the companies' size. As regards
the density of union membership, there is not any similar relationship.
There is a weak, but significant positive relation between modern forms
of variable pay and employees' representation at the cross-national level
that cannot be replicated at national level in Germany, Sweden, and The
Netherlands. There is a weak, but significant positive relation only in the
UK, although all other correlation coefficients have a positive algebraic
sign, too. Vice versa, consistent weak or small negative correlations
between modern forms of variable pay and the degree of unionisation
are both found in cross-national and national analysis. Significant
negative relationships are found in The Netherlands and particularly in
the UK, which shows that the more employees of an organisation are
unionised, the less modern forms of variable pay are applied in the
compensation system. In Sweden, a similar tendency exists, but lacks
significance, whereas there is not any link in Germany. These findings
might be an indicator of a slightly negative attitude of unions toward
variable pay in most of the European countries. The fact that modern
forms of variable pay tend to be found more frequently if the number of
employees' representatives is higher indicates that local employees'
representatives have not the same perspective towards modern forms of
variable pay as trade unions.

Work Organisation and Pay Systems – HPWO and Group Delegation

Modern forms of variable pay are more often found in high performance work organisations (*cf.* Figure 4.3). This result was also found at
national level indicating that modern forms of variable pay are significantly more often applied in organisations with task or time autonomy, a
greater task variety, responsibility, and effective participation. At national level the relations are all statistically significant and of almost
equal size. Modern forms of variable pay are also significantly more
often found in workplaces with a high intensity of group delegation (*cf.*
Figure 4.3). Approximately, half of the workplaces with a higher intensity of group delegation are linked with performance-based pay at team
and company level or income from shares. This result was also found at

national level in the analyses about Germany and UK. The Netherlands and Sweden do not show significant relationships.

**Figure 4.3. Percentages of modern variable pay
by HPWO (ESWC 2000) / by group delegation (EPOC)**

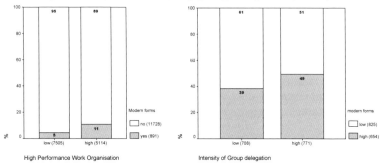

However, the type of pay system seems to depend less on the type of work organisation than expected. For example, there is only a very weak relation between team-based pay and teamwork or interdependent tasks. Whereas team-based pay is significantly more often found with team-work at cross-national level, the results for national sub-samples are different and could be replicated at national level regarding Belgium, Finland, Sweden, and the UK, which almost show equal positive relationships. There is not any relationship only in Germany and The Netherlands. It seems obvious that team-based pay is more frequently applied in organisations with teamwork. An individual-based compensation system in a team-based work organisation might cause a competitive behaviour and does not promote a group-supporting behaviour. For this reason, it is astonishing to notice a so small relationship. This lack of alignment could justify in part the reason why teamwork is sometimes less successful than expected.

Managerial Strategy and Pay Systems – Strategy for Product Innovation

The company strategy was not explicitly dealt with in the EPOC study, but questions regarding management initiatives over the last three years were asked. We used answers referring to product innovation as an indicator for an innovation strategy of the company. In every country, more than a quarter of managers reported that their company introduced product innovation strategy over the last three years. Establishments with an innovation strategy have more often modern forms of variable pay (46%) than those without (32%). These findings are also replicated

140

in the country-specific analyses: as a matter of example, the UK shows the highest correlation and The Netherlands the lowest – even the sole non-existent significant correlation.

Quality of Working Life and Pay Systems

Employees receiving traditional forms of variable pay such as piece rate or productivity pay are more likely to say that their work is less sustainable than those having other types of pay systems. Work is worded "sustainable", if employees think they will be able to do the (same) job when they are 60 years old. The analysis of the national sub-samples of the ESWC 2000 dataset offers similar results. Weak, but significant negative relationships are found in Belgium, Germany, and Sweden, whereas findings concerning Finland and the UK remain negative, but are not statistically significant. In The Netherlands, a relation between piece rate pay and sustainability does not appear to exist. Employees with modern forms of variable pay are not more satisfied with their jobs than those without. Additionally, base or fixed pay is associated with higher job satisfaction, and a weak negative relationship is found between job satisfaction and piece rate or produc-tivity pay. The national results basically provide the same pattern of findings, but due to smaller sample sizes, it is hard to find any signifi-cant relations. The negative correlation pattern between job satisfaction and piece rate pay in most of the covered countries (significant in Ger-many and the UK) is the sole consistent finding: it demonstrates that employees working on piece rate are less likely to be satisfied. Signifi-cant positive relations between HPWO and job satisfaction can be reported for the overall sample as well as for sub-samples of all the countries, showing the strongest association in Sweden and the weakest in Belgium. The weak positive relationship between job satisfaction and modern forms of variable pay and the strong connection between HPWO and satisfaction suggest that job satisfaction is more dependent on the type of work organisation than on the type of pay system. We can plausibly deduce from those results that HPWO increases the quality of working life and, therefore, leads to a higher job satisfaction. As pointed out earlier, we have to be cautious, as correlations do not prove causal inferences.

Modern forms of variable pay seem to be related with a negative per-ception of employees' working life balance. Employees with modern variable pay more often report that work and social commitments do not fit very well. Whereas modern forms of variable pay are negatively correlated with physical load and, therefore, are less likely to be found in workplaces with high repetitive and physically demanding tasks (blue collar job profiles), the correlation with health problems is significantly positive, albeit at a very low level. It means that people getting modern variable pay slightly more often report health problems than those who do not get it (*cf.* Figure 4.4).

Figure 4.4. Percentages of a) modern variable pay by health problems, b) HPWO by physical load (ESWC 2000)

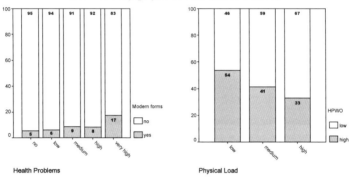

Results change when HPWO is taken into account. Most of the time, employees are reporting a positive working-life balance and feel they have a sustainable work, if they work in work organisations that are characterised by a high HPWO profile. They also report fewer health problems, physical load, and excessive demands. The strongest negative relationship exists between HPWO and physical load. Employees who work in high HPWO profile workplaces are more likely to answer that their work does only include low physical load. In general, HPWO apparently support a more positive assessment of working conditions and other factors that contribute to a higher quality of working life.

Organisational Performance and Pay Systems

While ESWC 2000 data does not provide any information about organisational outcomes, the EPOC questionnaire includes questions about indicators which measure the organisational effectiveness. Managers have been asked whether they could report any outcomes due to the introduction of direct participation. The criteria for the assessment of performance are the reduction in the numbers of employees and managers, the decrease in absenteeism and sickness rates, the increase in output, the improvements in quality, time and cost reduction. Establishments with modern forms of variable pay do report more effects – due to the introduction of group delegation activities concerning only two out of eight criteria – than those without modern forms of variable pay. Those two criteria are increases in output and the reduction in the numbers of managers (*cf.* Figure 4.5).

Figure 4.5. Percentages of performance by modern variable pay (EPOC)

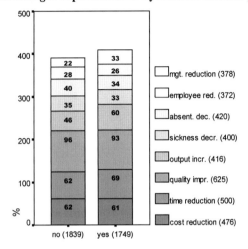

Variable pay (modern forms)

At the national level, the number of cases decreases to a certain extent, which makes a statistical interpretation of the results questionable for most of the criteria (ranging from 17 to 125 respondents), and only five out of 32 results are significant. These few significant results are not interpreted, as they might be due to sample effects or be influenced by unknown third variables; this is especially the case when correlation patterns differ between countries, which might also indicate institutional differences between countries.

After taking into account these predominantly insignificant relationships between modern forms of variable pay and performance, we conclude that pay systems on their own, seem to have only a minor influence on performance. In the next step, the influence of moderating variables such as aspects of work organisation and strategy are analysed, which might explain why there is not any relationship between pay systems and performance at a general level. On the basis of our assumptions, we expect that an inconsistent alignment between pay systems, work organisation, and strategy weakens the impact of modern pay systems on performance. Positive responses to the effectiveness must be considered as dependent on the alignment or fit of different elements within the organisational system. If certain aspects of work organisation, managerial strategies, and pay systems are consistently aligned, then they should foster positive outcomes.

Figure 4.6. Percentages of performance by modern forms of variable pay and low/high group delegation (EPOC)

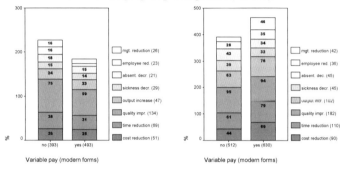

The analysis of data supports this alignment hypothesis: we associate modern forms of variable pay with performance indicators for high and low intensity of group delegation (*cf.* Figure 4.6). Companies with a low intensity of group delegation and with modern forms of variable pay more often report that the introduction of group delegation does not lead to reduction in time, improvement in quality, reduction in the number of employees and managers than companies with other forms of pay systems. Managers from companies with a high intensity of group delegation and with modern forms of variable pay more frequently answer that the introduction of group delegation does lead to cost and time reduction and also to a reduction in the number of managers. An increase in higher output has been also noticed, but findings are not statistically significant. Due to small sample sizes at national level, we did not carry out these analyses at national level, but only at cross-national level.

Figure 4.7. Percentages of modern variable pay by group delegation without/with innovation strategy (EPOC)

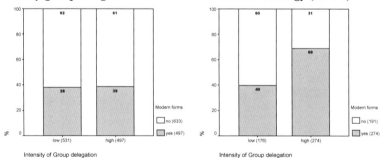

144

We have also studied the influence of innovation strategy on the relation between work organisation and pay systems. The key questions are the following: Does the influence of strategy make up for differences in the relationship between pay system and work organisation; does strategy play a key role in the alignment of those variables? Can the coincidence of pay systems and work organisation be considered as strategy-driven as it is postulated in the strategic fit approach? A low or high degree of group delegation seems not to influence the choice of companies deprived of an innovation strategy, whether they use modern forms of variable pay or not. Significant relationships have not been found neither at cross-national nor at national level. However, companies endowed with an innovation strategy and an intensive group delegation more frequently use modern forms of variable pay than companies with low group delegation. Strategy seems to play a key role in the introduction of modern forms of variable pay, when it is aligned with a high intensity of decisive power and control which have been transferred from management to employees (*cf.* Figure 4.7). At national level, it has only been the case for Germany. In the UK, The Netherlands, and Sweden there was not any noticeable relationship. To sum up, a positive relation between modern forms of variable pay and group delegation apparently only exists in organisations that implemented a strategy towards product innovation. These findings seem to support the assumptions made by the strategic fit approach.

Performance, Work Organisation, Strategy, and Pay Systems

In the following section, we extend the scope of contingency and take into consideration indicators for strategy, pay systems, work organisation, and performance for a further analysis. The examination of a contingent relationship is somehow difficult for two reasons: the selection of sub-samples and the application of filters to these samples reduce the number of cases when it comes to the investigation of the influence of moderating variables. The EPOC questionnaire contains jump rules that structure the way through the course of questions, *i.e.* respondents are asked if something applies for them and only if they agree they have to answer the following questions in that section of the questionnaire, reducing the number of respondents successively as they follow this decision tree. Due to the small number of cases, which ranges from 27 to 105, only huge differences or especially strong relationships become statistically significant.

Figure 4.8. Percentages of performance by modern variable pay, low/high group delegation without innovation strategy (EPOC)

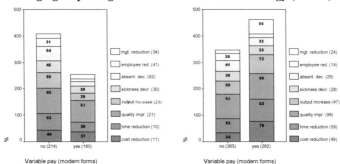

Companies with modern forms of variable pay, a low intensity of group delegation, and without an innovation strategy more frequently answer that the introduction of group delegation does not lead to time reduction, quality improvement, and output increases or to the reduction in absenteeism or in the number of employees. As expected, companies with modern forms of variable pay, a high intensity of group delegation, and deprived of an innovation strategy are more positively answering. Managers of the establishments state that the introduction of group delegation leads to cost and time reduction, output increases, and a reduction in the number of managers (*cf.* Figure 4.8). These findings point out again the importance of group delegation when it is combined with a set of aligned variables even without an innovation strategy.

Contrary to our expectations, companies with a high intensity of group delegation and an innovation strategy report similar effects of the introduction of group delegation regardless whether they apply modern forms of variable pay or not (*cf.* Figure 4.9). Statistical analysis did not show significant results for any of the outcome indicators. These findings do not support findings mentioned above, where the reported positive effects of the aligned variables feature something different. If these results have not been influenced by the small number of cases, it seems that innovation strategy may compensate for the effects of modern pay or group delegation, although high group delegation companies slightly more often report positive effects than companies with low group delegation.

Figure 4.9. Percentages of performance by modern variable pay, low/high group delegation with an innovation strategy (EPOC)

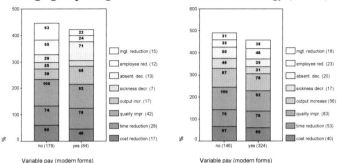

Summary and Conclusions

From our secondary analysis of the ESWC 2000 and EPOC survey, we can draw the following conclusions: some aspects of HPWO more frequently appear with modern forms of variable pay, this is consistent with the current research (*e.g.* Lay & Rainfurth, 1999; Pendleton *et al.*, 2001; Poutsma, 2001). Furthermore, every third company reports the use of group delegation (EPOC Research Group, 1997), and almost every third has taken innovation strategy initiatives. Moreover, EPOC data show that modern forms of variable pay and high intensity of group delegation much more often exist in companies with an innovation strategy, whereas there is not any link for companies without an innovation strategy. All the associations between pay system, work organisation, and strategy are rather low, but can be found in almost all the considered countries of the ESWC 2000 and the EPOC survey. Only a few other studies have analysed the relationship between strategy and pay systems, while finding no consistent relationships (*cf.* Bahnmüller, 2001; Thompson, 2002). This might be due, in part to the fact, that there is often a kind of "time lag" between changes in strategy and congruent changes in pay systems. This can result from sequential implementation, *e.g.* first a change in strategy, secondly in work organisation, and thirdly in pay system. Another reason might be the restrictions of collective bargaining, which cause time delay or might even block the alignment of pay systems. What can show that collective bargaining might delay or hinder alignment is the case of UK: with a deregulated free market economy, the relationship between innovation strategy and modern forms of work system is much stronger than on average – even stronger than in Sweden, Germany, and The Netherlands, especially, which can be characterised by socio-liberal markets and strong institutionalised participation rights. Interestingly, the UK also shows the strongest negative relationship between the density of union and modern forms of variable pay.

In the EPOC survey, each of these three variables – modern forms of variable pay, high intensity of group delegation, and innovation strategy – shows positive bivariate correlations with two or three out of eight outcome variables. This means, for example, that more companies in the EPOC survey report increases in output if they have an innovation strategy, high intensity of group delegation, or modern forms of variable pay.

Regarding employee-related outcomes, the ESWC 2000 data shows that HPWO has much stronger positive relationships with indicators of quality of working life, such as job satisfaction, sustainable work, or working life balance, than modern forms of pay systems. Correlations between HPWO and the indicators of quality of working life reach a medium level concerning job satisfaction, whereas they remain weak as regards modern forms of pay systems at a cross-national and national level. The results of existing studies concerning pay systems and/or work organisation together with organisational performance are very different between European countries as well as between different studies within a country (*e.g.* Eriksson, 2002; Nilsson, 1990). The same holds for the relation between pay systems and work satisfaction (*e.g.* Eriksson & Leander, 1995; Holman, 2002).

Why are most of the correlations so low concerning the relationships between pay systems, work organisation, and quality of working life together with performance? While interpreting these results, the following aspects have to be taken into account:

- With regard to indicators of quality of working life, it is known from research on stress that only low correlations can be expected due to interpersonal differences and the furthering and hindering influence of many different variables.

- Low reliability and validity of assessments might also explain the low correlations between the reported effects of group delegation and other variables.

- Many factors do influence the relationships between model variables in different directions and lead to low correlations, too. If some of them are controlled by holding them constant or including them in analyses, as we did in comparing correlations between different groups or by using regression analyses relationships increase; however this reduces sample size and correlations might not become significant.

From the analysis of the interdependencies between pay systems and/or work organisation and organisational performance, our results of the EPOC data show that an interaction effect between group delegation and modern forms of variable pay exists at least for three out of eight analysed outcomes: more companies with modern systems of variable pay report reduction in costs, throughput times, and management personnel as a result of group delegation, if they have high intensity of group delegation compared to those with traditional pay systems.

As research regarding high performance work systems shows inconsistent results at best (Godard, 2004), more research is needed, finding and analyzing moderating variables, which can explain these differences.

Company strategy seems to be a key moderator of the relationship between pay systems, work organisation, and organisational performance. Our results from the EPOC data show that the effects of pay systems depend on strategy:

- If a company has an innovation strategy and high intensity of group delegation, the type of pay system has not any impact on the group delegation effects.

- Only if an innovation strategy is combined with low intensity of group delegation, three out of eight outcomes of group delegation depend on the type of pay system. In this case, less companies report management, reduction in employees and decrease in absenteeism.

- If a company has not any innovation strategy, the effects of group delegation differ for both low and high intensity of group delegation, if modern forms of variable pay exist:

  - For low intensity of group delegation, less companies report group delegation effects concerning five out of eight outcomes (reduction in time and employees, increase in output and quality, decrease in absenteeism).

  - For high intensity of group delegation, more companies report group delegation effects regarding four out of eight reported outcomes (reduction in cost, time and management, increase in output).

The comparison between the effects of work organisation and pay systems indicates that work organisations show much stronger relations to quality of working life, such as job satisfaction and stress.

Our analyses indicate that the intensity of group delegation seems to be more important to achieve group delegation effects than pay systems. This supports the assertion that aspects of work organisation have stronger effects than pay systems not only on the quality of working life, but on performance outcomes as well. Furthermore, our data also support our theoretical assumptions that one should not only consider isolated variables to improve the quality of working life and performance outcomes; it is also necessary to align these variables on the basis of their explicit or implicit steering mechanisms for the employee's behaviour. Our data show that interaction effects exist between strategy, work organisation, and pay systems. This means that, if these variables are aligned, they do have stronger effects than if they are independently studied. Furthermore, if strategy, work organisation, and pay systems imply different goals and directions for the employee's behaviour, this might deteriorate performance and quality of working life. These counteracting effects can be viewed as one reason for the observed low bivariate correlation between work organisation, pay systems, performance and quality of working life. These relationships get much stronger, if one controls these counteracting effects and *e.g.* analyses the effects of work organisation with high degrees of direct participation and autonomy combined with modern forms of pay systems, such as team bonuses and/or profit sharing.

Further research is necessary to specify, to investigate on these mechanisms and to explain the reported inconsistent results together with national differences. Nevertheless, the results of our secondary analyses of the ESWC 2000 and EPOC data are promising, although these surveys were not designed to answer our research questions.

References

Almodovar, A., Zimmermann, M., Maqueda, J., Tejedor, M., Orden, V. de la, Fraile, A., Nogareda, C., Arévalo, A., Laguarta, A. (2005), *Working Conditions Surveys. Comparative Analysis Related to Data Sources, Data Availability and Findings Emanating from EU National Surveys on Working Conditions*, Luxembourg: Office for Official Publications of the European Communities.

Antoni, C., Berger, A., Baeten, X., Emans, B., Hulkko, K., Kessler, I., Neu, E., Vartiainen, M. & Verbruggen, A. (2005), *Wages and Working Conditions in the European Union*, Dublin: European Foundation for the Improvement of Living and Working Conditions.

Bahnmüller, R. (2001), *Stabilität und Wandel der Entlohnungsformen: Entgeltsysteme und Entgeltpolitik in der Metallindustrie, in der Textil- und Bekleidungsindustrie und im Bankgewerbe* [Stability and Change in Pay Systems: Pay Systems and Pay Policy in the Metal Industry, Clothing Industry and Banks], Munich, Mering: Hamp.

Emans, B. J. M., Antoni, C. H., Baeten, X., Kakonen, N., Kira, M., Neu, E. (2003), "Pay-for-performance in Europe: Prevalence and National Differences", Paper Presented at the 11th European Congress on Work and Organisational Psychology, Lisbon.

EPOC Research Group (1997), *New Forms of Work Organisation: Can Europe realise its potential? Results of a Survey of Direct Employee Participation in*

Europe, Luxembourg: Office for Official Publications of the European Communities.

Eriksson, G. & Leander, E. (1995), "Konsekvenser av individuell lönesättning - en enkätundersökning inom högskolan" [Consequences of individual pay – A survey within the university and college], Linköpings universitet [Linköping University].

Eriksson, M. (2002), "Lönesystem, produktivitet och kunskapsstimulans" [Pay system, productivity and knowledge encouragement], Chalmers Tekniska Högskola [Chalmers University of Technology].

Godard, J. (2004), "A Critical Assessment of the High-Performance Paradigm", *British Journal of Industrial Relations*, 42, p. 349-378.

Gomez-Mejia, L.R. (1992), "Structure and Process of Diversification, Compensation Strategy, and Firm Performance", *Strategic Management Journal*, 13, p. 381-397.

Holman, D. (2002), "Employee Wellbeing in Call Centres", *Human Resource Management Journal*, 12, p. 35-50.

Lawler, E. E. (1990), *Strategic Pay*, San Francisco: Jossey-Bass.

Lawler, E. E. (1995), "The New Pay: A Strategic Approach", *Compensation and Benefits Review*, 27, p. 5-14.

Lay, G. & Rainfurth, C. (1999), "Königsweg Prämie?" [Bonus systems – A silver bullet?], Report from the Innovation in Production Survey, No. 13, Fraunhofer Institut für Systemtechnik und Innovationsforschung (ISI).

Nilsson, T. (1990), *Bonus för industritjänstemän – lönar det sig?* [Bonus for industry white collar workers – Does it pay?], Stockholm: SIF [Swedish Union of Technical and Clerical Employees in Industry].

Paoli, P. & Merllié, D. (2001), *Third European Survey on Working Conditions 2000*, Luxembourg: Office for Official Publications of the European Communities.

Pendleton, A., Poutsma, E., Brewster, C. & van Ommeren, J. (2001), *Employee Share Ownership and Profit-sharing in the European Union*, Dublin: European Foundation for the Improvement of Living and Working Conditions.

Poutsma, E. (2001), *Recent Trends in Employee Financial Participation in the European Union*, Dublin: European Foundation for the Improvement of Living and Working Conditions.

Sisson, K. (2002), *Direct Participation and the Modernisation of Work Organisation*, Luxembourg: Office for Official Publications of the European Communities.

Thompson, M. (2002), *Pay and Performance in the UK Aerospace*, DTI/SBAC.

Tichy, N.M., Fombrun, C.J. & Devanna, M.A. (1982), "Strategic human resource management", *Sloan Management Review*, 23, p. 47-60.

Van het Kaar, R. & Grünell, M. (2001), *Comparative Study on Variable Pay in Europe*, Dublin: European Foundation for the Improvement of Living and Working Conditions.

http://www.eiro.eurofound.eu.int/2001/Study/TN0104201S.html

CHAPTER 4.2

Pay Systems and Pay Outcomes in Different European Countries

Conny H. ANTONI

This section puts forward national findings for the following countries: Belgium, Finland, Germany, The Netherlands, Sweden, and the United Kingdom. All the national reports mainly draw on findings from two types of databases: first and foremost, they result from national studies carried out in each country and, secondly, from cross-national European databases. There are three European databases: (1) the European Industrial Relations Observatory (EIRO), based on national reports made by EIRO national centres (Van het Kaar & Grünell, 2001); (2) the European Survey on Working Conditions (ESWC), based on a sample of employees (Paoli & Merllié, 2001); (3) the Employee direct Participation in Organisational Change (EPOC), based on a sample of companies (EPOC Research Group, 1997). While focusing on pay-related issues, Antoni and Berger (see Antoni *et al.*, 2005) reanalysed the ESWC and EPOC databases in order to picture the European situation as a whole. Additional analyses were carried out for the sub-samples of these six countries and the outcomes thereof are used below, together with the outcomes of the above mentioned national research projects, in order to get a picture of the situation in each country. Taken together, the studies give some insight into the relationships of pay-parameters, context-parameters, and (incidentally) performance parameters, as they are found in each country. The key points of interest for reviewing research literature and secondary analysis have been indicators of pay, pay system and their associations with personal conditions (age and gender), organisational conditions (size and sector), working conditions (contract type and working time flexibility), institutional factors (degree of union membership and employees' representation), aspects of work organisation, managerial strategy, quality of working life, and performance. The summary at the end of each national report reflects our efforts to make clear the way a national perspective on pay and pay systems contribute to the overall European picture.

References

Antoni, C., Berger, A., Baeten, X., Emans, B., Hulkko, K., Kessler, I., Neu, E., Vartiainen, M. & Verbruggen, A. (2005), *Wages and Working Conditions in the European Union*, Dublin: European Foundation for the Improvement of Living and Working Conditions.

EPOC Research Group (1997), *New Forms of Work Organisation: Can Europe Realise Its Potential? Results of a Survey of Direct Employee Participation in Europe*, Luxembourg: Office for Official Publications of the European Communities.

Paoli, P. & Merllié, D. (2001), *Third European Survey on Working Conditions 2000*, Luxembourg: Office for Official Publications of the European Communities.

Van het Kaar, R. & Grünell, M. (2001), *Comparative Study on Variable Pay in Europe*, Dublin: European Foundation for the Improvement of Living and Working Conditions.

http://www.eiro.eurofound.eu.int/2001/Study/TN0104201S.html

CHAPTER 4.2.1

Pay Systems and Outcomes in Belgium

Xavier BAETEN & An VERBRUGGEN

This chapter on pay systems and outcomes in Belgium is based on seven national studies (Baeten & Hoornaert, 2003a, 2003b; Baeten & Van den Berghe, 2002; Baeten & Verbruggen, 2005; Belgian Federal Government, 2004; De Witte & Morel, 2002; Steyaert, 2000), which encompass findings from cross-national European studies.

Most of the national studies have collected data by means of written and computer-based questionnaires that have been sent to both employers and employees. There is a strong focus on the circumstances and the prevalence of financial participation schemes. Another point of particular interest has been pay systems' outcomes. Both employees' satisfaction with the current pay system and gender-related issues, together with the effectiveness of pay systems from a HR point of view have been studied in Belgium. This complies with the stakeholder-oriented approach, which is specific to this book. Very recently, data about the prevalence of performance-based pay systems were also collected, both at the employers' and employees' level.

Modern forms of variable pay have often been part of political debates in Belgium. This is linked with Belgium's differentiated law system concerning financial participation. For instance, pay in profit sharing models is subject to tax at 25%, whereas tax only reaches 15% in share ownership systems. In order to be entitled to a favourable tax treatment, it is necessary to place some limits: shareholding may not be higher than 10% of the organisation's total pay costs or 20% of the total profit (Van het Kaar & Grünell, 2001). Nevertheless, the research is not wide-ranging concerning pay systems, performance, work organisation, and working conditions.

Indicators

The existence or not of different types of pay systems appears to be the main indicator. While focusing on work organisation, many studies have used indicators such as the presence or not of different forms of participation, autonomy, and flexibility. A key performance-related

155

indicator has been the turnover. Quality of working life was measured through wide ranging indicators such as satisfaction, absenteeism, and job security.

Prevalence of Pay Systems

In the ESWC 2000 survey, 4% of the Belgian employees answer they get modern forms of variable pay in comparison with 6% on average in all the 15 European countries included in this study. The occurrence of performance-related pay in Belgium is increasing. In 1998, only 26% of a representative sample of Belgian employees received one form or another of performance-related pay (Salarisenquête Vacature, 2002). In 2005, Vlerick Leuven Gent Management School conducted a research in which 10,902 employees participated: they were asked, whether they are entitled to variable pay, which was defined as "a system that makes your pay dependent on some results and mostly paid out once a year". In general, 27% of the employees are entitled to a bonus. This is quite comparable with the 1998 data, but it should be taken into account that variable pay, which is mostly paid out once a year, as it was defined in this study, is only one form of performance-related pay. Furthermore, there is a key difference in the occurrence of bonus schemes if the sector in which the respondents are employed is taken into account. 37% of the employees in the private sector are entitled to a bonus in comparison with only 9% in the public sector. Concerning the private sector, the occurrence of variable pay is linked with the hierarchical level. 14% of the blue-collar workers have a bonus, compared with respectively 29%, 58%, and 59% for clerical workers, middle management, and senior management (Baeten & Verbruggen, 2005b).

Another survey conducted by Vlerick Leuven Gent Management School more specifically focused on the variable pay schemes that were used. The sample consisted of 335 organisations and was representative as regards the size of the organisation. Rewarding individual performance is the most popular system (22% of the companies have a system in place for blue collars, 48% for white collars, 64% for management). The occurrence of profit sharing and stock-related compensation is very limited, both for blue collars (resp. 5% and 3%), white collars (resp. 11% and 10%), and management (resp. 29% and 26%). A positive link exists between the occurrence of performance-related pay and the inclusion of pay in collective bargaining. Within the group of organisations where pay is part of collective bargaining, 37% of them have performance-related pay. This percentage only reaches 24% for organisations where pay is not part of collective bargaining (Baeten & Verbruggen, 2005a). This is a key finding, which contradicts the general belief that unions have a negative impact on the occurrence of performance-related pay schemes. The previous data were found by means of a web-based questionnaire, which was sent to people in charge of HR. Although the occurrence of a broad-based financial participation is rather limited, stock options and profit sharing are by far the most popular systems of financial participation; they are particularly popular within organisations with high employee turnover. The occurrence of both is pretty much linked with the hierarchical level. A key difference apparently lies between HR beliefs and HR practices: senior management shows a positive attitude towards profit sharing and financial participation. However, only 54% of the 161 companies in the sample have at least one system. More generally, we have found that there is a huge gap between rhetoric and reality concerning the managements' attitude regarding workers' participation (Baeten & Van den Berghe, 2002).

Results from the analyses of ESWC 2000 data (Antoni *et al.*, 2005) suggest that there is a link between the level of income and pay systems. Employees who receive modern forms of variable pay, more generally belong to high-income groups. With regard to the relationship between gender and modern forms of variable pay, it can be said that men receive more often forms of variable pay than women. 5% of the male workers receive pay that relates to group or company performance or income from other shares, whereas only 2% of the female workers do so.

In Belgium, discriminatory regulations in Collective Labour Agreements – which mention women's pay as a percentage of men's pay – have been banned. However, apparently, there is still a difference between men's and women's earnings. A study, which was published in 1997 by the National Institute of Statistics, has shown that in 1996, female blue-collar workers earned 79% of what their male counterparts earned. This percentage is limited to 70% among a white-collar population. Fortunately, this difference has decreased between 1977 and 1996. To conclude, there are still differences between men's and women's earnings, but these differences are diminishing (Belgian Federal Government, 2004).

Findings from the analyses of ESWC 2000 data show that there is not any significant correlation between age and the prevalence of modern forms of variable pay. The distribution by age groups shows very small percentages ranging from 0% (65 years old or over) to 5% (15 to 25 years old) of workers which are paid with modern forms of variable pay.

As already mentioned above, modern forms of variable pay nearly do not exist in the public sector, but are more frequent in private sector establishments. The analysis carried out at national level did not evidence significant relations between modern forms of variable pay and size or other working conditions such as contract type and working time flexibility. Whether Belgian workers are receiving an income under a form of compensation – which refers to group or company performance – or an income coming from other shares has apparently nothing to do with the companies' size, the contract type or the flexibility of working times.

Recent findings from national studies contradict these findings: Baeten and Van den Berghe argue that financial participation is positively linked to the size of the organisation, which is listed on the stock exchange. Secondly, financial participation is more popular among full-time workers than among temporary and part-time workers (Baeten & Van den Berghe, 2002). As far as the link between companies' size and bonus schemes is concerned, bonuses for clerical workers seem to prevail in large organisations (*i.e.* 1,000 or more employees). 43% of the clerical workers in these organisations have a bonus, in comparison with only 26% of this group in organisations employing between 500 and 1,000 employees (Baeten & Verbruggen, 2005b).

Relation between Pay System and Work Organisation

The results brought by Antoni *et al.* (2005) show that employees with modern forms of variable pay – with team bonus and/or profit sharing and/or income from shares – are more usual in high performance work organisations (HPWO), characterised by time and task autonomy, task variety, responsibility, and effective participation. This finding is consistent with the results obtained in analyses conducted at cross-national level, although the association between HPWO and modern forms of variable pay is not as strong as at cross-national level. Percentages of employees with modern forms of variable pay range from 3% with a low degree of HPWO to 7% with a high degree of it.

Effectiveness of Pay Systems and System Alignment

Regarding the effectiveness of pay systems in terms of organisational performance indicators, Baeten and Van den Berghe (2002) show that a positive relationship exists between the occurrence of stock options and the organisation's return on equity. In addition, there is a negative relationship between general rewards satisfaction and absenteeism (Baeten & Hoornaert, 2003a).

On the basis of ESWC 2000 survey data, Antoni *et al.* (2005) assume that pay systems and the quality of working life are linked to each other. However, data analysis does not reveal any consistent results. Employees who receive traditional forms of variable pay such as piece rate or productivity pay are more likely to say that their work is less sustainable than those having other types of pay systems. With a Belgian sample size of around 1,500 respondents in comparison with the overall sample size of 21,000 employees, the weakness of cross-national correlations between types of pay systems and the assessment of general satisfaction also gets down and does not show any significance. Employees with modern forms of variable pay are not more satisfied with their jobs than those without. Job satisfaction – consistent with cross-national analysis –, is also significantly linked with HPWO in Belgium; as a result, it seems to be more dependent on the type of work organisation than on the type of pay system. Other findings regarding HPWO and indicators of quality of working life such as exaggerated demands, physical load, health risks, or health problems are getting the same way and are supporting this assumption. The correlations between modern forms of variable pay and quality of working life indicators are often weak and sometimes positive, whereas the association between HPWO and those indicators are stronger and negative. Figure 4.10 illustrates this difference. The association between modern forms of variable pay and physical load is negative, but is not statistically significant. The relationship between HPWO and physical load is also negative and significant. Employees less often refer to physically demanding tasks when they work in a high profile HPWO.

**Figure 4.10. Percentages of a) modern variable pay and
b) HPWO by physical load in Belgium**

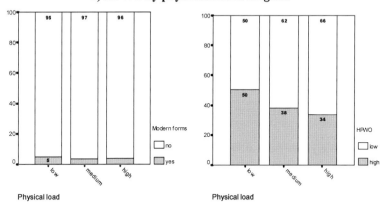

Employees are in favour of variable pay. Even at the lowest white-collar levels, only 26% prefer a pay which is only made of a fixed part. Most of the employees prefer a large variable part and disagree with the statement that everybody doing the same job should be paid equally, irrespective of their performance. However, we should take into account that employees tend to overestimate their own performance. Employees have a moderate behaviour towards cafeteria plans. However, they do

159

not fully agree with the statement that their benefits package complies with their personal needs. The most appreciated employee benefits are the following: retirement provision and medical insurance, followed by company car, disability insurance, additional time off, life insurance, private accident insurance (Baeten & Hoornaert, 2003b).

The higher the pay is, the more satisfied people are with their rewards package. Employees are more satisfied with insurance-related benefits, their job, the flexibility of working time, job security, and time off (satisfaction over 70%) (Baeten & Hoornaert, 2003a). 34% of the people surveyed want to reduce their working time and consider a flexible working time as fundamental (Baeten & Hoornaert, 2003b).

A positive relationship exists between the gross monthly pay, the satisfaction with employee benefits and the job. The regression analysis made clear that the satisfaction with the total rewards package is more strongly influenced by the satisfaction with cash, followed by the satisfaction with structure, communication on pay and reward issues (Baeten & Hoornaert, 2003a). Cash is clearly the most important reward element. It becomes even more important according to the hierarchical level. The higher the hierarchical level is, the less important seems to be time off. Employees are often quite satisfied with their pay level, their evolution, and their employee benefits. However, they are not satisfied with the way performance and competences are included in their pay (Baeten & Hoornaert, 2003b).

Another survey investigated on employers' opinions about the effectiveness of pay systems. The lower the hierarchical level is, the less effective pay systems seem to be in the opinion of HR executives. Surprisingly enough, the bigger the organisation is, the less effective pay systems apparently are. This might be linked with the need for (over)structuring and preventing a more individual and flexible follow-up. A promising finding was the one which states that pay systems' effectiveness register a better score in organisations with pay-for-performance. The main weaknesses in the opinion of HR executives are the following: line management and employee's involvement, discrimination, link with organisational strategy, relationship between pay and team performance (Baeten & Verbruggen, 2005a).

Summary and Conclusion

This chapter has reported the national research carried out in Belgium on pay, working conditions, and managerial policy, their relationships and outcomes as well as the results of the secondary analyses of the ESWC 2000 data. What has often been neglected in most of the national research has been especially focused on in the Belgian research: the relationship between employees' satisfaction and their type of pay or the kind of pay system they are the most in favour. Another focal point has been gender-related issues. In Belgium, a current well-elaborated statutory framework and the implementation of national tax policies reflect the particular interest raised by the issue of pay and financial participation.

Besides the regular use of measures at income level, such as the total amount of cash or gross monthly income, variables have been used in order to shed light on various components of pay systems. These are for instance stock options, insurance-related benefits or other financial or non-financial bonuses. The diversity of pay systems which have been examined in recent studies, range from performance-related pay schemes with a variable element in remuneration to reward packages put in place by the employees themselves (cafeteria plans). Aspects of work organisation have been studied while using indicators for different forms of participation, autonomy, and flexibility. Relevant performance-related indicators have been absenteeism and turnover, although indicators of organisational effectiveness have been scarcely used. Quality of working life was predominantly measured in terms of employee's satisfaction.

The occurrence of performance-related pay in Belgium seems to increase, although we do not have any comparative data in this respect. In 1998, only 26% of a representative sample of Belgian employees received one form or another of performance-related pay (Salarisenquête Vacature). In 2005, 37% of employees working in the private sector were entitled to a bonus scheme, which is only one tool of performance-related pay. A further striking result from national research is that employees are very much in favour of variable pay and pay differentiation. Even at the lowest white-collar levels, only 26% prefer a pay which is only made of a fixed part and most of the employees prefer a large variable part (Baeten & Hoornaert, 2003b). Stock options and profit sharing are by far the most popular systems of financial participation. Belgian employees only seem to have a moderate attitude towards cafeteria plans. The spread and use of financial participation such as profit sharing or share ownership schemes seem to be bound to hierarchical level and high-income groups. Senior management and white-collar workers are definitely more involved in the use of performance-related pay (Baeten & Van den Berghe, 2002). Employees more often report that they receive modern forms of variable pay when they are working in private sector establishments. Research results regarding contract type or company's size show some inconsistency. While the national research literature enables us to conclude that size and contract type matter, the analysis of the ESWC 2000 dataset reveals, however, that these variables and the incidence of modern forms of variable pay are not linked at all. Belgian results show that a gender gap remains in terms of level of payment. Female white-collar workers, especially, seem to experience great disadvantages in terms of income level in comparison with their male counterparts (Belgian Federal Government, 2004).

Findings from the secondary analysis of the ESWC 2000 data show that in Belgium, modern forms of variable pay such as performance-based pay at team and company level together with income from shares are significantly more usual in high performance work organisations; they are characterised by participation in decision-making and highly diversified and independent tasks which have been delegated.

Due to the lack of Belgian national and cross-national research which focuses on indicators of organisational performance, the results reported in this summary mainly refer to studies on the quality of working life, and on reward or job satisfaction in particular.

Concerning the link between modern forms of variable pay and job satisfaction, the findings from the sub-analysis of the ESWC 2000 dataset, in the case of Belgium, show that employees receiving performance-based pay at team and company level together with income from shares are not more satisfied with their jobs than those without. However, one of the key findings that can be derived from national research is the following: the higher the pay is, the more satisfied people are with their rewards package. Cash is clearly the most important reward element and seems to be linked with the hierarchical level: the higher the pay is, the more important cash becomes. Besides the importance of the gross monthly income, the most appreciated employee benefits are retirement provision and medical insurance, followed by company car, disability insurance, additional time off, life insurance, and private accident insurance. The impact of the general rewards satisfaction gets noticeable in its relation with other variables such as absenteeism. The research literature enables us to argue that there is a negative relationship between rewards satisfaction and absenteeism. However, the issues raised by the practice of variable pay – the misuse of bonuses to compensate for problems of job evaluation schemes or the lack of a system of transparency and communication – show that the way performance is linked to pay is a decisive factor for the assessment and credibility of pay-for-performance and the performance management process. Employers themselves are not really satisfied with the pay systems' effectiveness, mainly concerning line management's and employees' involvement, discrimination issues – *i.e.* equal pay – and the link pay-organisational strategy-team performance.

References

Antoni, C., Berger, A., Baeten, X., Emans, B., Hulkko, K., Kessler, I., Neu, E., Vartiainen, M. & Verbruggen, A. (2005), *Wages and Working Conditions in the European Union*, Dublin, European Foundation for the Improvement of Living and Working Conditions.

Baeten, X. & Hoornaert, S. (2003a), "Hoe tevreden zijn Vlaamse en nederlandstalige Brusselse werknemers met hun beloningspakket?", Research Report (unpublished).

Baeten, X. & Hoornaert, S. (2003b), "Onderzoek bij werknemers naar de tevredenheid en de voorkeuren m.b.t. het beloningspakket", Research Report (unpublished).

Baeten, X. & Van den Berghe, L. (2002), "Participatie van medewerkers: houdingen en feiten op het vlak van financiële en organizatorische participatie", in L. Peeters, P. Mathyssens & L. Vereeck (eds.), *Stakeholder Synergie. Referatenboek, Vijfentwintigste Vlaams-Wetenschappelijk Economisch Congres* (Hasselt, 14.03.2002), Faculteit Toegepaste Economische Wetenschappen, Limburgs Universitair Centrum, Diepenbeek, Garant.

Baeten, X. & Verbruggen, A. (2005a), "Motivating and Rewarding Nowaday's and Tomorrow's Workforce", Research Report (unpublished), Vlerick Leuven Gent Management School.

Baeten, X. & Verbruggen, A. (2005b), "Peiling: Verloning arbeiders, bedienden en kaderleden", Research Report (unpublished), Vlerick Leuven Gent Management School.

Belgian Federal Government (2004), Belgian Federal Government: website: http://meta.fgov.be/pc.pce/pceg/nlceg02.htm.

De Witte & Morel (2002), Salary Survey 2002, http://www.belgium.hudson.com.

Salarisenquête 2002, http://www.vacature.com.

Steyaert, S. (2000), *Gewikt en Gewogen. Evalueren en waarderen in organizaties*, Brussel: SERV/STV-Innovatie en Arbeid.

Van het Kaar, R. & Grünell, M. (2001), *Comparative Study on Variable Pay in Europe*, Dublin, European Foundation for the Improvement of Living and Working Conditions. http://www.eiro.eurofound.eu.int/2001/Study/TN0104201S.html.

CHAPTER 4.2.2

Pay Systems and Outcomes in Finland

Kiisa HULKKO & Matti VARTIAINEN

The analysis of Finnish research on pay and pay systems comprises twenty-three studies, which have mainly been published from 2000 onwards: those studies more deeply examine findings coming from cross-national European studies. The literature covered in this review joins economics and psychology of work. Different methods have been applied such as the use of existing statistics, interviews – face-to-face and by phone-questionnaires, and surveys in order to collect data. Wide ranging employees' groups have been studied from top management executives to blue-collar workers. A few studies examine pay systems in relation with the quality of working life, gender, and age. A more usual focus is set on the relation between pay systems and productivity outcomes, motivation, turnover, and personal performance. The most prominent concept which has been studied is the functionality of pay and reward systems.

The Finnish collective agreement culture can be described as centralised. Collective agreements are signed concerning increases in general salary, but some degrees of freedom exist at the local company-level bargaining. As a result, the pay consists of an interaction between central agreements and local bargaining. The relatively high number of Finnish studies might result from the quick increase in the incidence of variable pay from 1990s onwards. However, there is not full understanding between the employer's and employee's representatives concerning the issue where and how variable pay should be decided. Currently, most of the Finnish trade unions seem to approve of variable pay, despite the union's discrepancies concerning many related issues, such as the level at which decisions about variable pay should be made (company level or national level); the opinions within the trade union range from strong disagreements to a supportive point of view (Van het Kaar & Grünell, 2001). This might be sufficient to justify our willingness of clarifying in depth variable pay-related research questions.

Indicators

The Finnish compensation system consists of three bases and main pay components (*cf.* Table 4.1). Fixed pay is typically defined by agreements, as well as a part of variable pay, *i.e.* the rules of performance-related pay are approved of in central agreements, but locally applied. The results-based pay is fully decided at the organisational level. A review of the Finnish research literature revealed pay indicators which relate to fixed and variable pay and to the functionality of pay systems. Fixed pay indicators include, for example, job requirements, performance, seniority, general experience, and education. Variable pay indicators concern both performance-based pay and pay by results. Typically, results-based pay systems have several levels of measuring, *i.e.* individual, group, and company levels. Both fixed and variable pay were often studied grouped according to white-collar workers and blue-collar workers systems. There are quite a few indicators of organisational interventions. The studies of Nurmela *et al.* (1999) used the leadership style (fairness concept) and personnel's opportunities to influence decision-making, and Lautala (2001) used teamwork and involvement in variable pay system design. Indicators of the quality of working life included *e.g.* work motivation, employees' turnover, and stress. Performance indicators which have been recently used mainly relate to productivity and performance outcomes at various levels.

**Table 4.1. The bases, measurement,
and components of Finnish pay systems**

Bases of compensation	Measurement	Pay components
Results and outcomes	Result and outcome indicators - *What are the outcomes?*	Results-based pay *e.g.* profit-sharing, group bonus
Competences and performance	Appraisal of competences and personal performance - *How is work done?*	Person-based pay *e.g.* personal allowance
Job and task requirements	Job evaluation - *What is done?*	Job-based pay *e.g.* monthly base pay

Prevalence of Pay Systems

Pay is typically given according to job requirements and seniority or performance in Finnish organisations (Hakonen, Salimäki & Hulkko, 2005). There has been a trend towards job and performance-based pay systems. In 2004, nearly half of Finnish organisations used pay systems on the basis of job evaluations, and more than half of the organisations used competency or performance evaluations. Job and performance-based systems will become even more common in public sector especially where 100% of prevalence is set as the goal in collective agreements in 2006. At the municipal level, there is an ongoing project for implementing job- and performance-based pay system by 2007. However, seniority-based pay is still used in nearly half of the organisations, but it is declining.

Variable pay systems, payment by results in particular, are currently quite usual in Finnish workplaces. Firstly, they started to develop in the manufacturing sector in the mid-1990s. At the end of the 1990s, it gained pace in the private service sector. According to the Confederation of Finnish Industries (2005), 32% of private sector companies had results-based pay systems in use by the end of 2004, and they covered 52% of employees. Payment by results is more usual in industrial companies than in service sector companies covering 69% of industrial employees, 44% of service sector employees, and 40% of the employees in the building sector. Differences are also due to the business area – in energy and paper industries – where results-based pay covered more than 90% of personnel. Variable pay is more commonly a part of white-collar workers' pay package rather than blue-collar workers' (over 63% *vs.* 41%). Larger companies tend to use much more variable pay than smaller companies. 10% of the smallest companies, employing less than twenty people, still use variable pay systems. When variable pay is used, it covers all the personnel in half of the cases. In the second half of the companies, variable pay is mainly used for white-collar employees. Variable pay systems are more usual in large, capital intensive companies that have a larger part of salaried employees and high pay wages (Uusitalo, 2002). Profit sharing is also required by R&D intensity and the company's willingness to get some stability in the skilled workforce (Kauhanen & Piekkola, 2002). In addition, a major part of publicly traded companies introduced management stock option plans since 1990s.

Contrary to these findings, in the ESWC 2000 survey, only 10% of the Finnish employees answer that they have modern forms of variable pay in comparison with 6% on average among the 15 European countries included in this study (Antoni *et al.*, 2005). This proves how quick this development has been.

Payments by results are still scarce in the public sector as only 7% of municipal employees and 25% of governmental employees have such systems in 2003 (Lehto & Sutela, 2004). However, over the last couple of years, the introduction of new variable pay systems has gained more pace in public sector than in private sector (Ylöstalo, 2003).

ESWC 2000 data for the overall cross-national sample and for the Finnish sample confirm this finding. 14% of the employees in private owned companies report that their reward package includes variable pay schemes such as profit sharing, share ownership, or team performance-related pay. Less than 5% of the employees in the public sector did receive any of these variable components. An investigation on the relationship between pay systems and employment conditions (contract type, working time flexibility) reveals that the type of contract seems to play a key role when it comes to the incidence of modern forms of variable pay: unlimited and fixed term contracts are more usual. In comparison with other countries covered in this report, this correlation is particularly strong for Finland. In contrast with findings concerning other countries and at cross-national level, the association between modern forms of variable pay and working time flexibility is weak and has not any statistical significance. Therefore, employees working in workplaces with flexible working time schedules do not receive significantly more often modern forms of variable pay than others.

The analysis of the Finnish sub-sample from the ESWC 2000 dataset, which consists of around 1,500 interviewed employees, shows that most of the time, employees who receive modern forms of variable pay, belong to high-income groups. The proportion of employees belonging to the intermediate high-income level category who have modern forms of variable pay is about 14% and, respectively, 17% for the high-income group. Another finding, which is consistent with the overall results from cross-national analysis, is the existence of a gender gap in the incidence of modern forms of variable pay. 14% of male employees receive performance-based pay at team and company level or income from shares. This is twice as much as the proportion of female employees receiving forms of variable pay (7%). In a current study (Lehto & Sutela, 2004) including all the sectors, payment by results was used in 2003 in workplaces with 42% of men (covering 38% of men individually), whereas the respective proportions of women in workplaces were 23% and 20%. This results in pay differences between men and women. Men are not only more often paid bonuses, but the amount they are given is also bigger. Lehto's and Sutela's study shows that 13% of male pay and salary earners had received at least € 1,000 for the previous year, whereas the respective proportion among women was only 5%. This differential is repeated in the medium sized bonuses between 500 and € 1,000.

In all, women earn about 20% less than men on average in Finnish workplaces. Some differences cannot be explained by task, age or experience, or another known variable except by gender. Interestingly, women with higher educational background having well-paid jobs drag the most behind their male colleagues (*e.g.* Korkeamäki & Kyyrä, 2003; Vartiainen, 2002; Ylöstalo, 2003). Some findings show that pay system reforms which have introduced job evaluation and performance evaluation have decreased the gap in gender pay in six governmental organisations studied (Huuhtanen *et al.*, 2005). The decrease in pay gap cannot be said yet to result from pay system reforms in the whole organisations studied. The study was made by using pay data prior to reform and after.

Concerning age, we can conclude from ESWC 2000 data that there is not any significant positive correlation between age and modern forms of variable pay; nonetheless, findings from the review of the national research literature show that age is connected with higher pay in Finland (*e.g.* Ilmakunnas & Maliranta, 2003), especially among those with graduate and post-graduate degrees. This is due to seniority-based payments and the moving up to more demanding jobs.

Pay system development has been active in Finnish organisations at the beginning of 2000 – 70% of organisations surveyed said that they are developing their pay system and more than 60% were planning to do so in the three years to come (Hakonen, Salimäki & Hulkko, 2005).

Relation between Pay Systems and Work Organisation

The connection between modern forms of variable pay – team bonus and/or profit sharing and/or income from shares – and high performance work organisations (HPWO) found on average in all the 15 countries included in the ESWC 2000 survey, also exists among Finnish national data. There, a strong relationship does exist, and modern forms of variable pay are more usual in high-performance workplaces. 16% of Finnish employees who work in such workplaces report that their remuneration includes at least some element of modern variable pay, whereas only 7% of those who do not work in high performance workplaces receive modern forms of variable pay (Antoni *et al.*, 2005).

Private companies that have introduced group work use variable pay more frequently. Other changes made in work organisation are connected with the use of more variable pay (Lautala, 2001). In another study, 53% of organisations were willing to change reward systems in order to support the change of working methods and 49% wanted to boost new organisational structure such as team work (Hakonen *et al.*, 2001). There are some descriptive results concerning the use of organisation and team-level performance indicators as a basis of results-based bonuses (*e.g.* Nurmela *et al.*, 1999) and the use of team rewards in metal industries.

It's more common to have variable pay in companies that have high amount of local bargaining (Lautala, 2001). Organisations that systematically tend to develop pay systems in co-operation with employees more often have variable pay systems in use (results-based and performance-based pay) (Hakonen, Salimäki & Hulkko, 2005). The influence of participation in the compensation system design, its implementation and its effect on the acceptability and functionality of the system have also been studied: the relationship is positive as a result (Hakonen, Salimäki & Hulkko, 2005; Lautala, 2001; Nurmela *et al.*, 1999).

Effectiveness of Pay Systems and System Alignment

The effectiveness of results-based pay systems in particular has been widely studied in Finland. According to several studies, variable pay is connected with higher productivity of a company (*e.g* Kauhanen & Piekkola, 2002; Piekkola, Hohti & Ilmakunnas, 1999; Snellman, Uusitalo & Vartiainen, 2003). Payment by results for white-collar workers, in particular, is strongly associated with higher productivity (Uusitalo, 2002). Variable pay systems which work well are related to evaluated effects on unit performance such as the quality of products and the efficiency (Nurmela *et al.*, 1999). The use of variable pay (results-based and performance-based) is linked with the reward system alignment with company goals, and the effectiveness of the reward system (Hakonen, Salimäki & Hulkko, 2005). Fixed pay (where seniority payments are used) has also a positive effect on the whole productivity of the factory (Piekkola, Hohti & Ilmakunnas, 1999).

The use of variable pay is related to an increase in interest on work and commitment (Confederation of Finnish Industry and Employers, 2002). Companies which are using variable pay systems have lower quit rates; and the effect gets stronger in the case of white-collar workers (Uusitalo, 2002). The association is stronger between variable pay and turnover than with fixed pay level and turnover (Snellman, 2002). The characteristics of the variable pay system have an effect on how well the system motivates employees: if an employee's ability is not likely to affect payments, his motivation decreases, whereas if he participates in variable pay system design his motivation increases and so does individual and collective level performance measurement (Kauhanen & Piekkola, 2004).

The functionality of variable pay is related to commitment and work motivation according to Nurmela *et al.* (1999) and Vartiainen and Sweins (2002). Employees approve of variable pay systems even when they do not work so well (Nurmela *et al.*, 1999).

In other countries alike, employees in Finnish companies with modern forms of variable pay as part of their pay package are not more satisfied with their jobs than those without. The Finnish sub-sample of the ESWC 2000 dataset shows a strong correlation between satisfaction and high performance work organisation. This finding suggests that job satisfaction is assessed in relation with the kind of work organisation and is not predominantly influenced by the type of pay system. In the cross-national analysis, employees who receive piece rate or incentive work pay, more often report that their work is less sustainable than those having other types of pay systems. This finding from cross-national data analysis could be replicated, but was not significant at the Finnish national level. When Finnish employees were asked whether they could imagine carry on doing their current job up to the age of sixty, 14% of them, who received piece rate or incentive work pay said yes, whereas 18% said no. A study whose data are coming from Finnish employees' survey, and carried out by Kalmi and Kauhanen (2005) found quite similar connections between HPWO practices and the quality of working life outcomes. Modern forms of variable pay were not significantly related to other practices such as the possibilities to influence or outcomes such as job satisfaction.

Other indicators of the quality of working life, such as excessive demands, physical load, health risks, or health problems show weak connections with modern forms of variable pay for the Finnish subsample. Stronger and negative relationships only exist between HPWO and excessive demands or physical load. Working in a high profile HPWO workplace seems to be associated with less excessively demanding tasks (Antoni *et al.*, 2005).

A few researches have been conducted concerning the pay system – strategy relationship. Nurmela *et al.* (1999) and Vartiainen and Sweins (2002) suggest that the evaluated fit of performance-based pay or profit sharing and organisational strategy was related to the functionality of results-based pay. Employees were surveyed in both studies. Hakonen, Salimäki, and Hulkko (2005) asked 447 personnel managers or other people responsible for pay system development in their organisations to evaluate the fit between pay practices, company goals, the functionality and the effectiveness of pay systems. First of all, the evaluated fit was better in organisations using job evaluation, competence or performance evaluation, and modern forms of variable pay. The link was especially clear when organisations were using both modern forms of variable pay and competence or performance evaluation determining pay level. The fit was also explained by how systematic pay systems had been developed in the past. To conclude, they found that the better the evaluated fit was, the better the estimated functionality of pay systems and effectiveness of pay systems were.

Summary and Conclusion

In this chapter, the national research in Finland on pay, working conditions, and managerial policy, their relationships and outcomes as well as the results of the secondary analysis of the ESWC 2000 data were reported. Finnish studies have largely concentrated on the use of variable pay and its relation to the quality of working life indicators and performance. Some research also points out the relationship between work organisation and pay. Concerning fixed pay, most of the research focuses on the factors determining pay level for an individual.

Finnish studies use variable pay and fixed pay occurrence, and pay levels as indicators as well as the functionality of pay systems. A concept of reward system's functionality has been developed in some of the Finnish teams of research.

The systems of payment by results are common within Finnish organisations. In 2004, 32% of private sector companies had variable pay systems in use, and they covered 52% of employees. Payments by results are still quite rare in public sector as only 7% of municipal employees and 25% of governmental employees have adopted such systems in 2003. In the last couple of years, the speed of introducing new variable pay systems has been higher in public sector than in private sector (Ylöstalo, 2003).

The review of national literature showed that women tend to earn 20% less than men in similar jobs between and within companies. This gender gap is particularly strong for women who have well-remunerated jobs (Korkeamäki & Kyyrä, 2003; Vartiainen, 2002; Ylöstalo, 2003). The difference is also found in the use of results-based pay.

Pay and organisational factors are not narrowly linked to each other in Finnish research. The research is based both on economic data at the society's level and questionnaire-based data at the industry or company level. At the national level, information about the amount of fixed and variable pay is well covered. The use of various organisational forms and working climate within Finnish organisations are well known (*e.g.* yearly Working Life Barometer by Ministry of Labour). These two aspects are still scarcely related to each other. A few existing studies indicate a positive relationship between variable pay and group work as well as between the design of participative pay system, pay acceptance, and functionality.

Variable pay makes up about 2% to 6% of employees' yearly income (depending on the sector and the employee's group). It may not be a considerable amount of money, but it seems to have some positive effects on the productivity and the quality of working life when some requirements are met. We can find some hints of positive pay-system alignment effects, but further research necessarily needs to be carried out in the area of strategic rewarding.

References

Antoni, C., Berger, A., Baeten, X., Emans, B., Hulkko, K., Kessler, I., Neu, E., Vartiainen, M. & Verbruggen, A. (2005), *Wages and Working Conditions in the European Union*, Dublin: European Foundation for the Improvement of Living and Working Conditions.

Confederation of Finnish Industry and Employers (2002), *The Performance-based Pay 2002-report*.

Confederation of Finnish Industries (2005), Salary Survey, http://www.ek.fi.

Hakonen, A., Salimäki, A. & Hulkko, K. (2005), *Palkitsemisen tila ja muutos Suomessa 2004. Yhteistoiminnallinen kehittäminen, yhteensopivuus ja toimivuus* [Reward practices and current changes in Finland 2004. Cooperative development, contingency and functionality], Työpoliittinen tutkimus 280, Helsinki: Ministry of Labour.

Hakonen, N., Hakonen, A., Kuronen, T., Hulkko, K. & Palva, A. (2001), "Palkitsemisen tila Suomessa 2001" [Reward practices in Finland 2001] (unpublished).

Huuhtanen, M., Jämsén, S., Maaniemi, J., Lahti, C. & Karppinen, V. (2005), "Palkkausuudistus valtiosektorilla. Tutkimus työn vaativuuden sekä henkilön pätevyyden ja suoriutumisen arviointiin perustuvien palkkauksjärjestelmien toimivuudesta ja vaikutuksista sukupuolten välisiin palkkaeroihin" [Pay reform in Finnish government sector. Study on functionality of new pay systems and their effects on pay differences between genders], Helsinki University of Technology, Laboratory of Work Psychology and Leadership, Report 3/2005.

Ilmakunnas, P. & Maliranta, M. (2003), *Technology, Labor Characteristics and Wage-productivity Gaps*, Helsinki: ETLA.

Kalmi, P. & Kauhanen, A. (2005), *Workplace Innovations and Employee Outcomes: Evidence from a Representative Employee Survey. Research Paper 61*, SKOPE Publications.

Kauhanen, A. & Piekkola, H. (2002), *Profit Sharing in Finland: Earnings and Productivity Effects. ETLA Discussion Papers 81*, Helsinki: ETLA.

Kauhanen, A. & Piekkola, H. (2004), "What makes performance-related pay schemes work? Finnish evidence", *ELTA Discussion Papers 929*, Helsinki: ELTA/

Korkeamäki, O. & Kyyrä, T. (2003), "Explaining Gender Wage Differentials: Findings from a Random Effects Model", VATT-Discussion Papers No 320.

Lautala, S. (2001), "Tulospalkkaus yksityisellä sektorilla. Tutkimus palkkiojärjestelmien käytön syistä, edellytyksistä ja reunaehdoista" [Performance-based pay in private sector], Research Papers No 82, Helsinki: Labor Institute for Economic Research.

Lehto, A.-L. & Sutela, H. (2004), *Threats and Opportunities. Findings of Finnish Quality of Working Life Surveys 1977-2003*, Helsinki: Statistics Finland.

Nurmela, K., Hakonen, N., Hulkko, K., Kuula, T. & Vartiainen, M. (1999), "Miten tulospalkkaus Suomessa toimii? 40 toteutustapaa tutkineen hankkeen loppuraportti" [Functionality of performance-based pay in Finland. Final report of a study of 40 pay systems], Helsinki: University of Technology, Laboratory of Work Psychology and Leadership, Espoo.

Piekkola, H., Hohti, S. & Ilmakunnas, P. (1999), "Experience and Productivity in Wage Formation in Finnish Industries", Working Paper No 154, Helsinki: Labor Institute for Economic Research.

Snellman, K. (2002), "Has Profit Sharing Led to Fewer Separations", Working Paper No 187, Helsinki: Labor Institute for Economic Research.

Snellman, K., Uusitalo, R. & Vartiainen, J. (2003), *Tulospalkkaus ja teollisuuden muuttuva palkanmuodostus* [Profit sharing and changing pay formation in industry], Helsinki: Edita.

Uusitalo, R. (2002), "Tulospalkkaus ja tuottavuus", VATT-discussion Papers No 276.

Van het Kaar, R. and Grünell, M. (2001), *Comparative Study on Variable Pay in Europe*, Dublin: European Foundation for the Improvement of Living and Working Conditions. http://www.eiro.eurofound.eu.int/2001/Study/TN010 4201S.html.

Vartiainen, J. (2002), "Gender Wage Differentials in the Finnish Labor Market", Working Paper No 179, Helsinki: Labor Institute for Economic Research.

Vartiainen, M. & Sweins, C. (2002), *Personnel Funds in Finland – Their Functionality and Outcomes. Työpoliittinen tutkimus 243*, Helsinki: Ministry of Labor.

Ylöstalo, P. (2003), *Working Life Barometer 2003*, Helsinki: Ministry of Labor.

Prevalence of pay systems information from employer associations:

http://www.ek.fi

http://www.vn.fi

http://www.kuntatyonantajat.fi.

CHAPTER 4.2.3

Pay Systems and Outcomes in Germany

Conny H. ANTONI & Ansgar BERGER[1]

In addition to cross-national European studies, findings from seven national studies contribute to the German perspective on pay structures and systems. Except for one study (Bahnmüller, 2001) which explicitly concerns workers councils, all the studies used questionnaires sent to management representatives. Almost all the variables rely on single source subjective assessments of these respondents. Broad samples of workplaces from the manufacturing and the service sector were analysed, but the manufacturing sectors seem to prevail. Most of the studies focus on the relationships between pay systems, work organisation, and performance outcomes. Only one of them examines the link between a company strategy and pay systems (Bahnmüller, 2001). A common research question seems to be the testing of a contingency relationship between pay systems, work organisation, and performance. In terms of outcomes, these studies concentrate on organisational or corporate performance outcomes and the relative neglect of employee-related outcomes such as employee attitudes and well-being.

The relative small number of German studies concerning modern forms of variable pay might result from the fact that management and workers council have to give their consent to survey research within companies and fear that results might be used by one side or another to support their bargaining position.

Indicators

Concerning pay systems, the inexistence or not of different types of pay systems has been the main indicator. Here are the following indicators for work organisation which are used:

- Different forms of teamwork
- Delegation of responsibilities
- Cost and profit centres

---

[1] The authors would like to thank Jessica Jockers and Felicia Werk for their assistance in data analysis and literature research.

Similar types of indicators of organisational performance are used with regard to productivity and profitability. Only one study tried to develop an indicator for management strategies in terms of rationalisation strategy and company strategy (innovative, restrictive, or expansive).

Prevalence of Pay Systems

Secondary analyses of the EPOC and ESWC data (Antoni *et al.*, 2005) revealed a lesser degree of modern forms of variable pay and a higher prevalence of more traditional forms of pay such as piece rate pay in relation with other European countries. In the ESWC 2000 survey, 5% of the German employees report having modern forms of variable pay in comparison with 6% on average in all the 15 European countries included in this study. Data from the EPOC survey supports this difference, showing that 22% of German companies confirm the use of modern forms of variable pay, whereas 36% is the average of all the countries included in this survey. The prevalence of more traditional forms of variable pay – base or fixed pay – is higher than for the average of the European countries.

Over the last years, the prevalence of pay systems has changed in Germany: a trend leads to an increase in performance-based pay, profit sharing, and share ownership schemes; these trends towards flexible pay systems are more usual for non-pay-scale employees and companies that are not subject to pay scale agreements (Franz *et al.*, 2000). Bonus pay is also more frequently found in companies with teamwork than in companies without (Lay & Rainfurth, 1999).

An analysis of the spread of different pay systems in production areas shows the following distribution in percent of analysed companies (Bullinger, Bauer & Menrad, 2000; Jirjahn, 2002):

• Salary for white collar employees (93%)
• Time pay only (51%)
• Time pay plus efficiency bonus (43%)
• Bonus pay (29%)
• Individual piece rate pay (21%)
• Group piece rate pay (12%)
• Time pay plus bonus (10%)

The frequency of performance-based pay systems is also more usual in large-scale companies. The analysis of the frequencies of pay systems in percent of employees leads to the following pattern:

- Time pay only (37.4%)
- Time pay plus efficiency bonus (15.9%)
- Salary (13.5%)
- Bonus pay (12.5%)
- Group piece rate pay (10.6%)
- Individual piece rate pay (4.8%)
- Time plus bonus (3.5%)
- Standard pay (1.2%)
- Contract-based pay (0.7%)

The results show an increase in group piece rate pay and a decrease in individual piece rate pay, and the respondents identified bonus pay and time pay plus bonus or efficiency bonus with the most important future pay systems. Additionally, respondents believe that management by objectives and profit sharing will gain importance in the future in the context of pay systems (Bullinger, Bauer & Menrad, 2000).

Secondary analyses at cross-national level showed that employees who receive team bonus and/or profit sharing and/or income from shares are more frequently found in high-income groups. The analysis of the ESWC 2000 sub-sample for Germany suggests that the same connection exists between pay and income level. The percentages of those employees receiving variable pay components and belonging to the intermediate high-income group reach 6% and those belonging to the highest income category represent 13%. The gender difference that has been reported for all the countries also prevails in Germany. Once again, the proportion of male employees reporting modern forms of variable pay is twice as much as the proportion of female employees.

Further results from the ESWC 2000 survey for Germany show that there are not any significant associations between age and the prevalence of modern forms of variable pay. Data from the EPOC survey enable us to examine the relationships between modern forms of variable pay, conceptualised as bonuses for team volume of output, profit sharing, or share ownership schemes, and model variables that account for organisational and employment conditions, such as sector, size, and working time flexibility. Findings from both surveys are generally presented together in order to compare and validate results of the secondary data analysis.

The ESWC 2000 sub-sample for Germany reveals a significant positive correlation between modern forms of variable pay and sector. Employees working in private sector establishments more often report that team bonus, profit sharing, and/or income from shares are part of their remuneration. Furthermore, modern forms of variable pay are more frequently found in bigger companies (*cf.* Figure 4.11). In particular, companies with a total number of employees of more than 250 experience an increasingly higher proportion of employees with modern forms of variable pay (12%-14%). Findings from the secondary analysis of the EPOC data at cross-national and national level show similar results for both sector and size. Nearly one third of the workforce in private owned companies receive some forms of variable pay (29%). Despite the limits of the comparability owing to the use of different concepts and methodology, results support the assumption that modern forms of variable pay are significantly more usual in the private than in the public sector; and recurring in bigger companies as well.

**Figure 4.11. Percentages of modern variable pay by size
in Germany (ESWC 2000)**

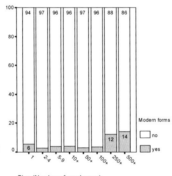

Size (Number of employees)

The investigation on the relationships between pay systems and employment conditions (contract type, working time flexibility) leads to findings which are consistent with results from the cross-national data analysis. At cross-national level, both contract type and working time flexibility are found to be more usually linked with pay systems that include modern forms of variable pay. In the case of working time flexibility, both ESWC 2000 and EPOC survey evidence weak, but positive significant correlations. Employment conditions that are positively associated with variable pay include work under an unlimited contract and flexible working times. The analysis of the German subsample of the ESWC 2000 data does not reveal any significant relationship with contract type. This suggests that the incidence of modern forms of variable pay has nothing to do with the fact that employees work on unlimited, fixed term, and temporary contracts. Findings about working time flexibility support the following assumption made on the basis of cross-national data: employees working in workplaces with flexible working time schedules significantly receive more often modern

178

forms of variable pay than others. The proportions of German employees receiving modern forms of variable pay and working time flexibility reach 8% according to the ESWC 2000 survey and 26% according to the EPOC survey; in contrast with 5% (ESWC 2000) and 19% (EPOC) for German employees having modern forms of pay without working time flexibility.

Relation between Pay Systems and Work Organisation

The association between indicators of work organisation and those of pay systems has been identified as one of the main goals of our project. High performance work organisations (HPWO) are defined as an indicator of work organisation. This label applies to companies that are characterised by time and task autonomy, task variety, responsibility, and effective participation. In comparison with the cross-national ESWC 2000 data analysis, that has already shown a significant positive correlation between modern forms of variable pay and high performance work organisations, the findings for Germany reveal an even stronger correlation. 10% of employees having team bonus, profit sharing, and/or income from shares are working in companies with a high profile of high performance work organisations (HPWO), whereas only 4% of employees receiving modern forms of variable pay are found in companies that incorporate a low-grade of HPWO characteristics. Results from the analysis of the German EPOC sub-sample support our assumption that modern forms of variable pay are linked with work organisations which give employees more influence on decision-making processes and participative rights. As an indicator of work organisation, group delegation is defined as the strongest form of direct participation and includes the transfer of decisive power and control from management executives or line managers to groups of employees. The proportion of managers reporting modern forms of variable pay together with a high intensity of group delegation in the workplaces of their company reaches 40%, in comparison with 24% for a low intensity of group delegation. This result suggests that bonus related to team performance, profit sharing, or share ownership schemes are more often found in workplaces with a high intensity of group delegation.

Concerning the relation between pay systems and work organisation, the literature review shows that HPWO leads to a higher level of pay. In addition, flattening the hierarchy structure and introducing self-regulating teams positively affect pay (Bauer & Bender, 2001). In contrast, the delegation of responsibilities in order to lower hierarchy levels has not any significant effects on pay (Bauer & Bender, 2001).

Changes in work organisation do not always lead to changes in pay systems: whereas 55% of the companies introduced teamwork from

179

1994 to 1999, only 31% changed their pay system. However, companies with teamwork more often point out the necessity of implementing entirely new pay systems (37%) than companies without teamwork (31%) (Bullinger, Bauer & Menrad, 2000). Furthermore, in companies with teamwork, the transition to dynamic pay systems is more frequent than in companies without teamwork. More specifically, the implementation of teamwork often leads to the transition from time pay to group piece rate pay, bonus pay, and time pay plus efficiency bonus. Hence, the percentage of time pay is smaller in companies with teamwork (42% with teamwork *vs.* 64% without teamwork). Therefore the percentage of bonus pay (41% *vs.* 16%), group piece rate pay (18% *vs.* 6%), and time pay plus efficiency bonus (53% *vs.* 33%) is higher in companies with teamwork than those without (Bullinger, Bauer & Menrad, 2000). Similar results have been found in a study of Heywood and Jirjahn (Jirjahn, 2002): innovative HRM systems that rely on teamwork, information sharing, and regular training for their employees were found to be associated with group piece rate, group premium pay, and profit sharing. Therefore, individual-based piece rates are found more frequently in traditional systems of mass production. Performance-based pay systems such as:

- time pay plus efficiency bonus
- time pay plus bonus
- individual piece rate pay and
- group piece rate pay

are found more often in companies with an average or high level of integration of indirect functions than in companies with a lower level of integration. Companies with teamwork, especially large-scale companies, have a higher level of integration than companies without teamwork (Bullinger, Bauer & Menrad, 2000).

Effectiveness of Pay Systems and System Alignment

We consider indicators of quality of working life in addition to indicators of organisational performance in order to study the relations between pay systems and their effectiveness. From the cross-national analysis of ESWC 2000 data (Antoni *et al.*, 2005), it could have been concluded that employees receiving modern variable pay do not report a higher job satisfaction. The findings concerning sustainability and satisfaction from the cross-national analysis could be mostly replicated for the German sub-sample. There is a small positive relation between modern forms of variable pay and satisfaction. However, this relationship is not statistically significant for the German data. There is a negative relationship between piece rate or productivity pay and the assess-

180

ment of the sustainability of work. The proportion of employees in Germany who receive these traditional forms of variable pay – linked to individual performance – and deny that they will be able to carry on doing their current job until the age of sixty, is much higher (11%) than the proportion of employees, which positively assesses the sustainability of their jobs (6%).

Other indicators of the quality of working life, such as excessive demands, physical load, health risks, or health problems only show very weak and negative correlations with modern forms of variable pay. According to the German sub-sample, excessive demands remain the exception to this rule. Employees who receive modern forms of variable pay more often report (11% *vs.* 5%) a mismatch between their skills and job demands than those getting traditional pay. Negative correlations between HPWO and the quality of working life indicators indicate that employees working at a high profile HPWO in the workplace in Germany report less often physical load, health risks, or health problems. Figure 4.12 illustrates the association between HPWO and health risks.

Figure 4.12. Percentages of a) HPWO by health risks in Germany (ESWC 2000) and b) performance by modern forms of pay (EPOC)

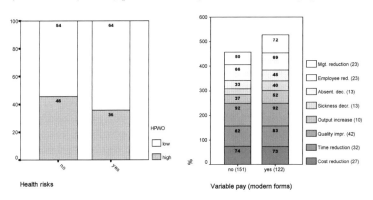

The effectiveness of a pay system is often measured in terms of productivity. In companies which partially or completely use bonus systems, the productivity per employee is higher than in companies with fixed pay; furthermore, the percentage of scrap is lower in companies which consider quality as an indicator of bonus systems (Lay & Rainfurth, 1999). The most important goal of changes in pay systems which have already been implemented is the increase in productivity (Franz *et al.*, 2000). Bullinger, Bauer and Menrad (2000) argued that from a management perspective, contract-based pay, group piece rate pay, and time pay plus bonus or efficiency bonus seemed to be the most satisfying of pay systems for the employees. Unfortunately, this study does not provide any data from the perspective of the employees themselves, in order to examine the differences between perspectives.

The EPOC dataset contains indicators of performance, such as the reduction in numbers of managers or employees, the decrease in sickness or absenteeism, the improvement in quality, the increase in output, and the reduction in time or costs. The analysis of the German subsample of EPOC data does not show any statistically significant relationship between the various effect criteria and the type of pay system, although companies with modern forms of variable pay apparently more often report effects than companies without (cf. Figure 4.12). A measure of global effect could not be statistically tested, because only a few respondents answered all the questions in this matter, which make the sample size below the required minimum of respondents for carrying out a statistical analysis.

The relation between system alignment and effectiveness has also been studied in the literature: the type of work organisation has not any impact on the assessment of the current wage system or on changes in the base pay system, but it does influence the assessment of future capability of the current pay system. Furthermore, it is suggested, that changes in pay systems are more likely when cost pressure and changes in work organisation are combined with changes in the achievement climate of the company (Bahnmüller, 2001). Companies without teamwork and without bonus systems rated their productivity per employee lowest. Companies with teamwork or bonus systems rated their productivity per employee being at a medium level. Companies with teamwork and bonus system reported the highest productivity per employee, which is consistent with the findings mentioned above concerning organisational fit (Lay & Rainfurth, 1999).

On the basis of the EPOC survey, Antoni et al. (2005) decided to choose innovation strategy as an indicator of managerial strategy and to investigate on the alignment of three and four model variables, such as the fit between modern forms of variable pay, group delegation, and innovation strategy, which represent indicators of pay systems, work organisation, and strategy. Innovation strategy is defined as activities which have been put in place by the management in the workplace, towards product innovation in the last three years. Interestingly, the fact of having low or high group delegation does not seem to influence the choice of modern forms of variable pay in companies deprived of an innovation strategy. However, companies with an innovation strategy and intensive group delegation more often have modern forms of variable pay than companies with low group delegation (67% vs. 9%). The finding of the German sub-sample is pretty similar to results for the whole sample size.

Summary and Conclusion

This chapter has reported the German national research on pay, working conditions, and managerial policy, their relationships and outcomes as well as the results of the secondary analyses of the ESWC 2000 and EPOC data.

The main indicators of pay and pay systems in these studies are income level and the existence or not of different types of pay systems or components. The interpretation of the questions and, consequently, of the data which refer to these various components is not always crystal clear. For example, do all the respondents in the ESWC 2000 study, who answer that they get piece rate or productivity payments, but not base or fixed salary, really differ from those who answer that they also get base or fixed salary? Or do components reflecting skill in the EPOC study refer to grading aspects (skill requirements) or to variable pay components rewarding individual skills? More information is needed about the structure and dynamics of base pay – *i.e.* criteria for grading – as well as about variable pay *e.g.* criteria and relative volume of variable components.

Many studies have used the existence or not of different forms of teamwork, participation, task variety and task autonomy as indicators of work organisation. Some have included several of these aspects into an aggregated HPWO variable.

Indicators of organisational performance revolving around productivity and profitability prevail in studies concerned with workplaces to the relative neglect of employee-related outcomes, which are vice versa in the primary focus of surveys targeting individual employees and working conditions. Some company specific studies use both types of indicators.

Organisational or institutional factors and their relation with pay systems have not been studied so much yet. It can generally be concluded from the secondary data analysis of the ESWC 2000 and the EPOC survey that the incidence of modern forms of variable pay is higher in bigger companies and private sector companies.

German research is limited regarding the effects of age and gender issues on pay systems. Concerning gender, mostly discrimination has been studied. Results from the German and the European samples evidence that women tend to receive lower pay than men. Age was almost exclusively studied around the topic of seniority which is related to higher pay.

Concerning the relationship between pay systems and employment conditions there are also few results. The incidence of modern forms of variable pay is higher when flexible working time is applied in the company. In the ESWC 2000 sample full-time workers seem to have a bit more often modern forms of variable pay than temporary or part-time workers; however, there is nothing similar in the German sub-sample.

The review of the German research and our secondary data analyses of the German samples from the ESWC 2000 and EPOC study do support some hypotheses of our research model. More or less one common result we reach is that aspects of high performance work organisations (HPWO) are found more frequently with modern forms of variable pay. Findings from both surveys make us conclude that modern forms of variable pay are more often found in companies where decisive power and control have been transferred from the management to the employees. However, a time lag apparently exists between changes in work organisation and the corresponding changes in pay systems (Bullinger, Bauer & Menrad, 2000). Flattening the hierarchical structure and introducing self-regulating teams positively affects pay (Bauer & Bender, 2001).

In most of the studies, managerial strategy is not dealt with; the few indicators which have been reported appear to be quite questionable. Consequently, the relationship between pay systems and managerial strategies has merely been studied. The results do not show consistent relationships so far. This might be due, in part, to the fact that there is often a kind of "time lag" between changes in strategy and congruent changes in pay systems.

Concerning the quality of working life aspects, there is not any relationship between pay and job satisfaction, but job satisfaction correlates with aspects of high performance work organisations (HPWO).

Concerning the relationship between pay systems and organisational performance, the German EPOC data do not show any significant findings, which might be due to small sample sizes. However, other German studies do report higher productivity and quality for bonus systems than for fixed pay, if they are combined with teamwork particularly.

References

Antoni, C., Berger, A., Baeten, X., Emans, B., Hulkko, K., Kessler, I., Neu, E., Vartiainen, M. & Verbruggen, A. (2005), *Wages and Working Conditions in the European Union*, Dublin: European Foundation for the Improvement of Living and Working Conditions.

Bahnmüller, R. (2001), *Stabilität und Wandel der Entlohnungsformen: Entgeltsysteme und Entgeltpolitik in der Metallindustrie, in der Textil- und Bekleidungsindustrie und im Bankgewerbe* [Stability and change in pay systems: Pay systems and pay policy in the metal industry, clothing industry and banks], Munich, Mering: Hamp.

Bauer, T.K. & Bender, S. (2001), "Flexible Work Systems and the Structure of Wages: Evidence from Matched Employer-Employee Data", Discussion paper

No. 353, IZA (Forschungsinstitut zur Zukunft der Arbeit / Institute for the Study of Labor).

Bullinger, H.-J., Bauer, S. & Menrad, W. (2000), *Entgeltsysteme in der Produktion: Ergebnisse einer Unternehmensstudie in Deutschland* [Pay systems in production: Results of a study about companies in Germany], Stuttgart: IAO (Fraunhofer Institut für Arbeitswirtschaft und Organisation).

Franz, W., Gutzeit, M., Lessner, J., Oechsler, W.A., Pfeiffer, F., Reichmann, L. & Roll, J. (2000), *Flexibilisierung der Arbeitsentgelte und Beschäftigungseffekte* [Transition to flexible pay and effects on employment], ZEW (Zentrum für Europäische Wirtschaftsforschung / Centre for European Economic Studies).

Jirjahn, U. (2002), "The German Experience with Performance Pay", in M. Brown & J.S. Heywood (eds.), *Paying for Performance. An International Comparison*, New York: M.E. Sharpe, p. 148-178.

Lay, G. & Rainfurth, C. (1999), "Königsweg Prämie?" [Bonus systems – A silver bullet?], Report from the Innovation in Production Survey, No. 13, Karlsruhe: Fraunhofer Institut für Systemtechnik und Innovationsforschung (ISI).

CHAPTER 4.2.4

Pay Systems and Outcomes in The Netherlands

Ben J.M. EMANS[1]

Most of the information about the situation related to pay systems and practices in The Netherlands stems from two longitudinal research projects both financed by the national government and conducted by the research institute OSA. Both projects consist of surveys (with large representative samples) which are repeated every two-year. The first one, which uses a panel sample of employing organisations, is about labour demand, with questions referring to the need for personnel, pay systems, absenteeism, labour time, contract types, and the educational background of employees. In 1999, about 2,700 companies representing nine sectors including government, education, business, and the building sector were surveyed (Bekker, Fouarge, Kerkhofs, Román, De Voogd-Hamelink, Wilthagen & De Wolff, 2003; Fouarge, Kerkhofs, De Voogd-Hamelink, Vosse & De Wolff, 2001). The other one, with a panel sample of employable people, is a survey about labour supply, comprising a representative sample of 4,780 Dutch employable people in 1998 (Fouarge, Grim, Kerkhofs, Román & Wilthagen, 2004; Fouarge, Kerkhofs, De Voogd, Vosse & De Wolff, 1999). From this research, a number of figures surface about payment parameters such as pay level and the prevalence of variable pay systems on the one hand, and contextual parameters such as the age of employee, gender, organisation's size and sector on the other hand. In addition to these empirical results, a number of more focused studies, often ordered by the government, provides pieces of additional information. Finally, a third source of empirical findings is found within two large European databases. One, known as the ESWC-data (European Survey on Working Conditions, Paoli & Merllié, 2001), is based on a sample of employees, including 1,276 Dutch employees. The other, known as the EPOC-data (Employee direct Participation in Organisational Change), is based on a sample of companies, including 500 located in The Netherlands (EPOC Research Group, 1997). Focusing on pay-related issues, Antoni and Berger (see

---

[1] The author would like to thank Peter van der Meer for his fruitful comments on an earlier draft of this text.

187

Antoni *et al.*, 2005) reanalysed the ESWC and EPOC databases in order to picture the European situation as a whole. Additional analyses were carried out on the Dutch sub-samples and the outcomes thereof are used below, together with the outcomes of the above mentioned national research projects, in order to obtain a picture of the situation in The Netherlands. The examination of these studies, if taken together, gives some insight into the relationships between pay-parameters, context-parameters, and (incidentally) performance parameters, as they are found in The Netherlands.

A couple of caveats one needs to bear in mind when reading the following sections are worth noting. First, the data underlying the outcomes presented below do not directly refer to the current situation, but to (recent) history. The periods in which they were collected, range from 1994 to 2002. As a result, we cannot exclude that the conclusions given could be to a certain degree outdated. Secondly, what is inherent in any attempt to include findings from different sources is the problem raised by different sources, that is, sources based on different definitions and articulations of key variables. Consequently, the outcomes of different pieces of research are not perfectly comparable at all. This problem was clearly raised in the efforts of integration described below and it could only be solved by refraining from any fine-grainiess in the presentation of empirical findings and focusing on what is common in those findings.

The problem was the most strongly raised where different definitions of 'variable-pay system' had to be brought together under one single umbrella (actually there are as many definitions as sources where data about those systems can be found). In their analyses of the ESWC and EPOC files, Antoni and Berger (Antoni *et al.*, 2005) set up a parameter, called 'modern form of variable pay'. That parameter reflects the occurrence of pay formulas that incorporate bonuses for team output, profit sharing, and/or share ownership schemes. In short, in these formulas, individual pay levels are linked with performance or value creation, by the company as a whole or by a subunit within the company. In the national surveys performed in The Netherlands, similar parameters were applied, indicating the occurrence of formulas associating individual pay with either the company or the subunits.

To conclude these preliminary lines, some general characteristics of the Dutch society will be pointed out. They describe the context one needs to bear in mind when reading about pay practices.

The Dutch Context: Three Characteristics

The Dutch society is sometimes characterised as a 'consensus society' or as a society based on an 'organised consensus', or as a 'polder model' society. These terms refer to the efforts Dutch people tend to invest endlessly in compromising efforts, whenever they are involved in conflicts of interest (see Emans, Laskewitz & Van de Vliert, 1994, where this aspect of the Dutch society is explained and linked with the country's history as well as with its high rankings on two organisational cultural dimensions: 'femininity' and 'individualism' (Hofstede, 1980)). This cultural peculiarity is reflected in high levels of participation of employees in organisational decision-making. Participation rights are well institutionalised. For instance, workers councils have a strong position and can be found in nearly all the companies (Van het Kaar, 2004). As regards decision making on payment systems this is reflected in highly centralised practices of collective bargaining. It is a relevant contextual aspect for understanding Dutch pay practices, because most of the time, these are the outcomes of long winded debates involving many participants. Among other things, the relatively compressed pay distribution among Dutch employees has probably something to do with this.

The label 'part time economy' provides another characterisation of the Dutch society, or more specifically its economy. Compared to other countries, high percentages of Dutch workers, especially the female workers, are working under part time contract. In 2002, 6.2% of male employees and 51.7% of female employees had a job of less than 24 hours per week (Fouarge *et al.*, 2004). This is an important thing to keep in mind when looking at payment practices, because it reduces the straightforward relationship between net hour pay and personal income.

Finally, a third feature of the Dutch society is its tendency to kick out low productive people from the labour market. A legal system of allowances for low-ability people enables (or enabled: things are changing) employers to dismiss painlessly employees who do not work well. New legislation, operative starting January 2006, has been developed in order to redress this state of affairs. It should be kept in mind, however, that the employed people form less than 80% of the employable population. As a result, figures about payment practices do not apply to a substantial part of the employable workforce.

Prevalence of Pay Systems

The Netherlands is one of the few countries in Europe in which the labour unions are (moderately) positively disposed to adopt variable pay. Statistics of 1998 (more recent data were not available) reflect this attitude since one third of the collective pay agreements included variable pay (Van het Kaar & Grünell, 2001). Nevertheless, variable pay systems are not a key issue in The Netherlands. This is reflected, for instance, by the fact that only 22% of the employees are subject to variable pay related to individual performances (Verboon, De Feyter & Smulders, 1999), and that only 31% of the employing organisations apply such a system (Bekker *et al.*, 2003). For variable pay related to company performances, the figures are even lower: 15% of the employees (Verboon, De Feyter & Smulders, 1999) and 18% of the employing organisations (Bekker *et al.*, 2003). A slightly lower figure surfaced in the ESWC survey: almost 9% of the Dutch employees report that they receive modern forms of variable pay (in comparison with 6% on average in all the 15 European countries included in this study, Antoni *et al.*, 2005). Figures from a survey performed in 1994/1995 with a sample of 36 profit companies (Thöne, Tiessen, Wendt & De Zeeuw, 1996) indicated that only 5.1% of the total volume of those companies' expenses had something to do with variable pay. The amount of variable pay for senior personnel depended on the firm's profits for the majority (69%) of the companies. For a lower personnel, the figure is 25%.

The ESWC 2000 data, when analysed cross-nationally, show that modern forms of variable pay, such as team bonus, profit sharing, and/or income from shares, are more frequently found among higher income groups. Accordingly, most of the time, employees in Dutch enterprises report that modern variable pay is an element of their reward package if they belong to groups of higher income levels. The proportions for employees with modern forms of variable pay range from 5% in the lowest income group to 17% in the highest income group.

Gender differences in the dispersion of modern forms of variable pay could be found by analyzing the Dutch ESWC 2000 sub-sample. The proportion of male employees with team bonus, profit sharing, and/or income from shares is three times higher (13%) than the proportion of female employees (4%). The national research literature shows that men receive higher hourly income as well as higher additional payments than women (Fouarge *et al.*, 1999, 2001). Meanwhile, their working time per week is higher as well (Verboon, De Feyter & Smulders, 1999). Another gender difference appears when it is argued that female employees have less often something to do with variable pay systems than men (for similar outcomes from the ESWC study: see above).

From ESWC 2000 secondary data analyses, it can be concluded that there is not any significant correlation between age and the prevalence of modern forms of variable pay. Nevertheless, national studies show that pay level and age are positively related: the older the employees are, the higher the income will be. However, the level of additional payments is far less related to age (Fouarge *et al.*, 1999, 2001).

Other findings at cross-national level which could be replicated with Dutch data deal with size and sector. Both ESWC 2000 and EPOC datasets show that a positive correlation exists between modern forms of variable pay and the size of the company. The higher the number of persons employed in a company is, the higher the percentage of employees receiving pay related to group or company performance or income from shares is (Antoni *et al.*, 2005). Other studies from Verboon, De Feyter and Smulders (1999) and Fouarge *et al.* (2001) show that small firms have more part-time workers, apply less variable pay systems and have lower average pay levels compared to large ones (Bekker *et al.*, 2003). Finally, what is somewhat surprising given the natural link between big companies and collective labour agreements, is that incomes tend to be lower in companies who sign some collective labour agreement, compared with companies that do not so (Fouarge *et al.*, 2001). An explanation may be that collective labour agreements served as a tool for the social partners in The Netherlands in their efforts to slow down, for reasons of international competitiveness, income rises in The Netherlands and to resist the international competitiveness.

The secondary analysis of ESWC 2000 data as well as the review of the national research literature reveal that modern forms of variable pay nearly do not exist in the public sector, whereas there is a strong association between team-based pay, profit sharing, share ownership schemes, and private owned companies. The proportion of public sector companies that use modern variable pay schemes is 5% in comparison with 23% of private sector companies. Differences between sectors occur as regards all the aspects of payment practices. The outcomes of the study by Berkhout *et al.* (2001) are especially worth noting, as their estimates of inter-sector income level differences are devoid of the obscuring effects of other inter-sector differences, such as differences in age, gender, and education level of workforces. Their (and others') outcomes show that the Dutch public administration relatively pays well (especially its lower educated employees). It is the same for employers in the sectors of finance and education, but they contrast with employers in the retail, transport, and building sectors. This pattern matches with figures about monthly pay found by Fouarge *et al.* (2001). Individual pay-for-performance systems are mostly found in the business and finance sectors and to a lesser extent in the manufacturing sector (as far as the profit economy is involved) and in the education and health care sectors (as far as the non-profit economy is involved, Fouarge *et al.*, 2001; Van Sas, 1999; Verboon, De Feyter & Smulders, 1999).

Results from cross-national data (ESWC 2000 and EPOC) suggest a weak, but significant positive correlation between both contract type and working time flexibility and modern forms of variable pay. However, in the Dutch sub-samples of both surveys, these connections have not been found. Results from the EPOC survey show, for instance, that the proportion of companies using modern forms of variable pay without having flexible working times is approximately as high (22%) as the proportion of companies using those forms of pay without having flexible working times (21%). Another finding from the review of national studies is that flexibility in labour contracts reduces the hourly income of the employees involved (Zant *et al.*, 2000).

For the vast majority of firms performance and skills form an important factor for promotion and compensation. Correspondingly, performance appraisal systems tend to be used widely. In (no less than) 80% of the companies, a system for performance-related pay only exists for only a minority of the workforce. The prevalence of compensation practices based on performance and skills appeared to correlate positively with the prevalence of high levels of pay, promotion opportunities, and perks as well as with other high performance practices such as high-norm selection practices, career guidance practices, and training opportunities (Horgan, 2003).

Relation between Pay Systems and Work Organisation

A secondary data analysis of the Dutch part from the ESWC 2000 dataset was carried out in order to investigate on the relationship between pay systems and aspects of the work organisation. More specifically, the impact of the profile of 'high-performance work organisations' (HPWO), defined by time and task autonomy, task variety, responsibility, and effective participation, was studied. Modern forms of variable pay appeared to be more frequently found (in 13% of the cases) in high-HPWO companies than in low-HPWO companies (5% of the cases). However, the Dutch EPOC data do not support this finding: aspects of work organisation as measured with the intensity of group delegation, are not significantly related to modern forms of variable pay (group delegation is defined as the strongest form of direct participation and includes the transfer of decisive power and control from management executives or line managers to groups of employees). Team bonus, profit sharing, or income from shares is found in 16% of companies with high levels of group delegation. In companies with low levels of group delegation this figure is about as high (17%) (Antoni *et al.*, 2005).

Effectiveness of Pay Systems and System Alignment

Concerning the impact of pay systems, we have first, the outcomes of Van Silfhout's survey (2000) about employees' and managers' expectations. Both groups expected performance-based pay systems as well as job-based pay systems to have both positive and negative outcomes. Among the positive outcomes that were expected from individual pay-for-performance systems there were the following: increase in productivity, increase in appreciation, and personal gain. Among the negative outcomes that were expected from individual pay-for-performance systems were: uncertainty, feeling of pressure and dissatisfaction for the lesser performers. Among the positive expected outcomes of job-based pay systems were: the enjoyment of work and jealousy prevention. Among negative outcomes associated with team-based pay-for-performance were: discontent due to differences in performance (Van Silfhout, 2000).

The latter findings are both corroborated and qualified by the outcomes of a study of Van Vijfeijken (2004), who showed that the outcomes of team performance-based pay systems depend on specific conditions that are related to the type of the team task and the type of performance appraisal which is used. Dependent on those conditions, the outcomes can be negative as well as positive.

For the Dutch sub-sample of ESWC 2000 data, Antoni *et al.* (2005) report a correlation which is close to zero between employees receiving traditional forms of variable pay (such as piece rate) and their rating of their work being sustainable or not. In addition to this finding, employees with modern forms of variable pay did not turn out to be more satisfied with their jobs than those without. There is, though, a strong positive relation between job satisfaction and high performance work organisations. This suggests that the assessment of job satisfaction depends more on the type of work organisation than on the type of pay system.

Other indicators of quality of working life, such as excessive demands, physical load, health risks, or health problems only show weak and non-significant correlations with modern forms of variable pay. The Dutch sample indicates that health risks is one exception to this rule: among the employees who report that their health is at risk, 12% say they enjoy modern forms of variable pay, whereas from the employees who do not report health risks, the figure only reaches 8%. With the use of indicators derived from the EPOC survey, Antoni *et al.* (2005) have been able to investigate on the relationships between pay systems and organisational performance. The EPOC dataset contains indicators for performance, such as the reduction in numbers of managers or employees, the decrease in sickness or absenteeism, the improvement in quality, the increase in output, and the reduction in time or costs. In the Dutch sample, differences in these effect criteria were found between companies with modern forms of variable pay and companies without (see Figure 4.13). However, due to many missing cases and resulting small sample size, statistical significances could not be established.

Figure 4.13. Percentages of modern variable pay by performance in The Netherlands (EPOC)

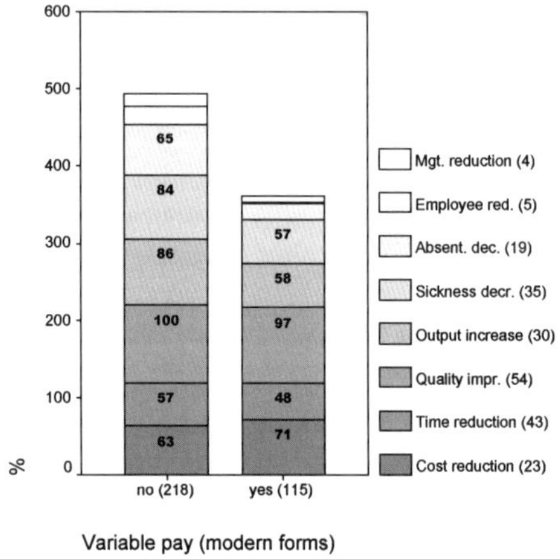

Variable pay (modern forms)

The EPOC survey provides data on management activities which aim at enhancing product innovation; as a result, it enabled Antoni *et al.* (2005) to calculate an innovation strategy index. In the Dutch sample, companies with a high innovation strategy index, in comparison with other companies, appear to have more often modern forms of variable pay. However, in contrast with the corresponding findings at the cross-national level, this finding was not statistically significant. The introduction of pay-for-performance systems can serve several strategic purposes. One is financial and consists of adapting the pay volume to the company's profits. The other is a HRM one: the purpose consists of motivating workers to get higher productivity. In The Netherlands, the second strategic purpose, rather than the first one, seems to play a role in decision-making on pay systems. This was reflected in the interview outcomes of Thöne *et al.* (1996), as well as in the low variable/fixed pay ratios found by Thöne *et al.* (1996), which hardly show any financial significance. The research outcomes, mentioned above, about the expected outcomes of pay-for-performance systems (Horgan, 2003; Van Silfhout, 2000) tell the same story. Decisions about pay levels can stem from many different strategic considerations. One of them is the consideration of rising the firm's attractiveness for prospective employees. In

2000, this consideration played a role in 30% of the Dutch firms (Fouarge *et al.*, 2001).

Summary and Conclusion

The overall picture that emerges from the research findings described above reveals that the use of performance-based variable pay within Dutch companies does not seem to be very popular. Meanwhile, the degree of popularity varies according to the types of employees as well as the types of employers. In short, the probability that a Dutch employee is subject to a pay-for-performance system is highest when he is a full-time employed, well paid male worker who works in a large-sized, private company where performance management forms a key part of the HRM strategy. In the preliminary lines, the Dutch society was described as a consensus society. Inherent in the consensus tendency is the pursuit of equality – low differentiation in rewards –, rather than equity – reward differentiation which is related to whatever kind of interpersonal differentiation. The figures about pay-for-performance prevalence show that, for moving from equality to equity in the Dutch situation, quite a number of conditions have to be fulfilled.

References

Antoni, C., Berger, A., Baeten, X., Emans, B., Hulkko, K., Kessler, I., Neu, E., Vartiainen, M. & Verbruggen, A. (2005), *Wages and Working Conditions in the European Union*, Dublin: European Foundation for the Improvement of Living and Working Conditions.

Bekker, S., Fouarge, D., Kerkhofs, M., Román, A., De Voogd-Hamelink, M., Wilthagen, T. & De Wolff, Ch. (2003), *Trendrapport Vraag naar Arbeid 2002* [Trends in labour demand 2002]. OSA-publicatie A200, Tilburg: OSA, Tilburg University.

Berkhout, E., De Graaf, D., Heyma, A. & Theeuwes, J. (2001), *Loondifferentiatie in Nederland: de vraagkant* [Pay differentiation in The Netherlands: The side of labour demand]. OSA-publicatie A183, Tilburg: Katholieke Universiteit Brabant, Organizatie voor Strategisch Arbeidsmarktonderzoek.

Emans, B., Laskewitz, P. & Van de Vliert, E. (1994), "The Netherlands", in M.A. Rahim & A.A. Blum (eds.), *Global Perspectives on Organisational Conflict*, Westport, CT: Praeger, p. 53-66.

EPOC Research Group (1997), *New Forms of Work Organisation: Can Europe Realise its Potential? Results of a Survey of Direct Employee Participation in Europe*, Luxembourg: Office for Official Publications of the European Communities.

Fouarge, D., Grim, R., Kerkhofs, M., Román, A. & Wilthagen, T. (2004), *Trendrapport aanbod van arbeid 2003* [Trends in labour supply 2003]. OSA-publicatie A205, Tilburg: OSA, Tilburg University.

Fouarge, D., Kerkhofs, M., De Voogd, M., Vosse, J.P. & De Wolff, C. (1999), *Trendrapport aanbod van arbeid* [Trends in labour supply]. OSA-publicatie A169, Den Haag: Servicecentrum uitgevers.

Fouarge, D., Kerkhofs, M., De Voogd-Hamelink, A.M., Vosse, J.P. & De Wolff, C. (2001), *Trendrapport Vraag naar Arbeid 2000* [Trends in labour demand 2000]. OSA-publicatie A177, Den Haag: Servicecentrum uitgevers.

Hofstede, G. (1980), *Culture's Consequences: International Differences in Work-related Values*, Beverly Hills, CA: Sage.

Horgan, J. (2003), "High Performance Human Resource Management in Ireland and The Netherlands", Thesis University of Groningen.

Paoli, P. & Merllié, D. (2001), *Third European Survey on Working Conditions 2000*, Luxembourg: Office for Official Publications of the European Communities.

Thöne, T.J.F., Tiessen, R., Wendt, H. & De Zeeuw, L.S. (1996), *Variabele beloning: alleen op- of ook neerwaarts? Praktijk en beleid in Nederland vergeleken met Japan, de V.S. en het V.K.* [Variable pay: Upward and/or downward? Practices and policies in The Netherlands compared with Japan, USA and UK]. OSA-werkdocument W143, Den Haag: Sdu.

Van het Kaar, R. (2004), *EIRO Comparative Study: Developments in European Works Councils – Case of The Netherlands*, European Industrial Relations Observatory (EIRO): http://www.eiro.eurofound.eu.int/2004/11/word/nl040 9103s.doc

Van het Kaar, R. and Grünell, M. (2001), *Comparative study on variable pay in Europe*, Dublin: European Foundation for the Improvement of Living and Working Conditions. http://www.eiro.eurofound.eu.int/2001/Study/TN0104 201S.html.

Van Sas, E.M. (1999), *Prestatiebeloning en het poldermodel, een analyse van persoonsgebonden variabele beloning in CAO's* [Pay-for-performance and the Poldermodel; an analysis of individual pay for performance in collective labour agreements], Utrecht: AWSB/SER.

Van Silfhout, R.V. (2000), "Inequality in Pay within Organisations: Normative and Instrumental Perspective", Thesis Katholieke Universiteit Brabant.

Van Vijfeijken, H.T.G.A. (2004), "Managing Team Performance: Interdependence, Goals and Rewards", Thesis, Technische Universiteit Eindhoven.

Verboon, F.C., De Feyter, M.G. & Smulders, P.G.W. (1999), *Arbeid en zorg, inzetbaarheid en beloning: het werknemersperspectief* [Labour and care, employability and compensation: The employees' point of view], Hoofddorp: TNO Arbeid.

Zant, W., Alessie, R., Oostendorp, R. & Pradhan, M. (2000), *Flexibiliteit op de Nederlandse Arbeidsmarkt; een empirisch onderzoek op basis van OSA-vraag en aanbodpanels* [Flexibility of the Dutch labour market: An empirical investigation based on OSA-panels of labour demand and supply], Tilburg: OSA (Organizatie voor Strategisch Arbeidsmarktonderzoek).

CHAPTER 4.2.5

Pay Systems and Outcomes in Sweden

Elizabeth NEU

The following part about Swedish pay systems and outcomes is based on national empirical studies, in addition to the findings of cross-national European studies. In the Swedish national studies, data stems from questionnaires and interviews that examine the relationships between different pay systems and the following three variables: work organisation, working conditions, individual and organisational performance.

In the Swedish research, there is not any common definition of the different pay systems, which makes comparisons somehow difficult. The broad term *individual pay* is widely used to point out the development which made a shift from "traditional" and collectively agreed pay based on occupation and seniority towards "modern" and individually agreed pay based on competence and performance.

Different kinds of individual pay forms are implemented in all the sectors of the Swedish labour market. However, it is still usual for the collective agreements to include some kind of guaranteed pay rises for each individual employee. Collective agreements without such a guarantee are more usual in the public sector than in the private one (National Mediation Office, 2004). However, the term *individual pay* does not say anything about the nature of pay systems. Individual pay can therefore be both fixed and variable.

In Sweden the differences in pay between women and men differ according to sectors. For white-collar workers in the private sector, women earn 77% of men's pay, and in sales the percentage reaches 79%. In the building sector as well as in the engineering one, women earn between 83% and 89% of men's pay. In public health care the number is 98% and among teachers, women earn 101% of men's pay (Sweden Statistics, 2004).

One particular approach adopted by the Swedish research is the analysis of the attitudes of employees towards individual pay as well as the motivational effects of such pay systems and additional sources of this kind: this approach will be discussed below. In these studies, self-reports are used and the stress is mainly put on the relations between pay systems and productivity, work motivation, and work satisfaction as well as satisfaction with the pay system. The cooperation between colleagues and its relation with pay systems has also been analysed.

Indicators

Indicators of pay and pay systems have been the existence or not of various types of pay systems. The cooperation between colleagues has also been measured to identify and explain the influence of pay systems. Productivity was not only defined in terms of organisational efficiency or outcomes, but also in terms of customer satisfaction.

Prevalence of Pay Systems

Generally speaking, Scandinavian countries do not have many re-stricting laws concerning modern forms of variable pay in comparison with other European countries. Therefore, you would expect to find a higher degree of variable pay systems in Sweden than in some other countries. However, due to the Sweden Statistics (2001) variable pay is not very usual. The Work Environment survey is conducted every two years and covers between 10,000-15,000 employees from different sectors and occupational groups. In 2001, a total of 88% of the popula-tion answered that they only had fixed pay. 3% had some kind of bonus or piece rate and 4% had profit sharing in addition to the fixed pay. 1% had pure performance-related pay and 4% had some "other pay form". Secondary analyses of ESWC 2000 survey data give a slightly different picture: almost 10% of the Swedish employees answer that they receive modern forms of variable pay in comparison with 6% on average in all the 15 European countries included in this study (Antoni *et al.*, 2005).

However, according to Van het Kaar and Grünell (2001), the relative importance of variable pay in the employees' total salary is generally said to be 25% in Sweden. It is also stated here that a great part of the collective agreements signed by the Swedish Trade Union Confedera-tion (Landsorganisationen, LO) provide for pay systems typically based on a 90% fixed pay component and a 10% variable bonus which depend on the quality of the production and other economic factors. Conse-quently, it is somewhat unclear to what extent modern forms of variable pay are spread on the Swedish labour market.

In the Nilsson study (1990) a written questionnaire has been sent to a stratified sample of 488 local (company level) representatives of the Swedish Union of Technical and Clerical Employees in Industry. 20% of the companies covered by the survey had some kind of bonus pay system. The most common was profit sharing, which the employees received once a year. Another rather common system was "performance bonus", which was also paid once a year, but calculated by group or divisional performance. None of the bonus systems was calculated on an individual basis. Bonus pay systems were far more common within private industry than in public owned industry (Nilsson, 1990). In general, the prerequisites of wide ranging pay systems seem to be at hand, but the lack of empirical studies is obvious.

From the Swedish sub-sample of the ESWC 2000 dataset Antoni *et al.* (2005) report, that employees, who receive team-based pay, income from profit sharing, or share ownership schemes also receive more frequently higher income. The highest proportion of employees with modern variable pay components is to be found among the high-income group (16%).

Gender differences in the prevalence of modern forms of variable pay are following the same logic as already shown at cross-national level. Male employees report more than twice as female employees that they receive modern forms of variable pay. The analysis of the Swedish data reveals that there is no significant correlation between age and modern forms of variable pay.

Moving onto the examination of the relationship between pay systems and organisational factors such as size and sector, the Swedish sub-samples of ESWC 2000 and EPOC surveys give contradictory findings. The data from the ESWC 2000 survey support the assumption of a positive connection between modern forms of variable pay and size – as it was found at cross-national level – whereas the EPOC data show a negative, albeit non-significant, correlation between these two variables. In this specific case, managers from establishments with a smaller number of employees more often report the use of modern forms of variable pay.

Consistent results can be found concerning the prevalence of modern variable pay according to sectors. Interestingly, both sub-samples show an average positive correlation between modern variable pay and sectors. Team-based pay, income from profit sharing, or share ownership schemes are more usual in private owned companies. The percentages of employees with modern forms of variable pay who work in private sector companies are 16% in comparison with 4% for public sector companies. The ratio for the Swedish sub-sample of the EPOC survey appears to be even more impressive. 44% of companies which use modern variable pay belong to the private sector in contrast with 4% of those companies which belong to the public sector.

Secondary data analysis at cross-national level showed that pay systems and employment conditions are related in a way that employees, which work under unlimited contracts or in companies with flexible working times are more likely to report that they receive modern forms of variable pay. The analysis of Swedish data from the ESWC 2000 survey gives similar results for contract type and working time flexibility, although the positive correlation between modern variable pay and working time flexibility is not statistically significant. The percentages of employees with modern variable pay are highest for those who work under temporary (20%) and unlimited contracts (11%).

When the absolute numbers are taken into account, the data reveals that the employees surveyed were predominantly working under unlimited contracts, whereas the high proportion of fixed term contracts only covers a small number of employees. The Swedish data from the EPOC survey show that modern forms of variable pay are significantly more often found in workplaces with working time flexibility. This weak, but significant correlation is displayed in percentages for companies with modern variable pay schemes (28%) and those without working time flexibility (37%).

Relation between Pay Systems and Work Organisation

The conclusion which could be drawn from the ESWC 2000 survey data is that forms of work organisation that give employees opportunities to participate and to decide on issues which are directly linked with their job, are more usual when modern forms of variable pay are used. Swedish data supports this conclusion regarding the association between modern forms of variable pay and HPWO. The proportion of employees getting team bonus, profit sharing, and/or income from shares and working in workplaces with a higher degree of time and task autonomy, task variety, responsibility, and effective participation is higher (14%) than the proportion of those employees working at low profile HPWO's (8%).

Contrary to these findings, Swedish data from the EPOC survey reveal a negative correlation between modern forms of variable pay and the intensity of group delegation. Percentages are higher for companies using modern variable pay schemes with a low intensity of group delegation (38%) than for those companies in which employees are granted high grade of decisive power and control over work-related issues (29%).

Effectiveness of Pay Systems and System Alignment

With regard to the relationships between pay systems and indicators for the quality of working life, Antoni *et al.* (2005) report a positive relation between modern forms of variable pay and a general job satisfaction; they also report a negative association between piece rate or productivity pay and the sustainability of work for the Swedish sub-sample of the ESWC 2000 survey. The employees receiving traditional forms of variable pay such as piece rate are more likely to say that their work is less sustainable than those having other types of pay systems. Percentages of employees with piece rate or productivity pay rating the sustainability of their job negatively are 7%; in contrast, 4% of those employees say that it is conceivable to go on doing the same job up to 60 years old. Swedish employees, who receive modern forms of variable pay, also report significantly more often that they are satisfied with their jobs than those without.

In two independent studies (Bergman & Höglund, 2003; Wennberg & Martinsson, 2001) it was concluded that higher level of job satisfaction and well-being seemed to be linked with a performance-related pay system and not a piece rate system. The divisions which had implemented a performance-related pay system based on the performance of the division, raised a higher level of employee's job satisfaction and well-being in comparison with the division that had kept the piece rate system. It can be deduced that piece rate pay systems cause stress, whereas the performance-related pay system does not in this case.

Regarding the attitudes towards individual pay forms, a study within the public sector shows that about 60% of the respondents are satisfied with the pay system (Strandås, 2003). However, there are only small effects of pay systems on work motivation in self-reports (Andersson & Larsson, 2003; Eriksson *et al.*, 2002; Lundberg, 2002; Sverke, Näswall & Hellgren, 2005; Wallenberg, 2000a, 2000b). Another study within the public sector (Eriksson & Leander, 1995) shows that men are more receptive towards individual pay than women. In most of the cases in this study, individual pay meant that the individual has a fixed monthly pay, which was increased once a year. In this case, the pay rise was based on ten different factors like "education", "performance in teaching", "performance in research" etc., which can be said altogether to make up for the individual's competence and performance. Men more positively rated the impact of the implementation of individual pay than negatively. However, a lot of respondents said that job satisfaction and cooperation between colleagues had decreased because of the individual pay system.

The reasons which have been reported to justify a decrease in the level of cooperation are the following: the feelings of unfairness in pay system, the bad leadership, and the stress (Nilsson, 2000):

- 93% of metal workers answered that cooperation (defined as helpfulness and sharing of knowledge) between colleagues is fundamental for the quality of work and the efficiency
- 45% said that the level of cooperation had not changed over the last few years
- 37% said that the level of cooperation had increased
- 15% said that it had decreased over the last few years

Regarding what could justify the increase in the level of cooperation, the metalworkers thought that "experience of group organisation" and "better education and information" have been the most important reasons. When they were asked whether their willingness to cooperate had changed because of the existence of the performance appraisal by the supervisor, they gave the following answers:

- 40% answered that their willingness to cooperate had increased
- 15% answered that it had decreased
- 45% answered that it hadn't changed

Granqvist and Regnér (2003) highlight the importance of regular meetings or "talks" between employee and supervisor where performance and pay issues are dealt with; they find a statistical relationship between the occurrence of those talks and an increase in pay. The impact on women is higher than men. Further on, they evidence that employees who individually negotiate with their supervisor on average gets 5% more in terms of pay increase than employees who do not negotiate individually.

In their reanalyses of ESWC 2000 data, Antoni *et al.* (2005) set up other indicators of the quality of working life. Indicators, such as excessive demands, physical load, health risks, or health problems show only weak and non-significant correlations with modern forms of variable pay for the Swedish sub-sample. In contrast with this result, the connection between HPWO and physical load is also negative, but very much stronger (*cf.* Figure 4.14). The proportion of employees working in high profile HPWO workplaces and reporting less physically demanding tasks is by far the highest proportion.

Besides indicators for the quality of working life which derived from the ESWC 2000 survey, the EPOC survey provided indicators of organisational performance and managerial strategy. There are only a few statistically significant relationships between the various effect criteria and the type of pay system. Unlike the findings obtained at cross-national level where positive significant correlations for the reduction in number of managers and output increase have been reported, Swedish data show negative relationships between modern forms of variable pay and a decrease in sickness and absenteeism together with an increase in quality improvement. These results suggest that modern forms of variable pay are sometimes related to negative outcomes for the employee's quality of working life. This might be due to the fact that in some organisations, variable pay systems are related to the performance of the employee himself – or herself –, but also to the performance of his or her colleagues and therefore connected to competition and stress.

Figure 4.14. Percentages of a) HPWO by physical load (ESWC 2000) and b) performance by modern variable pay (EPOC)

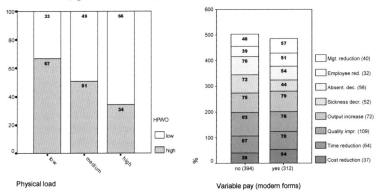

Physical load   Variable pay (modern forms)

Nilsson (1990) reports that the productivity of a service company has increased due to the bonus system (performance bonus in this case). The improvements were:

- Higher quality on customer service (measured by fewer complaints);
- The time between the customer's complaint and the employee's action decreased;
- The billing for customer service increased.

In another study (Eriksson, 2002) two divisions within three different companies were compared. Among the divisions, there is the first one with a pay system defined as "traditional" and based on work content. In contrast, the second division with a pay system defined as "modern" and based on an assessment of individual competence, knowledge, and experience. Consequently, a total of three independent comparisons were conducted with the purpose of exploring the relationship between pay system and productivity. In none of the cases, the author could find such a relationship.

Antoni *et al.* (2005) decided to use innovation strategy as an indicator of managerial strategy; it is defined in the EPOC questionnaire as activities towards product innovation, which have been carried out by the management in the last three years. Results for the Swedish sub-sample match up with findings obtained at cross-national level. Workplaces with an innovation strategy have more often modern forms of variable pay. The proportion of companies using team bonus, profit sharing, and/or share ownership schemes and following an innovation strategy is higher (42%) than the proportion of companies without an innovation strategy (26%).

The analysis of Swedish data with regard to an alignment between pay systems, work organisation, and strategy shows different results in comparison with cross-national level. The existence or not of an innovation strategy does not change the nature of the relationship between modern forms of variable pay and the intensity of group delegation. In both cases, there is only a non-significant negative correlation which indicates that companies with a high intensity of group delegation have less often modern variable pay than those with a low intensity of group delegation (*e.g.* 37% *vs.* 51%) with an innovation strategy.

Summary and Conclusion

In this chapter, we report national research in Sweden on pay, working conditions, and managerial policy, their relationships and outcomes as well as the results of the secondary analyses of the ESWC 2000 and EPOC data. In general, however, there is few research on pay systems in Sweden. The research that tries to investigate on relationships between pay systems and specific factors like performance, work organisation, and working conditions nearly does not exist. An explanation for this can be the long tradition of central negotiations, in Sweden, between trade unions and employers' associations regarding pay and other working conditions. Pay levels have been collectively decided for employees from the whole of sectors and mainly on the basis of occupation and trade union membership. Sweden is said to have one of the most highly centralised systems of pay bargaining worldwide (Bender & Elliot, 2003). Therefore, issues regarding pay have been mainly political and not scientific; accordingly, to a great extent, studies on pay systems have been carried out by organisations from the labour market, and not by academic institutions.

However, from the 1980s onwards, the pay negotiation process has become a more decentralised one. The collective agreements still cover a great number of employees, but increase much more the freedom of action of each company than before. This change has permitted the development of new pay systems, but this process is slow, and the prevalence of variable pay systems is not very common. The parties of the labour market have not actually agreed on the desirability of the "new" pay systems, and sometimes people involved in the debate get heated. We need further research to know more about the various effects of certain types of pay systems.

Indicators of pay and pay systems have been the existence or not of different types of pay systems. The broad term *individual pay* is widely used to indicate a change from collectively agreed pay to modern forms of pay systems. Like in other countries indicators of pay and pay systems have been primarily the existence or not of different types of pay systems. In addition, cooperation between colleagues has been measured to identify and explain the influence of pay systems, and productivity was not only defined in terms of organisational efficiency, but in terms of customer satisfaction. Contrary to other countries in Sweden the broad term *individual pay* is widely used to indicate a change from collectively agreed pay to modern forms of pay systems.

Due to unclear definitions of various pay systems, comparisons between different studies are somehow difficult. It could be said that today, most of the employees in Sweden get some kind of individual element in their pay (National Mediation Office, 2004). It means that their pay, in one way or another, is determined on the basis of individual performance or competence. In general, the importance of variable pay elements in employees' total salary is around 15% (Sweden Statistics, 2001) and 25% (Van het Kaar & Grünell, 2001).

From a secondary data analysis of Swedish sub-samples from the ESWC 2000 and EPOC surveys, it can be concluded that modern forms of variable pay prevail more among male employees belonging to high-income groups, and working predominantly under unlimited contracts in private owned companies, in workplaces with flexible working time schedules. There are inconsistent findings between the two surveys concerning the company's size.

Studies evidence that feelings of unfairness in pay systems, bad leadership, and stress can impair the cooperation between colleagues. However, the existence of a certain type of pay systems does not seem to affect this cooperation (Nilsson, 2000).

Whereas the ESWC 2000 dataset supports the hypothesis that modern variable pay is linked with high performance work organisations, the Swedish sub-sample from the EPOC survey shows that modern forms of variable pay systems are not found more often in workplaces with a high intensity of group delegation.

There are not any consistent results about the effectiveness of pay systems. In a few studies, attempts have been made to investigate on this issue, but the conclusions remain contradictory. Swedish data from the EPOC project shows while using indicators for quality of working life that job satisfaction and the sustainability of work is rated higher by employees receiving modern forms of variable pay. Indicators of organisational effectiveness that are negatively related to modern forms of variable pay are the decrease in sickness and absenteeism together with an increase in quality improvement. No matter an innovation strategy exists or not in the companies, the relationship between modern forms of variable pay and strategy tends to be negative, but without statistical significance.

References

Andersson, Å. & Larsson, T. (2003), "Individuell lönesättning och motivation" [Individual pay and motivation], Ekonomprogrammet C-nivå, 2003:080, Luleå tekniska högskola [Luleå University of Technology].

Antoni, C., Berger, A., Baeten, X., Emans, B., Hulkko, K., Kessler, I., Neu, E., Vartiainen, M. & Verbruggen, A. (2005), *Wages and Working Conditions in the European Union*, Dublin: European Foundation for the Improvement of Living and Working Conditions.

Bender, K.A. & Elliott, R.F. (2003), *Decentralised Pay Setting. A Study of the Outcomes of Collective Bargaining Reform in the Civil Service in Australia, Sweden and the UK*, Aldershot: Ashgate Publishing Limited, England.

Bergman, A. & Höglund, U. (2003), "Lönesystem och arbetsmiljöfaktorer – kan man finna några samband?" [Pay system and work environment factors – Are there any relationships?], Research report, Luleå Tekniska Universitet [Luleå University of Technology].

Eriksson, A., Sverke, M., Hellgren, J. & Wallenberg, J. (2002), *Lön som styrmedel – konsekvenser för kommunanställdas attityder och prestationer* [Pay as a control-tool – Consequences for public service employees' attitudes and performance], Arbetsmarknad & arbetsliv, nr 3, Stockholm: Arbetslivsinstitutet.

Eriksson, G. & Leander, E. (1995), "Konsekvenser av individuell lönesättning – en enkätundersökning inom högskolan" [Consequences of individual pay – A survey within the university and college], Research report, Linköpings universitet [Linköping University].

Eriksson, M. (2002), "Lönesystem, produktivitet och kunskapsstimulans" [Pay system, productivity and knowledge encouragement], Research report, Chalmers Tekniska Högskola [Chalmers University of Technology].

Granqvist, L. & Regnér, H. (2003), "Den nya lönebildningen. En forskningsöversikt och analys av lönebildningen för akademiker" [The new pay structure. A research overview and analysis of the new pay structure for academics], SACO [the Swedish Confederation of Professional Associations].

Lundberg, L. (2002), "Individuellt belöningssystem och motivation inom offentliga sektorn" [Individual reward-systems and motivation within the public sector], Research report, Luleå Tekniska Universitet [Luleå University of Technology].

National Mediation Office [Medlingsinstitutet] (2004), *Annual report*, http://www.mi.se

Nilsson, T. (1990), *Bonus för industritjänstemän – lönar det sig?* [Bonus for industry white-collar workers - Does it pay?], Stockholm: SIF [Swedish Union of Technical and Clerical Employees in Industry].

Nilsson, T. (2000), *Individuell lönesättning för kollektivanställda. Metallarbetarna på ABB* [Individual pay for blue-collar workers. The metal workers at ABB], Stockholm: SIF [Swedish Union of Technical and Clerical Employees in Industry].

Strandås, K. (2003), *Lön för mödan? Hur fungerar den individuella lönesättningen för Kommunals medlemmar?* [Is the pay worth the bother?], Kommunal.

Sverke, M., Näswall, K. & Hellgren, J. (2005), *Bättre löner i staten. Enkätundersökning om lön, motivation och arbetsvillkor bland statligt anställda* [Better pay in the government. A survey on pay, motivation and working conditions among governmental employees], Stockholm: OFR.

Sweden Statistics (2001), *"The Work Environment"*, Statistical database, http://www.scb.se

Sweden Statistics (2004), *"Women and Men in Sweden"*, Statistical database, http://www.scb.se

Van het Kaar, R. and Grünell, M. (2001), *Comparative Study on Variable Pay in Europe*, Dublin: European Foundation for the Improvement of Living and Working Conditions. http://www.eiro.eurofound.eu.int/2001/Study/TN0104 201S.html.

Wallenberg, J. (2000a), *Lön – Mål eller medel?* [Pay – Means or end?], Landstingsförbundet [The Federation of Swedish County Councils].

Wallenberg, J. (2000b), *Löner och arbetsplatsförhållanden för Kommunals medlemmar* [Pay and working conditions for public service employees], Kommunal.

Wennberg, F. & Martinsson, P. (2001), "Alternativa lönesystem inom byggbranschen: en utvärdering av NCC Entreprenads resultatlönesystem för yrkesarbetare I Luleå" [Alternative pay systems within the construction industry. An assessment of NCCs performance-related pay system for workers in Luleå], Research report, Luleå Tekniska Universitet [Luleå University of Technology].

CHAPTER 4.2.6

Pay Systems and Outcomes in the UK

Ian KESSLER

The literature review about British pay systems and outcomes is based on fourteen studies, which engross the findings from cross-national European studies. There are two national panel surveys, which cover pay systems and one comparative study at European level. The first of the panel surveys is the Labour Force Survey (LFS), which is a quarterly sample survey of households living at private addresses in Britain. Its purpose is to provide information about the British labour market that can be used then to develop, manage, evaluate and report on labour market policies. The LFS is based on a systematic random sample design, which is representative of Britain. Each quarter's LFS sample of 60,000 private households is made up of five waves; each one approximately comprises 12,000 households. Each wave is interviewed in five successive quarters, so that in any one quarter, one wave will be receiving their first interview, the other wave their second, and the last wave will receive the fifth and final interview.

The second panel survey is the Workplace Employment Relations Survey (WERS). The WERS 1998 is the fourth of the series of surveys, which began in 1980. As shown in the title, it focuses on employment relation practices in the workplace or at the establishment level. In 1998, workplaces employing 10 or more employees were covered. Managers and worker representatives in over 3,000 workplaces were interviewed. In addition, almost 30,000 employees in these workplaces filled in a questionnaire about their working life. Panel data for all the surveys is also available, which could be analysed as well, if respective resources were provided. Within this report, only the indicators used in these studies are analysed. Furthermore, some of the studies reported below, which have actually sought to relate pay systems to one or more of the other three variables, use data from these two surveys to a certain extent (Blanchflower & Oswald, 1988; Cully, Woodland, O'Reilly & Dix, 1999). These studies have varied in their approach, some focus on practices as they relate to reward and work organisation, others more on employee's attitudes and behaviours. A number of studies have revolved around notions of the high performance workplace and the high commitment model. There is some concentration by industry or sector. Thus, we have studies that focus on the aerospace and call centre industries. Some of them are also concentrated on particular types of pay system.

Indicators

Regarding pay system, the existence or not of different types of pay systems has been the main indicator. With work organisation, many studies have focused on the existence of different forms of teamwork as an indicator, although some studies have also put a stress on work variety, features associated with skill development and use. In terms of organisational performance similar types of indicators are used, *which* tend to revolve around productivity and profitability. Occasionally, more novel indicators such as share price movement are used.

Prevalence of Pay Systems

The highly developed stock markets and the supportive position of the government (translated into tax incentives for profit sharing and share ownership models) provide a stable foundation stone for variable pay and this is reflected by a high frequency of the forms of variable pay in comparison with other European countries (Van het Kaar & Grünell, 2001).

In the ESWC 2000 survey, 8% of the employees in the UK report they receive modern forms of variable pay in comparison with 6% on average in all the 15 European countries included in this study (Antoni *et al.*, 2005). From the UK sub-sample of the ESWC 2000 dataset, Antoni *et al.* report a positive correlation between modern forms of variable pay and higher income classes. The prevalence of employees who report that they receive modern variable pay as components of their reward package is especially high among the highest income group (21%). In contrast, percentages of employees with modern variable pay among other income levels range from 4% to 8%.

The gender gap in the use of modern variable pay is in UK less striking than in the other countries or at cross-national level. However, there is a significant difference between male (10%) and female employees (4%) concerning the impact of modern variable pay schemes. An investigation on the link between modern variable pay and age reveals a slightly negative correlation which has not any statistical significance.

The examination of the connection between modern forms of variable pay and size, showed both for the ESWC 2000 and EPOC UK sub-samples a significant positive association. Team bonus, profit sharing, and share ownership schemes are found more frequently in bigger companies (up to 65%), although more than 50% of all the companies whose workforce is over than four employees, have modern forms of variable pay. A high proportion of companies using team or company performance-related pay schemes or income from shares belongs to the private sector (62%), whereas the percentage of public sector companies with modern variable pay only reaches 15%.

The use of the ESWC 2000 data for the UK sub-sample in order to investigate on the relationships between pay systems and employment conditions (contract type, working time flexibility) reveals a positive association for employees who receive modern forms of variable pay and work under more permanent contracts, such as unlimited or fixed term contracts. Unlike the findings at cross-national level, this positive correlation is not statistically significant. Findings for the UK from both survey sub-samples, support the overall result that employees who report that their remuneration includes modern forms of variable pay are working more often in workplaces with flexible working time schedules. Nonetheless, the differences do not seem to be very impressive.

Relation between Pay Systems and Work Organisation

Findings about the relationship between pay systems and high performance work organisations (HPWO), as found for the whole sample of the ESWC 2000 survey match with results for the UK sub-sample. Secondary data analysis shows that employees with team bonus, profit sharing schemes, and/or income from shares are significantly more present in workplaces with a higher grade of time and task autonomy, task variety, responsibility, and effective participation. The proportion of employees receiving modern forms of variable pay and working at high performance work organisations reaches 14% in comparison with 5% for those employees working in workplaces that only incorporate these characteristics to a lower degree.

Among three surveys made within establishments in 1997, 2000, and 2002 with around 200 establishments per year, Thompson (2002b) analyses the relationship between high performance work organisation (HPWO) and performance. HPWO includes work practices such as semi-autonomous team working, continuous improvement teams, responsibility for one's own quality of work, job rotation, information sharing programs and briefing groups, employee relation practices, such as harmonised terms and conditions, regular social gathering for employees and induction programs, as well as performance-based rewards and broad job grading structures. He reports that HPWO is linked with better organisational and employee performance outcomes. For example, those companies with a significant score on the HPWO index in 1997 had average sales in 2002 of £133k per employee in comparison with £67k for those with a low score on the index.

In a further study, Thompson and Heron (2003) examined the relationship between pay systems, characteristics of the work organisation and organisational commitment, citizenship and innovative behaviour in a survey of over 400 employees in research and development departments of six high technology firms. Findings show that pay is positively associated with commitment, but negatively with innovative behaviour. Innovative behaviour was the strongest element related to characteristics of the work organisation, *i.e.* job design.

In line with cross-national findings reported by Antoni *et al.* (2005), there are results concerning the relationship between modern forms of variable pay and the intensity of group delegation, which serves as an indicator of work organisation in the EPOC survey. Group delegation is defined as the strongest form of direct participation and includes the transfer of decisive power and control from management executives or line managers to groups of employees. Modern forms of variable pay are more often found in workplaces with a high intensity of group delegation. The percentage of companies with modern forms of variable pay and with a high intensity of group delegation is 88% and the percentage of companies with a low intensity reaches 77%. Again, the general high level of percentages about the prevalence of modern variable pay in the UK is striking (Antoni *et al.*, 2005). Contrary to this, two surveys carried out in 135 British manufacturing plants in 1986 and 1990, Wood (1996) did not find any association between the use of High Commitment Management Practices (HCMP), such as teamwork and job design to ensure a complete use of worker skills, and the use of performance pay. But the study shows a tendency towards a greater use of HCMP in relation with payment system changes as well as a neglect of HCMP with the payment of individual bonuses.

Effectiveness of Pay Systems and System Alignment

Regarding the relationship between pay systems and the quality of working life, Holman (2002) found in a survey of 557 customer service representatives carried out within three British call centres, that the fairness of payment is linked to an extrinsic job satisfaction, but not to anxiety, depression, and an intrinsic job satisfaction.

Antoni *et al.* (2005) did a secondary data analysis for the ESWC 2000 survey with variables that indicate the self-assessment of the quality of working life, in particular employee's satisfaction with his current work and the individual sustainability of work – measured with the rating of employees – whether they think that they can carry on doing the same job up to 60 years old. Both indicators of the quality of working life, job satisfaction, and the sustainability of work show in the UK sub-sample a negative correlation with traditional forms of variable pay (piece rate or productivity pay), whereas only the connection between these forms and job satisfaction is statistically significant. Modern forms of variable pay, such as team bonus, profit sharing schemes, or other income from shares do not seem to be associated with a higher job satisfaction at all. Percentages of employees reporting modern forms of variable pay and various degrees of satisfaction do not show considerable differences and range from 6% to 8%.

Taking other indicators of quality of working life into account, such as excessive demands, physical load, health risks, or health problems data analysis reveals two significant relationships between modern forms of variable pay, physical load and health problems. The proportion of employees receiving modern forms of variable pay and reporting about health problems is the highest by far (*cf.* Figure 4.15).

Figure 4.15. Percentages of a) modern variable pay by health problems (ESWC 2000) and b) performance by modern variable pay (EPOC)

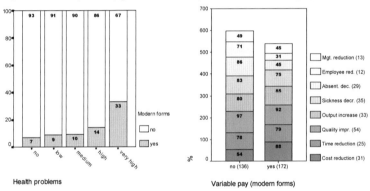

The effectiveness of pay systems is measured in the EPOC survey with indicators such as the reduction in numbers of managers or employees, the decrease in sickness or absenteeism, the improvement in quality, the increase in output, and the reduction in time or costs. There are only a few statistically significant relationships between the various effect criteria and the type of pay system (*cf.* Figure 4.15). For the UK sub-sample of the EPOC dataset, the most prominent effect that has been reported is cost reduction. Negative relationships have been found between modern forms of variable pay, the decrease in absenteeism and the reduction in numbers of employees.

In a survey of 67 UK manufacturing firms Paterson, West, Lawthom and Nickell (1997) did not find statistically significant relationship between either comparative pay, *i.e.* the extent to which base pay is higher or lower than competitors', individual or collective incentive compensation systems and changes in productivity or profits. In an analysis of the WERS survey, profit sharing has been lined with a lower rate of employee's dismissal (Cully *et al.*, 1999), but no other relationship of statistical significance between various organisational outcomes and profit sharing schemes or employee share ownership scheme was detected. Similarly, Blanchflower and Oswald (1988), using the WERS survey, report that establishments with employee share ownership schemes did not have superior financial performance than those without.

In contrast with these findings which do not show any impact of the employee share ownership, there are studies reporting that in the retail sector, the introduction of employee share ownership has been associated with a faster subsequent growth on average share price (Richardson & Nejad, 1986) and other financial criteria (Bell & Hanson, 1987). Furthermore, Wilson, Cable and Peel (1990) found in a panel study of 52 British engineering firms that quit rates tend to be lower in firms that introduced employee share ownership, while considering that everything else is putting on an equal footing.

Beside pay systems, work organisation, and indicators of effectiveness, a fourth variable has been particularly interesting: managerial strategy. As one aspect of managerial strategy the variable innovation strategy derives from a question about initiatives taken by the management of the workplace towards product innovation in the last three years, which is included in the EPOC survey (Antoni *et al.*, 2005). On average, European level EPOC data show a positive connection between modern forms of variable pay and companies that introduced an innovation strategy. The analysis of the UK sub-sample replicates this association. The proportion of companies which uses modern variable pay schemes and follows an innovation strategy is significantly higher (75%) than for companies without any strategy towards product innovation (49%). Concerning UK, it has also been found that the existence or not of an innovation strategy leads to a shift in the strength of the correlation between modern forms of variable pay and the intensity of group delegation. The companies which incorporate an innovation strategy tend to show a stronger association between a higher intensity of group delegation and a higher prevalence of modern variable pay; however, these positive correlations are not statistically significant. Percentages are higher for companies using modern variable pay with a high intensity of group delegation (88%) in comparison with companies with a low intensity (77%).

One of the few national studies, which analyses the relationships between company strategy, pay systems, employee and company's outcomes is based on a survey of more than 200 establishments in the aerospace industry (Thompson, 2002a). Company strategy was categorised as either cost or customer/service driven. Regarding pay systems, individual performance-related pay, team- or group-based rewards, employee share ownership and profit share schemes were analysed. With respect to the employee's outcomes, absenteeism, turnover, value added, and profit per employee were measured; regarding organisational outcomes, profit margins, profit growth, and levels of customer retention. Findings show a negative relationship between a customer-focused strategy and the use of team-based pay, but business strategies were not related to other types of pay system. Furthermore, significant relationships between companies with individual performance-related pay and low levels of absenteeism, low employee turnover, and high added value per employee exist. Significant relationships were also found between team-based pay, high profit margins and high growth in profits. Regarding employee share ownership schemes, it has only been reported a relation with high levels of customer retention, but there was not any relationship with any other variable which had been examined.

Summary and Conclusion

This chapter reports the British national research on pay, working conditions and managerial policy, their relationships and outcomes as well as the results of the secondary analyses of the ESWC 2000 and EPOC data. Studies have varied in their approach in terms of practices to be focused on, because they relate to reward and work organisation and others are more based on employee's attitudes and behaviour. Generally speaking, however, work, which focuses on practices, is more usual; this can be linked with the fact that many studies, which have touched upon our model have revolved around notions of high performance workplace and high commitment model. These approaches have derived from a number of practices labelled as 'high commitment', which have often included particular pay practices.

Without any doubt, a diversity of indicators have been used in relation to each of the variables in our model. In the case of pay structures and system, the existence or not of different types of pay systems has been the main indicator, while some reliance has been placed on the 'fairness' of approaches to pay. With work organisation, many studies have used the presence of different forms of teamwork as an indicator, although some have also concentrated on work variety, features-associated skill development and use. Only one study more explicitly, used features of lean production systems as an indicator. In terms of organisational performance, similar types of indicators are used, which tend to revolve around productivity and profitability. Occasionally, more novel indicators such as share price movement are used. The sole vari-

215

able, which does not appear prominently in these studies, is management strategies. Within only one study, an attempt was made to develop an indicator of management strategies. This suggests that distinguishing and measuring different management strategies may raise some problems.

Undoubtedly, the studies reviewed show some concentration on the variables in their analysis. This concentration is made under various forms. First, there is some concentration by industry or sector. As a result, some of our studies focus on the aerospace and call centre industries. Secondly, there is some concentration on particular types of pay system. No doubt that the research is more concentrated on the relationship between profit sharing and employee share ownership and other variables, than on other pay systems and their link with these other factors. A secondary analysis of the UK data shows that modern forms of variable pay prevail more among high-income groups and especially among male employees. Large-sized establishments from the private sector use more frequently schemes of modern variable pay. Employees that have flexible working time schedules more frequently report that they receive income from team or company performance-related pay or other income from shares.

Compared to other European countries, forms of variable pay are more frequent in the UK, which might be due to the highly developed stock markets and the supportive position of the government (Van het Kaar & Grünell, 2001). Nonetheless, it is startling to see that few researches have been carried out on this topic in the UK, because variable pay systems are mostly defined and established by the employers and not subject to collective pay agreements in the UK (which makes it less understandable, that only few organisations assess their variable pay systems).

Some findings extract from the literature review of British research showed that there is not any association between the use of HCMP (High Commitment Management Practices) and the use of performance pay; however, there is a tendency of greater use of HCMP in relation with payment system changes (Wood, 1996). Secondary data analysis revealed a connection between modern variable pay and forms of work organisation that gives employees a more decisive power and control, measured in terms of HPWO and direct participation (group delegation).

In terms of outcomes, this review has clearly shown that organisational or corporate performance outcomes have been concentrated on to the relative neglect of employee-related outcomes associated with employee health and welfare. This is linked with the fact that most of this work has been linked with the high performance/high commitment model. This model has tended to appear significantly in debates amongst academics concerned with strategic human resource management: this is an approach, which is initially interested in studying whether and how HR practices have an impact on organisational or corporate performance. Findings have been somehow contradictory: on the one hand, they report lower levels of absenteeism and employee turnover for IPRP (Individual Performance-Related Pay) schemes and a link between team pay with high profit margins and higher growth in profits (Thompson, 2002a). On the other hand, they do not report any relationship between comparative pay or incentive compensation systems and changes in productivity or profits (Paterson, West, Lawthom & Nickell, 1997). Additionally, HPWO (High Performance Work Organisation) was linked to better organisational and employee performance outcomes (Thompson, 2002b).

Finally, it is necessary to precise that the studies outlined have not shown many significant relationships between pay systems, structures, and the other variables in our model.

References

Antoni, C., Berger, A., Baeten, X., Emans, B., Hulkko, K., Kessler, I., Neu, E., Vartiainen, M. & Verbruggen, A. (2005), *Wages and Working Conditions in the European Union*, Dublin: European Foundation for the Improvement of Living and Working Conditions.

Bell, D. & Hanson, C. (1987), *Profit Sharing and Profitability*, London: Kogan Page.

Blanchflower, D. & Oswald, A. (1988), "Profit Related Pay: Prose Discovered", *Economic Journal*, 98 (392), p. 720-730.

Cully, M., Woodland, S., O'Reilly, A. & Dix, G. (1999), *Britain at Work*, London: Routledge.

Holman, D. (2002), "Employee Wellbeing in Call Centres", *Human Resource Management Journal*, 12, p. 35-50.

Paterson, M., West, M., Lawthom, R. & Nickell, S. (1997*), Impact of People Management Practices on Business Performance*, London: IPM.

Richardson, R. & Nejad, A. (1986), "Employee Share Ownership Schemes in the UK", *British Journal of Industrial Relations*, 24, p. 233-250.

Thompson, M. (2002a), *Pay and Performance in the UK Aerospace*, Society of British Aerospace Companies (SBAC), Oxford: Templeton College.

Thompson, M. (2002b), *High Performance Work in UK Aerospace, Audit 2002*, Society of British Aerospace Companies (SBAC), Oxford: Templeton College.

Thompson, M. & Heron, P. (2003), "What Do Knowledge Workers Want? The Employment Relationship and Innovative Performance", Research paper, Oxford: Templeton College.

Van het Kaar, R. and Grünell, M. (2001), *Comparative study on variable pay in Europe*, Dublin: European Foundation for the Improvement of Living and

Working Conditions. http://www.eiro.eurofound.eu.int/2001/Study/TN0104 201S.html.

Wilson, N., Cable, J. & Peel, M. (1990), "Quit Rates and the Impact of Participation, Profit Sharing and Unionisation: Empirical Evidence from UK Engineering Firms", *British Journal of Industrial Relations*, 28 (2), p. 197-213.

Wood, S. (1996), "High Commitment Management and Payment Systems", *Journal of Management Studies*, 33, p. 55-77.

European Case Studies

Conny H. ANTONI

In this chapter, we move onto single companies. The pay audit tool described in chapter 2 is firstly applied in retail banking companies within several European countries, then in European subsidiaries of a multinational company. By means of these national and cross-national case studies, contemporary pay practices in Europe are getting clearer. As the most existing research focuses on pay systems for managerial employees, concerning operational employees, our knowledge is quite limited. To bridge this gap in the research, the following case studies focus on operational employees. These case studies also illustrate the use of the pay audit tool developed by the authors.

In the retail banking case studies, the audit tool set up by the authors was applied in three different banks in Belgium, Finland, and Germany. This enables us to get insights into the way national and company specific conditions influence pay, and hold under control the influences of sectors, because the sector was kept constant.

Furthermore, we used the audit tool to study the pay systems in a European multinational company. Audits were carried out in the Belgian, French, Dutch, and German subsidiaries of this company; various influences and approaches to pay we find in these countries were examined. Therefore, these case studies enable us to get glimpses of the way national conditions influence pay, while controlling for company factors such as ownership structure and corporate strategy, as the company was kept constant.

CHAPTER 4.3.1

Case Studies – National Companies

Conny H. ANTONI, Xavier BAETEN, Ansgar BERGER,
Kiisa HULKKO & An VERBRUGGEN

Only a few studies have focused on the influence of company strategy on pay systems and work organisation, or on the way collective bargaining influences the ability of companies to align pay systems and work organisation with their strategy. As these aspects were not dealt with in the ESWC 2000 and only marginally studied in the EPOC survey, secondary analyses of these datasets give limited insights. An analysis of the EPOC survey shows a very weak negative correlation between modern forms of variable pay and the degree of trade union membership. However, the data suggest that the alignment of a company strategy, pay systems, and work organisation have an impact on the company effectiveness. That is why further research is needed on these matters and, particularly, whether and how companies want to align strategy, pay systems and work organisation, and how conditions of collective bargaining influence their ability to do so. In a first step, it was decided to carry out three studies in Belgium, Finland, and Germany. The methods used and their results are described in the following sections.

As quite a little is known about European companies with respect to the issues mentioned above and given the limits of the resources, case studies were the best method to gain a better understanding of the various actors and interest groups, their goals, intentions, actions and opinions regarding strategies, pay and work organisation, and the way these latter influence company practices, outcomes, and working life.

These case studies analyse the model variables and their influencing factors in a company setting, describe their dynamics, mutual interdependencies and consequences, from the perspective of key actors and interest groups or stakeholders of a company.

The control of the effects among sectors and the obtention of similar data from different countries make necessary the set up of three case studies from the banking sector and especially put the stress on the retail banking. The banking sector was chosen for practical reasons, in terms of availability of contacts, and because it has been subject to consolidation processes for the last couple of years. Therefore, it was expected to illustrate new strategies, reorganisation of work processes and pay systems. Due to limited resources, the field of research was restricted to three case studies. Belgium and Finland are among the smallest countries of the EU: Belgium is part of the EU since the outset, whereas Finland entered the Union later on and quite recently experienced dramatic economic changes. Germany represents one of the largest and most traditional European countries, with recent significant changes in the banking sector; in 2003, a new collective labour agreement was introduced in that sector concerning modern forms of variable pay.

The case studies are based on the audit tool set up by the authors. They use interviews with individuals and focus on groups representing key stakeholders of pay systems. Available documentary material on current pay systems and practices was also analysed. In all three cases, HR, line management and employees' representatives were interviewed as key stakeholders, while using common guidelines. On average, interviews lasted about two hours. All the groups, *i.e.* HR management, line management, and employee representatives, were asked to describe company strategy, pay systems, and work organisation, to explain why something is done, the way it is done, the way it works, the impact of it, and what should or will be changed in the future. In particular, the interviews sought to discover whether and how collective bargaining conditions further or hinder the strategic alignment of pay systems and work organisations. The stress was put on pay systems for operational, *i.e.* non-managerial, employees who were subject to collective bargaining.

In particular, the following topics were covered:

- Strategy – characteristics of company, HR and pay strategy, reasons for the existence of different pay schemes, links between compensation strategy, general HR strategy, and company philosophy, objectives and strategy;

- Work organisation – for instance, description of tasks and task interdependence, individual and group consultation, and delegation;

- Pay systems and practice – characteristics of base pay as well as variable pay (each existing system separately described) in terms of structure, rules, and processes in system and practice;

- Alignment of pay systems to strategy and work organisation and the effects on company performance (*e.g.* costs, quality, output), employee behaviour (*e.g.* turnover, absenteeism, innovative action), and attitudes (*e.g.* work climate, commitment);

- Vision of pay systems, strategy, work organisation, and their alignment;
- Collective bargaining – influences on current pay systems and future developments.

Case Study: Belgium

The case study is based on the analysis of documentary material on current pay systems and respective practices, as well as two interviews with a HR manager and a union representative; the focus is set on a group interview with line managers. They are the key stakeholders of pay systems in a Belgian bank.

At corporate level, the representative of the human resources department was interviewed in order to gain an understanding of the company's philosophy and strategy in general, HR and pay strategy especially, as well as other factors affecting pay systems. The pay systems were described in depth and assessed during the interview with the HR representative. The line managers and one union representative were interviewed in order to assess the various scopes and effects of pay systems and to consider future developments which are necessary to the improvement of pay systems.

The financial institution which matters, employed more than 10,000 employees in 2003, nearly half of which belong to the category of operational employees. Some 45% are managerial employees and 1% is part of the top management. Three out of four employees (76%) are post graduated, and about 25% of employees work under a part-time contract. The study only focuses on the operational employees and, more specifically, on those working in the retail division as client advisors; they are about three to four per office. They have to handle 80% of the financial service products on offer.

Strategy

The financial institution was formed as a result of a huge merger between Belgian banks some years ago. After the merger, the organisation's focus was mainly internally oriented, as it sought for synergies and economies of scale. Recently, the bank's strategic focus has changed from an internal to an external (customer) orientation. The different stakeholders are fully aware of this new direction. The financial institution provides banking and insurance products; it aims at being a universal bank insurance provider as well. The most important products are loans, insurance, savings accounts, and investments. The main client focus includes private persons, self-employed people, and small and medium-sized enterprises (SMEs).

The values of this financial institution are professionalism, service, honesty, openness, and enthusiasm. Another key element, which could be added to these values, is independence. The business model is set up around strong customer relationships, but the considerations of cost also play a significant role. This means that the strategy is rather mixed.

Within the HR strategy, the focus on internal cost still prevails. The second strategic HR element is the long-term relationship between the company and the employee. At first glance, these priorities might seem contradictory. However, encouraging part-time work can facilitate both strategies. Two examples of this long-term relationship are the pension plan (with defined benefits) and the opportunity given to a low performer employee to stay by means of job rotation. The third strategic HR element is the openness of communication and the fourth is competence management. This is linked with career management, *i.e.* there are assessment centres for each career phase. In practice, line management, the HR department, and the union representative are satisfied with performance management and the assessment process. The only comment in this regard was that line management needs more coaching in giving feedback to employees and in assessing them. However, there have been some recent developments in tackling this issue. The fifth strategic HR element is the need for differentiation, followed by a flexible work organisation (*e.g.* flexible working hours).

There is not any formal or clearly defined pay or reward strategy. The most important characteristics underlying the reward systems are cost, employee performance, and long-term employability. There is a clearly defined positioning of pay rates, determined by the total (financial) compensation. The bank believes in the payment of market rates on average. For high performers, there is a 75 percentile positioning.

Work Organisation

The operational employees always use the same set of instruments and software, which makes the work quite repetitive. Roles and functions are clearly defined and, as a consequence, the task is poorly diversified. On the other hand, there is a regular contact with customers, which contributes to task diversity. The work requires a rather high level of qualification, as many tasks which are purely clerical have disappeared in today's computerised work environment. Job rotation is an issue as regards employees who are getting older and bear in mind the strategic element of long-term employability. However, the financial institution does not know precisely which way to take in this respect.

In addition, work in this type of retail bank office is more a team-based activity than an individual one, and the company is also trying to flatten the hierarchical levels.

At an individual level, there is a consultative work, as well as yearly attitude surveys which focus on satisfaction and involvement. Employees are also encouraged to make suggestions, and this can even be linked with a bonus. In terms of individual consultation, customer relations are the most common issue. This illustrates the strategic alignment of work organisation. Goal setting, training, and development are also popular consultation issues. Delegation is a much more difficult issue due to the risk management. In the sectors involving financial services, procedures are fundamental for security reasons.

To sum up, the financial institution is trying to reduce the number of hierarchical levels. The work of employees in the retail division is characterised by a small degree of variety and autonomy, but teams play a key role and consultation is omnipresent. However, delegation is limited. We can conclude that some elements of high performance work organisation exist, but certainly not all the characteristics.

Pay Systems

The pay system of the financial institution is rather conservative. It is more focused on financial rewards, while limiting the employee's choices on determining the reward package, and limiting risk sharing between employer and employee. However, the HR representative considers that reward is strongly linked with performance, *i.e.* financial as well as non-financial results, and competencies. Furthermore, both individual and team performance play a role.

There are two pay systems: the first one for management and the second one for the clerical employees. We focus on the latter. The base salary concept for operational employees is mainly driven by collective agreements at sector and company level. The sector plays the most important role and has defined four grades. In the meantime, the organisation had already added two categories in order to recognise different levels.

Within the grades, age is the determining entry factor for the yearly rise as well. Promotion to another (higher) category is mainly competence-based. Seven competencies have been defined: skills and knowledge, customer relations, commercial attitude, self-management, output drive, teamwork, and entrepreneurship. Employees can only move to another grade when their overall competency profile has increased. Performance appraisal results, years of experience, and the last promotion also play a role in moving to another grade. There is a limited overlap between the different grades. The HR manager is dissatisfied with the method of setting base pay increases within grades for operational employees, because the system is only based on age, which prevents any attempt of differentiation. The line managers therefore claim that it does not matter whether operational employees well or badly perform, because their efforts are not rewarded. However, the union representative was satisfied with the system as it guarantees a complete objectivity. Nonetheless, the union representative also thinks that the employees often view the system of "same pay for the same job/age" as unfair.

According to the HR department, promotions, *i.e.* shifts to another grade, are transparently granted. The problem with the previous vague zone of transition between operational and managerial employees has been solved, and the financial rewards surrounding promotional steps are crystal clear. The only disadvantage the HR department (and the union representative) notices is the lack of transparency and objectivity – according to the union representative – of the criteria for promotion (on the basis of competencies) and the assessment of those criteria. Line management also claims that the potential for subjectivity in granting promotions is a significant weakness of the system. The line management generally thinks that "the one who asks the most will receive the most".

Variable pay systems for operational employees are mainly profit-based and team-based. There is profit sharing depending on the earnings per share. The amount is fixed per grade, *i.e.* every employee within the same grade receives the same amount. It is difficult to give precise data, but, in general, profit sharing for operational employees amounts to a sum between € 2,000 and € 3,000.

Team pay is based on the profitability of the cluster to which the employee belongs. A number of retail bank offices form a cluster. Their bonus is delivered on the basis of the profitability ranking of the cluster, in comparison with the overall profitability of all the clusters. The budget for the cluster bonus is calculated in relation with the total profit-sharing budget; on average, 15% is allocated to the cluster bonus.

Operational employees are not entitled to an individual bonus. However, 10% of these workers may be entitled to an exceptional bonus. The base amount is € 500, but it can be doubled. This bonus can only be granted to employees who have exceptionally performed, *i.e.* employees who have performed beyond the job requirements. Line management has almost complete discretion in granting these bonuses, as there are not any predefined criteria of distribution. Overall, operational employees' variable pay is rather limited; the profit share can be considered as semi-fixed pay because it is distributed on a monthly basis and has always been paid out. Actually, even if profitability drops, there would still be profit sharing. This means that the real variable pay at the top of fixed pay may amount to only 4% of base pay.

Negotiability with regard to grade assessment at the level of the operational employees' pay systems nearly does not exist.

By means of sounding boards and consultation platforms, the workforce can be involved in the design and operation of their pay system. In any case, none of the above mentioned variable pay components were the subject of a collective labour agreement. Yearly, there is a conversation between line management and the individual employee on the performance evaluation outcomes. Promotion to another grade is also communicated in writing. Each individual receives a personal overview of his or her total remuneration package each year. According to the line managers, the reward system is transparent and clear. However, as mentioned above, the union representatives were less satisfied. For example, they claim that the criteria for promotion and the granting of bonuses are opaque and subject to the line manager's discretion. The financial institution wants to counter this feeling of subjectivity, and is currently trying to introduce more objective patterns into the assessment procedures. The unions themselves do not see an obvious solution to the problem of subjectivity.

Line managers and the union representative point out that the difference in total cash between operational and managerial employees is too large, which is due to the limited amount of variable pay given to operational employees. As it will be shown, the budget devoted to bonuses for operational employees is very low, in comparison with the budget devoted to managerial employees. Nonetheless, both the HR department and union representatives are satisfied with the settlement of variable pay, albeit for different reasons. The HR department says that the variable pay system covers three important aspects (individual, team, and company) and has a strong strategic link with the organisation. The union representatives realise that the system behind variable pay is essentially solid, but lacks the necessary transparency and objective criteria for assessment. Line management is dissatisfied with the system as it stands.

Alignment and Effectiveness of Pay Systems

A direct link between managerial strategy and pay systems is difficult to discern. The variable part of pay aims at rewarding performance and results, as set out in the cluster goals (customer satisfaction, financial results, credit risk management, operational risk management, longterm goals/actions). Customer satisfaction is to be measured once a year (April/May) via a postal inquiry. There is an attempt to encourage teamwork through the cluster bonus. However, many employees see the cluster as a 'bridge too far' when it is used for the granting of bonuses, given that individuals are unable to control the results of the cluster.

The union representative evaluates the alignment of pay system with the organisation's strategy as satisfactory, particularly for managerial employees, but to a lesser extent for operational ones. However, line management believes that pay systems and strategy are not linked. HR is neither satisfied nor dissatisfied with the strategic alignment.

According to the HR department, the current pay systems have a negative effect on motivating operational employees, but a positive one on managerial employees. They also argue that pay only motivates in the short term. However, line management states that pay has a clear positive effect on the motivation of operational employees, e.g. stimulus by incentives. The union representative believes that pay has not any effect on the motivation of operational employees, because the variable part is too low; but it has a slightly positive effect on motivating managerial employees.

The HR department and line managers agree to say that pay does not have an influence on recruitment – line management even argues that it has a negative effect on attracting people. Possibilities for self-development within the organisation, career planning, and security are more important aspects recruited people take into account. People select a specific function or job, and agree with the pay that comes with the job. The union representative, on the other hand, thinks that pay has an overall positive effect on recruitment. People also apply for a job on the basis of the company's image as a good payer. HR thinks that pay does not affect the retention of staff, but the line managers and union representatives are convinced that it does, both in terms of turnover and commitment.

Line managers and union representatives report that pay negatively affects the work climate and cooperation, while the HR department ascribes a positive effect to pay. It states that pay issues never trigger social conflicts, which is confirmed by the union representative. Most of the conflicts are caused as a result of discontent with criteria for promotion. It is worth noting though that the line managers believe that pay does cause social conflicts.

According to HR and the union representative, pay does not seem to have any influence on the well-being in general, i.e. absenteeism, stress, and job satisfaction. HR thinks that there might only be an effect where there is a huge discrepancy between the pay and the job. However, the line managers argue that pay has a strong effect on job satisfaction.

The HR department attributes a significant positive effect on skill and competence development to pay. The line managers also admit that positive effect, albeit to a slightly lesser extent. Union representatives state that pay does not have that effect for operational employees, but it does for managerial employees.

There is a link between pay systems and performance. The different stakeholders have different opinions about the aspects which are influenced by pay. The HR department focuses on cost, production and service quality, and the increase in the total output. However, HR believes that pay systems are positively related to performance in the case of managerial employees, whereas there is not any link for operational employees. The line managers and union representatives agree with the positive effect on production and quality in service, but according to them, pay has a minor negative effect on the number of employees and management.

A noticeable difference between the assumptions of the HR department and line management is the effect of pay on the customer orientation. According to HR, it has a highly positive effect, both with regard to complaints and customer satisfaction. However, the line management states that there is not any effect at all on both of these aspects. Union representatives agree that pay has a moderate positive effect on the customer's orientation.

Vision / Future Developments

The HR department and the union representative are neither satisfied nor dissatisfied with the pay system in general. The system in itself is good, but some aspects could be improved, such as the criteria for promotion. The attitude of the line managers is more positive: they argue that the organisation is fully aware of the weaknesses of the system, and that actions are being taken in this respect. The line management is much more in favour of the system for managerial employees and would like it to be adapted for operational employees. The relation between fixed and variable pay should be 80-20, which is far from the current 96-4 for operational employees. 10% should be used for rewarding cluster performance, and 10% for individual performance. Line management is against a system that is purely based on age for pay increases.

The union representatives are in favour of a strict implementation of the systems in collective labour agreements. In the future, they are willing to show openness towards performance-related pay for operational employees. The problem of subjectivity in assessing performance is crucial. The unions also suggest the introduction of cafeteria plans.

Important strengths that must be maintained for the future include: the openness in communication and other practices, the social responsibility of the financial institution towards its employees (special rates on certain products, supplemental pension, luncheon vouchers, extra child benefits in June, part-time retirement, extension of the investment period for options, education possibilities), and the experienced functioning of the HR department.

Influence of Collective Bargaining Conditions

Finally, the case study sought to determine whether collective bargaining has an influence on the strategic alignment of operational employees' pay systems. Although it is almost impossible to isolate collective bargaining from other influences, it has been found that operational employees' pay systems are not linked to the organisation's strategy – according to the stakeholders – because of the lack of differentiation, and because salary increases are based on age. Meanwhile, operational employees' pay systems are strongly influenced by collective bargaining at a sectoral level. This might mean that collective bargaining has a negative influence, where generic sectoral influences mean that company-specific strategic issues are not taken into account. However, it is clearly shown in the study that union members are realising that such pay systems lead to dissatisfaction in the case of the best performers. On the other hand, the amount and the system of variable pay are not subject to collective bargaining. These could be used for a more strategic alignment. Currently, although the systems are changing, top management does not allocate sufficient funds to have a motivating impact on operational employees.

Case Study: Finland

The second case is a Finnish bank, specialised in investments and savings. It provides services to both retail customers and companies, though the particular branch office studied provides services only to retail customers. The compensation and benefits (HR) manager at corporate level was interviewed in order to gain an understanding of the company's philosophy and strategy in general, HR and pay strategy in particular, as well as general factors affecting pay systems. The pay systems and their development trends were mapped and described. The documentary material on current pay systems and the interview with the compensation and benefits manager gave an insight into the way pay systems should be; the principles underlying these systems are studied here. One branch manager, two employees, and a shop steward of the branch office were also interviewed, focusing on work and pay practices as well as development trends. The study sought to identify how pay matters stand in practice, and how they influence the company's performance, and the employee's behaviour and attitudes.

Strategy

The banking sector in Finland has a more or less common business strategy concerning financial products. In future, more emphasis will be put on long-term investment products since growth expectations lie in this area. Basic banking products are increasingly accessed through the Internet or other self-service media. In this study, the bank's strategic goal consists in becoming the most customer-oriented and the most competent financial service among banking groups in Finland. It aims at offering customers any financial service they need, depending on strategic partners when it is necessary. Efficiency, expertise, and good service are the key elements to success. This strategy implies offering reliable advices to private customers in the management of their accounts. The HR strategy supports the business strategy, for example, by identifying, developing competencies, and by providing a business school for career development.

Pay policy is embedded in the HR strategy. Regarding the base pay level, the company aims at average sector rates (the financing sector is among the highest paying sectors in Finland), by making regular market comparisons. Due to extensive variable pay systems in the last couple of years the company probably has paid slightly above average, if one takes total compensation including performance-based pay into account.

The strategy seems to be well aligned with the salary systems. Each year goals are checked and adapted, if necessary, at the management level. However, the overall HR strategy is not well known at the branch office level. Despite this, the pay strategy is clearly formulated and closely linked with what is considered to be significant.

Work Organisation

Work organisation in retail banking is based on teamwork although work tasks are individually executed while meeting customers. However, employees are organised in groups, headed by a manager. Weekly meetings are held for all the staff and for each group, dealing mostly with managerial issues such as the achievement of goals and the quality of customer service. Managers also meet each employee individually every week to discuss work-related and personal matters.

Work organisation is aligned with the overall strategy. The organisation was quite recently restructured to match requirements. Retail customer branches were organised into customer service groups that daily handle banking transactions, customer relationship groups offering services related to the management of customers' finances, and customer acquisition groups that mostly operate outside branches looking for new customers. The new service organisation makes it possible to comply with banking duties on time and to engage more efficiently and in-depth in financial advisory services.

In the branch office which was studied, there are three groups and twenty-one employees. One group consists of five employees in the customer service. Customers would meet a member of this group when getting into the office in order to take money from their account, pay a bill, etc. The two other groups of employees, each consisting of seven to eight staff, are experts in loans and investments. Customers would meet these employees only by appointment, *e.g.* if they are considering to buy a house or shares in an investment fund. The two groups of experts have their own managers, while the branch manager heads the customer service employees. Thus, in this branch, currently, there are three different employee's roles or jobs (plus the role of manager): employees with a service counselling role in customer service, and employees with a customer counselling role or financial expert role in both groups of experts.

In the specialised customer relationship roles, employees take care of their own clients and are set individual targets. The first meeting with a customer may last one and a half hours, which implies three to four customers per day. The teams are decided on the basis of facilitating the flow of customer service and employee's skills. Project groups and ad hoc groups are formed when it is necessary.

The company's Cooperation Board holds several meetings during the year. Its purpose is to promote and develop cooperation between the employer and the employees, and among the staff. The board has fifteen members, seven of which represent the clerical staff, two representing managers and specialists, and six representing the employer. Staff representatives also participate in the meetings of the company's Board of Directors, and are entitled to be there and have their say.

The possibilities of participation are quite the same in different branch offices. The participation system is set up and implemented in each office by management. The weekly meetings at branch, group, and individual levels have been mentioned above. The quality of products and the customer relations are examples of items on the agenda. However, employees noticed that "maybe there are too many meetings, while considering that we have our own targets". There is also a regular practice of surveys on work climate within the bank and a suggestion scheme. It is possible to influence decision-making and a certain level of autonomy exists concerning work scheduling, quality of work, and client deals. When employees have ideas about improving work processes, "they can always suggest and try out new ideas". Groups are able to apportion work targets to each individual, according to competence or efficiency.

Pay Systems

The systems are different for the various professional groups. The basic salary system forms the most significant part of the employees' incomes. Individual performance is assessed and this influences the salary. There are two basic pay systems: one for management, and one for the clerical employees. In the branch office studied, three managers are not part of the clerical employees' pay system. In addition, there are two types of clearly defined variable pay systems: a bonus system and a personnel fund. Next, only the pay system for clerical employees will be described.

All the staff groups in the bank are covered by a bonus system. Unit or team results and personal performance are the criteria for receiving a bonus payment. Long-term collective rewards are given through a personnel fund. Profit-sharing bonuses are yearly paid to the personnel fund according to a system agreed upon in advance, based on the company's operating profit.

The salaries of clerical bank staff are determined according to a company classification on the basis of a comprehensive evaluation of job demands, *i.e.* the complexity of tasks. The system is locally agreed on within the bank, but it looks like the collectively bargained system used in other banks. It consists of six pay grades (30, 40, 50, 60, 70, and 80); the jobs are assigned to a grade according to job demands. For example, grade 60 is the most common group and consists of special occupational tasks in customer service, and requires a versatile knowledge of professional skills. Grade 80 jobs have independent and special tasks that include the responsibility of some function. Grades 30 and 40 are practically obsolete nowadays.

In addition to grades, different steps exist, depending on job seniority, *i.e.* the number of working years in the job: three, six, nine, and twelve years. The minimum monthly income varies by 22% from grade 50 (without job seniority allowances) to grade 80 (without job seniority allowances). Within a grade, the monthly income varies by 15% from non existent job seniority allowances to all the job seniority allowances. The variation within a grade can even be higher, up to 25%, when merit pay increases are used. These increases are not included in the collective agreement and are allocated as part of a performance management process. Employees get an evaluation of their performance on a scale from one to five during a performance review with a superior. Each manager ensures that their own subordinates are fairly assessed in comparison with other employees. The pay increases are allocated to those getting the best evaluations in each manager's group.

In addition, the variable pay system consists of two different components. First, there is a collective bonus system in the form of a personnel fund. The idea which emerges from the personnel funds is that the company staff establishes, owns, and regulates the fund, which is based on the profit share paid by the company. All the staffs belong to the fund except for top management. Usually, shares are paid to the fund if a company's annual profit exceeds a pre-fixed threshold and meets possible other criteria. The fund's board is in charge of looking after its members' shares and investing them profitably. The first personnel funds were established in 1990 after legislation (814/1989) was passed by parliament. Recently, each employee has been entitled to draw money from the personnel fund.

The second part of the variable pay system is a group- or individual-based annual bonus. Each person has performance goals, and the branch office has overall goals. The obtention of a bonus requires an employee to go beyond the targets. At least five performance measures are selected for each employee. The bonus is, however, subject to management consideration – no direct link to performance measures is established. First of all, when the yearly result is calculated, the company board decides on the amount which can be paid in bonuses altogether. Then, the bonuses are allocated to business areas, business units and, finally, to branch offices. The branch office manager can then allocate bonuses according to individual performances. This practice was implemented at the beginning of 2004. Before 2004, the bonus system was tightly linked with office-level and individual-level performance measures. The change was made because management wishes to have more control over the costs and be free to award high performers.

Alignment and Effectiveness of Pay Systems

The pay system is clearly aligned with the strategy of the company and the work organisation. The salary system has an effect on motivational aspects and performance, while the variable pay system encourages performance and effort. The influence of the basic pay system is more indirect, though it does appear to encourage employees to stay in the bank, as well as work motivation, flexibility in terms of time and tasks, and recruitment of new employees. It also has an effect on competence development. Some competencies, such as investment and sales, are valued in the grading system, which may have increased training attendance in this area. However, the set up of new grades may also have had a negative effect on work climate.

The bonus system has an effect on performance, *e.g.* productivity and service quality, since the link with performance goals is obvious. The bonus system used in the previous years was a tool for managers to communicate important goals and motivate their personnel. "It is a nice extra sum (bonus), though uncertain." Employees may be advised on, "Now we have hardly achieved our goals, so let's see what we can do to achieve them." Bonuses have at least a temporary motivating effect when they are paid out. However, there may be a weak negative effect on well-being since bonuses contribute to work loading. Recently, the amount of sick days has increased. Individual bonuses also may have some negative effects on work climate when *e.g.* it is known that a couple of employees receive maximum bonuses and others very little. The fairness of bonus distribution may be a subjective and therefore possibly contentious issue.

The personnel fund is viewed as an equitable system since it rewards all the employees for the company's success. Otherwise, it is quite difficult to see its impact on the quality of working life or performance indicators. Strategically, such reward systems are designed for motivating the staff and being neutral in terms of cost structure. The success of the payment systems, *e.g.* the new bonus system, is assessed in a yearly personnel survey.

Vision / Future Developments

In this case, the more probable trend will be an increasing emphasis on variable pay and results-based pay, though this will happen gradually. A collective bargaining system slows down the trend. The common trend for some time has been to determine increasingly pay on an individual basis, partly because of labour shortages. According to some interviewees, the grading system could also have more grades. That would make pay increases more frequent. Changes in pay would also be welcomed under the form of smaller and perhaps fixed-term individual raises. Future development seems to be in considering incremental and small steps. Nobody mentioned a need for radical changes, although some people complainted about the top-down definitions of targets.

Influence of Collective Bargaining Conditions

The bank in question has already practised local bargaining during 30 years and has obtained its own agreement ever since. However, collective bargaining at sector and national levels influences the overall pay increases, agreement period, and the general content of the agreement. The interviewees think that the agreement has been of advantage to the company's employees over the years, and does not hinder pay system development. The bargaining relationship is good, and results greatly depend on the negotiators. One of the advantages of local bargaining is that negotiators are close to each other, and it is consequently easier to understand mutual benefits. Unions favour a collective pay setting in collective bargaining. This moderates the trend towards an individualisation of pay, as it is difficult to introduce variable pay components in collective agreements.

Case Study: Germany

The following case is a German bank specialised in investment funds and loan products. The human resources (HR) manager – at corporate level – was interviewed to gain a better understanding of the company's philosophy and strategy in general, HR and pay strategy in particular, as well as general factors affecting the pay systems. The current pay systems and development trends are mapped out. The documentary material and the interview with the corporate HR manager give an insight into what the pay systems should look like; the principles underlying the compensation systems are studied here. Two HR specialists, the head of the staff council, three managers from different line functions and three small groups of employees (four to six people per group) were also interviewed, focusing on work and pay practices as well as development trends. The study sought to identify the way payment matters stand in practice and the way they influence company performance, and employee's behaviour and attitudes.

Strategy

Due to a recent merger, a new company strategy has been developed in a participative way, while defining top quality and increasing market share as the primary company's goal. The strategy to reach these goals is to focus on core competencies, achievement and innovation, leadership by delegation and modelling, developing and challenging employees, and open communication. Core values are trust, achievement, and responsibility. Based on this company strategy, the HR department has developed a strategy, which explicitly states that compensation is based on performance, success, and market conditions, and emphasises that performance will be rewarded. Furthermore, it notices that transparent and fair performance evaluations are based on result-oriented and measurable goal agreements. The company has a common pay strategy for pay scale and non-pay scale employees, including base pay and performance-based pay components for both groups. It is only the relation between base and variable pay which differs between the groups, as non-pay scale employees have a higher percentage of variable pay. It is intended to pay market rates for both base and variable pay.

Work Organisation

Different types of work organisation exist in the bank: there are interdependent tasks within business processes requiring cooperation within process teams, as well as independent tasks of individual employees. An ongoing change program is identifying core business processes and forming teams with defined performance goals for obtaining feedbacks. That is why the delegation of tasks, competencies, and responsibilities to process teams are not a common standard yet.

Pay Systems

There are two different pay systems: one for pay scale and one for non-pay scale employees. About 60% of the 2,600 employees are subject to pay scale, while the remaining 40% are non-pay scale employees. Only the pay system for the operational employees subject to the pay scale will be described in the following section. Their base pay is determined by the pay scale agreement. Nine different grades are defined by general job descriptions, and employees are assigned to grades accordingly. Besides the general job descriptions in the pay scale agreement, which are sometimes ambiguous and partly outdated, company specific examples exist which relate jobs to grades. The number of employees working at these different grades varies: only 15% of pay scale employees are among the first five grades, 29% in grade six and about 20% in grades seven, eight, and nine, respectively. The minimum monthly income in a grade varies from € 1,711 in grade one, step one to € 3,357 in grade nine, step one. The maximum monthly income in a grade varies from € 2,018 (grade one, step four) to € 3,777 (grade nine, step three).

Within grades, seven steps are defined, depending on job seniority, *i.e.* the time during which you have done the job (one to two, three to four, five to six, seven to eight, nine, ten or eleven years). In the bank, only steps between three and seven are actually in use. Within a grade, the monthly income varies by a minimum of 12% (grade nine) and a maximum of 33% (grade five), depending on the number of job seniority allowances which are applied. Most of the employees are at the highest step of each grade. In addition, at every pay scale, employee gets an extra thirteenth month of income, due to the pay scale agreement. Further extra-pay components exist on an individual basis, which are not part of the pay scale agreement, but may or may not be linked with pay scale rises.

A variable pay component in the pay system also exists, which is not part of the pay scale agreement. Its payment depends on business success. The respective supervisor is in charge of deciding on whether individual pay scale employees get a variable pay component or not; the supervisor is given the budget – depending on the business success – in order to distribute it among the employees. Although this pay component is supposed to vary, it has always been paid to everybody in the past, notwithstanding individual performance, as a kind of fourteenth month of income. Some people were even rewarded more than a fourteenth month, subject to the management discretion. It amounts to 7% for pay scale employees. Due to difficult market conditions in the last two years, the bonus budget remained constant for the first time. As a consequence, increases in bonus for some people meant decreases in bonus for others, due to the fixed bonus pool.

Alignment and Effectiveness of Pay Systems

As the company has quite recently adopted a new strategy, both work organisation and pay systems are still in a transitory process and not aligned yet with the strategy. However, the aim is to achieve alignment with company and HR strategy. With respect to work organisation, business processes have been identified and process teams formed in order to delegate respective tasks and to set result-oriented and measurable goal agreements, which can be combined with performance bonuses, depending on the degree of goal achievement. Previous variable pay components were only varying in terms of degrees of rises, as there was not any strict total bonus limit. This has been modified so that there is now a fixed bonus pool – depending on the company success – which will be distributed according to individual and team performance.

With respect to the effects of the existing pay system, the employee representative is satisfied and believes that it contributes to job satisfaction, particularly if one compares it with payments and benefits of other companies. In contrast, HR management is dissatisfied and wants to change the system to make variable pay more dependent on performance and, thus, consistent with the company and the HR strategy. Line management and the employees are found between these positions as they value the advantages of the current system, but notice drawbacks as well.

The employee's representative, HR and line management believe that base pay grading criteria promote competence and skills development, because base pay depends on job demands; hence, more competencies and skills are required to apply for better-paid jobs. The employees do not recognise this link, as competence development is not directly linked with pay increases. Most of the stakeholders have some doubts about the motivational effects of the current pay practice, as bonus payments have been independent from performance in reality, but the new system will change this. However, the employee's representative believes that a stress on achievement also exists without variable pay.

The employee recruitment and retention has never been a problem; company benefits, culture, and job security are believed to contribute to this, as well as pay does. Most of the stakeholders do not believe that the current pay system is related to employee's well-being, social conflicts, or performance. All the stakeholders criticise current pay practices, particularly the granting of bonuses, for lacking transparency and flexibility.

Besides the need for strategic alignment, this is another reason for the company to change the goal agreements and bonuses based on the degree of goal attainment. Goals and indicators based on business processes will improve feedback and performance management, both for self-regulation and supervisors. Nevertheless, in the new system, supervisors will still assess the individual contributions to the team performance and determine individual bonuses. These individual bonuses will have to be discussed with the HR department so that decisions made on bonuses are well informed. Social conflicts have not been triggered by the current pay system and practice, probably because everybody gets bonus payments. Additional extra payments were not supposed to be communicated between employees and, until recently, did not imply that other employees have to get reduced bonus payments.

Vision / Future Developments

Although co-determination also applies to non-pay scale employees, which do not have a leading managerial position, it seems easier to change pay systems there, compared with pay scale employees. Therefore, it is intended to introduce bonuses, based on the degree of goal attainment, for non-pay scale employees first and then move onto pay scale employees.

Influence of Collective Bargaining Conditions

The influence of trade unions is viewed as weak, but the staff council has a policy of its own, based on the specific situation of the company. Recent changes in the staff council make the assessment of its policy towards the new performance-based pay strategy of the company difficult. These changes towards more performance-based pay and other changes, *e.g.* in pension plans, might not be supported, because up to now almost everybody was rewarded, irrespective of performance and some people will lose these privileges. Owing to federal laws of co-determination, which make the consent of the staff council necessary, the new pay strategy, with bonuses based on the degree of goal attainment, will be implemented for non-pay scale employees first. If the system turns to be successful, management plans to introduce it for pay scale employees as well.

Summary and Discussion

These three case studies sought to study in depth the perspectives of different stakeholders, whether and how their companies want to align strategy, pay systems, and work organisation, and how conditions of collective bargaining influence their ability to do so. With respect to pay systems, a stress was put on non-managerial employees subject to pay scale agreements. To do so, employees and their representatives as well as HR and line management were asked their opinions about strategies, pay systems, and work organisation, and about the way these influence company practices, outcomes, and working life. Despite the differences which exist between these three different banks located in Belgium, Finland, and Germany as regards the company specific strategies, work organisations, and pay systems, they also have a lot in common.

In all the cases, efficient performance, competence, and open communication play a role in the company strategy. General company, HR and pay strategy are well aligned in Finland and Germany, whereas, in the Belgium bank, pay strategy, in particular, seems to be less clear-cut and aligned. The level of competence of the employees is rather high and competence development plays a major role in all the banks.

The work itself is mainly individually based in all the cases, but employees are organised in teams. They have common goals, although work restructuring is still in process in the German case. Task delegation seems to be limited in the Belgian case; nonetheless, consultation and open communication exist. In the two other cases, individual and collective goal setting seem to help delegation to various degrees, depending on leadership styles.

In the Belgian and Finnish banks, work organisation seems to be aligned with strategy, while, in the German case, the work organisation is currently being reorganised to achieve a better degree of alignment.

With regard to pay systems for operational employees and base pay in particular, grading depends on job demands in all the banks, as it has been set out in the collective labour agreements. Pay increases within grades depend on age in Belgium and job seniority in Finland and Germany. In the Finnish case, pay increases within grades also are merit-based. Changes in grades require further competencies (Belgium), or a change in task demands or jobs in the two other cases. All the banks offer variable pay, which is currently not subject to collective labour agreements, but it is paid at the top of pay levels defined by collective bargaining. In the German case, recent collective labour agreements in the banking sector allow the introduction of some variable pay. In the Belgian case, a part of the profit sharing devoted to operational employees will be included into the pay scale from 2005 onwards. Various forms and combinations of variable pay are in use: individual and/or team bonuses and/or profit sharing. Only Belgium has not any individual bonus yet, but it will introduce it in 2005. Team or cluster bonuses and profit sharing exist as additional elements (in Belgium and Finland), or serve as a pool for individual bonus assignment (in Germany). This might reflect the fact that people mainly work individually, but it might also reflect the existence of interdependencies regarding common goals particularly. In Belgium, team and individual performance-based pay are or will be directly linked with the attainment of performance goals. In Finland and Germany, performance is measured, but bonuses are subject to the management's discretion.

Table 4.2. Pay systems for operational employees in the bank case studies

	Belgium	Finland	Germany
Base pay: grading	Job demands	Job demands	Job demands
Base pay increases: within grade	Age	Seniority Merit	Seniority
Base pay increases: to another grade	Competencies	Changing task demands / job	Changing task demands / job
Variable pay: individual	Exceptional bonus – performance	Individual bonus	Exceptional bonus – performance
Variable pay: team	Cluster bonus – performance	Team bonus	None
Variable pay: profit sharing	Profit sharing	Personnel fund	Flexible in theory 14th month of income in practice

Management obviously tries to align strategy, work organisation, and pay system in all the banks; but this alignment has only been fully achieved in the Finnish case. Different stakeholders seem to assess differently the effects of pay systems, which is particularly apparent in the Belgian and German case studies whereas the views seem to fit more in Finland. Collective bargaining at national or sectoral level seems to hinder or at least slow down the alignment of strategy, work organisation, and pay system in all the cases, as it favours a collective pay setting, which makes difficult the inclusion of regulations allowing companies to tailor their pay systems and to implement variable pay components, at the expense of fixed elements particularly. The same is somewhat true, albeit to a lesser degree, at company level, where company specific issues can be taken into account. As a result, the alignment of pay systems is easier for managerial employees. Consequently, either they are already better aligned or pay systems are changed first, as it happens in the German case. The determination of pay levels and pay increases by collective bargaining at sectoral level put some limits on the financial resources for further variable pay elements beyond the collectively agreed pay and, thus, limits the ability of carrying out a strategic alignment of variable pay components or systems.

Table 4.3. Alignment of strategy, work organisation, and pay systems in case studies

	Belgium	Finland	Germany
Company strategy	Customer orientation	Customer orientation Competence	Customer orientation Core competence focus Innovation
HR strategy	Efficient performance Long term employability Competence, flexibility Open communication Differentiation	Efficient performance Competence Good service orientation	Efficient performance Delegation Competence Open communication
Pay strategy	Cost Performance Long term employability Paying average market rates	Performance goal-oriented Paying average market rates	Performance goals Success Market conditions Paying average market rates
Work organisation	High employee competence level Competence development Individual-based work, organised in teams Consultation Open communication	High employee competence level Competence development Individual-based work, organised in teams Consultation and delegation Open communication	High employee competence level Competence development Individual-based work, organised in teams Consultation and delegation Open communication
Alignment HR – pay strategy / practice	Less clear-cut pay strategy Less well aligned	Very good	Restructuring in process
Company strategy and work organisation	Well aligned	Well aligned	Restructuring in process
Company and pay strategy and work organisation	Work in progress	Well aligned	Work in progress

Which kind of conclusion can we draw from these results? The three cases indicate that management is apparently willing to have the strategic alignment of work organisation and pay systems, both for operational and managerial employees. Collective bargaining is viewed as a tool to slow down this process. Nevertheless, there is a trend towards more emphasis on variable pay, such as pay-for-performance and/or profit sharing. As mentioned above, in the German case particularly, company strategies are changed first, then work organisation and finally pay systems, if a consensus between management and the staff council can be achieved. In terms of strategy, it makes sense to define goals first, before changing structures and processes, according to the principle of organisation theory that structure follows function. As pay systems are based on job demands with respect to base pay and process goals for variable pay, it is logical to design and implement work structures and processes before modifying the pay systems. If these arguments are taken into consideration, it is expected that changes in pay systems usually lag behind changes in strategy and work organisation. Furthermore, pay is regulated by individual contracts, local, sectoral or national collective labour agreements and legislation, which need to be considered or modified before bringing changes into pay systems; this postpones the deadline while assuming that consensus can be achieved and the changes can be implemented at all. The addition of other pay components to current systems is an alternative to avoid changes in current pay agreements. This 'add on' strategy has become quite common, concerning the implementation of variable pay components particularly. However, the increasing competition and the cost pressures limit the use of this alternative, because personnel costs are becoming so considerable, so that more and more companies cannot afford themselves such an option anymore. Nonetheless, a complete change in pay systems without increasing costs at sectoral level has been time consuming. These practical considerations might explain the low alignment between pay systems, work organisation, and company strategy.

Another interesting aspect among the case studies is the huge differences in terms of assessment of the effects on pay systems by various stakeholders, especially in Belgium and Germany. These results question the validity of studies based on expert effect ratings of a sole stakeholder group and illustrate the advantages of the multiple perspective approach adopted in the pay audit tool.

CHAPTER 4.3.2

Case Studies – Multinational Company

Xavier BAETEN, Conny H. ANTONI,
Ben J.M. EMANS & An VERBRUGGEN

Introduction

In the previous chapters, a synthesis was made of research results on the occurrence of pay systems and their outcomes in different countries. The results of case studies in the banking sector have also been discussed. However, the study of pay systems within one (multi-national) company throughout Europe tends to fill another important research gap, which can give important additional insights in terms of control of some environmental factors, such as the influence of the ownership structure, corporate strategy, etc. Another research gap lies in the group in question. Most of the research is focused on pay systems devoted to managerial employees, rather than operational employees.

This chapter tries to fill these gaps on the basis of the results of an in-depth study on pay systems which targets operational employees within a multinational company during 2003 and 2004. The following countries took part in the study: Belgium, France, Germany, Luxemburg, The Netherlands, and United Kingdom. In some countries we could not get all the data we were looking for. These countries (Luxemburg, United Kingdom) are not included in the analysis. The main results will be discussed per country. At first and in line with the model which was developed in chapter 3.1, an overview will be given over the relevant contextual factors (*i.e.* external environment, culture, strategy, work organisation), both at corporate and national level. Information will be given about the organisation's pay strategy and vision where it is possible to do so. Consequently, pay systems (base pay and variable pay) will be analysed. To conclude, the stakeholder approach will be adopted in the assessment of pay systems' functioning from the point of view of HR, line management, and the employees (representatives). This is one of the most interesting aspects of the research. It does not only allow us to set up an inventory, but also to provide information on the way the system works in practice and which kind of influence it yields on its stakeholders.

The figure below describes the general structure, which was developed by the SALTSA research group and which was used as the general structure in the development of the case studies.

Figure 4.16. General structure of pay systems as applied in the case studies

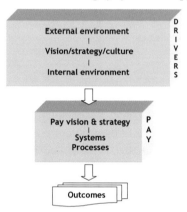

This chapter will also use the *pay tree*-concept which was introduced in chapter 2 in order to structure clearly the description and grasp all the key characteristics.

The Organisation

The research object of our study is a multinational in the fast moving consumer goods industry, which has activities of distribution and production facilities all over the world. Most of the organisations in the sector alike, this multinational organisation results from many mergers and takeovers, for some of them quite recent. The organisation is listed on the stock exchange.

The organisation experiences many changes, mainly driven by its takeover activity. At the moment of our study, the main priorities at the global strategic level were the internal growth, operational efficiency, and targeted acquisitions. Customer-drivenness is also a key strategic feature. The organisation's values are customer intimacy, innovation and differentiation, quality, teamwork, and people-orientedness. The decision-making process, as far as HR is concerned, is decentralised, leaving the subsidiaries with a significant degree of freedom. However, there is a current shift towards more centrally defined policies and central steering.

Belgium

The Belgian branch of the multinational organisation employs more than 3,000 employees, more or less equally spread among blue- and white-collar workers.

Pay Context

The *external environment* in Belgium, in which the organisation has been active during our study, was characterised by a limited economic growth and limited inflation. A very important macro contextual factor is the high pay cost, due to important social security provisions and relatively high tax rates. As a consequence, organisations in Belgium are prone to look for tax-friendly remuneration alternatives, such as meal vouchers and retirement plans.

In order to hold labour costs under control, the Belgian government has decided that pay increases at the national level should keep up with the evolutions in the neighbouring countries (the 'pay norm'). In the case of operational employees, pay increases are subject to collective labour agreements. This means that organisations are endowed with limited discretionary power concerning the differentiation between employees.

Unions in Belgium are powerful and strongly influence pay settlement, both at the national and sectoral level. This also places some limits on the attempts to differentiate on the basis of performance. Furthermore, the Belgian context is characterised by a separation between labour law and social security regulations for blue and white collars. There are also separate collective agreements for both groups.

Moving onto the internal environment and, more specifically, onto the organisational *culture*, elements from both a clan and a market culture (Kerr & Slocum, 1987) can be found. The Belgian organisation is characterised by result-orientedness, employee-orientedness, low turnover, open systems, loose control, and pragmatism. However, there is an ongoing shift from clan to a more market-based culture[1].

Regarding the *strategy*, the situation is rather complex. Corporate strategy was based on the "single" business, but it is departing from the "single" business to more related businesses. At the business unit level, a product leadership[2] strategy is in place (Treacy & Wiersema, 2000).

---

[1] The main features of a market culture: The organisation does not promise security, the individual does not promise loyalty, independence, and individuality, little socialisation.

[2] The main characteristics of the product leadership strategy are: conquering, the best in the market, fluid and flexible organisation, ever-changing business structure, per-

The HR strategy focuses on an active partnership, performance and competence management, a close link between rewards and performance, health and safety, communication.

While having a closer look at the *financial* data, since 2004 a positive evolution in return on equity can be found. However, work still remains to be done as regards financial performance and, more specifically, concerning return on sales.

Pay Vision and Strategy

Market positioning is a first key characteristic of an organisation's pay strategy. In the Belgian subsidiary and for the operational employees, the strategy is to pay at market level. This might be caused by the powerfulness of unions. While shedding light on the pay structure, it obviously aims at rather introducing high risk sharing, while focusing more on non-financial rewards, centralising more, and adopting some kind of cafeteria approach[3]. Currently, risk sharing is still rather limited, there is more centralisation, and there is not any choice. The most important gap between the actual and the preferred situation stands in the criteria and differentiation of fixed and variable pay systems. The purpose is the establishment of a strong link between pay and performance (both at individual and team level) as well as competencies. Nowadays, age/seniority is the main criterion, and collective bargaining also plays a very important role.

To sum up, there are important gaps separating pay strategy from practice and the intended pay strategy.

Pay Systems

Pay systems are not the same for blue-collar workers and operational white collars. Therefore, each group's pay system will be discussed separatly.

Blue Collars

Generally speaking, blue-collar workers are entitled to fixed and variable pay (the latter under the profit sharing form), but to some add-ons as well, like overtime pay and shift work supplement. There is also a stock purchase plan.

---

formance-oriented, future-driven, stimulate creativity, results, measuring and rewarding new product success.

[3] A cafeteria plan provides the employee with choices with regard to the composition of his/her reward package. For example, the choice can be made between a contribution to the pension plan and death insurance. Going one step further, it might also be possible to buy and sell holidays.

The *fixed pay* system's underlying framework is a point factor evaluation scheme, both at the sectoral level and the organisation's level. The sectoral system is based on education and experience, whereas the system of the organisation is purely job-related. There are ten grades and most of the employees are located in four out of ten grades. Increases in fixed pay are based on seniority.

Interestingly, blue-collar workers are also entitled to *variable pay*. The system is based on corporate performance with regard to production, hours worked, and absenteeism, which transforms it into gain sharing. It is named after "productivity premium". The amount is the same for all the employees and it is quite substantial. There is a yearly payout in cash, and the system is subject to collective bargaining.

White Collars

In the case of white-collar workers as well, the underlying framework for the fixed pay system is a point factor job evaluation scheme; however, it does not work in the same way as for the blue collars. A reference scheme has been developed in which different jobs are linked with grades. There are eight grades. The absolute majority of employees are in grades 6-9. Decision-making on white collars' base pay is mainly the subject of collective bargaining at company level. Age is the main criterion underlying increases in fixed pay. However, pay increases are put to an end at the age of 47.

There are three systems of *variable pay*. The first is the productivity premium, the same as in the case of blue-collar workers and also subject to collective bargaining. The second system is an ad hoc bonus, which is given to employees living up to the organisation's values in an extraordinary way. There is not any fixed timeframe for this bonus with regard to payout, and it is not part of a collective labour agreement. The members of the management team have to make a proposal which identifies team members who could be eligible for this bonus. The gross amount of bonus is € 1,250. This bonus is rather extraordinary.

For white collars working in sales, there is a sales premium which depends on the compliance with sales targets. The target level is € 2,500.

Finally, there is also a seniority premium which is paid out yearly and which amounts to 2.6% per year of seniority. This means that after 40 years (which is the limit), people get a bonus equivalent to a month of salary. This means that seniority has a double effect: on fixed pay as well as on this premium. As a consequence, not surprisingly, the intended pay strategy is much more performance-oriented.

The following pay 'add-ons' hold for both blue- and white-collar employees: add-on to holiday allowance, transport allowance.

Pay Processes and Procedures

At the level of pay processes and procedures, management's discretion is limited. Line management as well as employees' input seem to be rather limited. Despite all, degrees of local freedom remain important. HR wants the pay process to be more democratic, *i.e.* increase in the management discretion, which means an increasing involvement of line management and employees. There is also a trend towards more and open communications. Huge differences apparently separate individual employees from unions concerning performance-related pay. This makes decision-making and employees' involvement more complex.

As far as the evaluation of the systems is concerned, the company's subsidiary in Belgium takes part in an employee satisfaction survey on a yearly basis. Market data are gathered on a two-year basis.

Evaluation

Starting with the *processes and procedures*, the system is successful in terms of transparency and clarity. Nothing is surprising about that because the structure is well detailed and has been subject to a collective labour agreement. However, the unions still complain that white collars are deprived of a say in their job evaluation scheme (employee's involvement) and that blue collars' job evaluation is outdated. They are convinced that the assessment of performance after the age of 47 does not make any sense because it is not linked with pay at all. Furthermore, unions argue that direct heads wrongly assess.

Regarding the *functioning* of the pay system, HR is rather negative because of the inflexibility of the bargaining structure, the classification method itself, and the fact that the wrong criteria are driving base pay. According to them, variable pay is not sufficiently important and performance-driven. The unions think that the system is objective, but are worried about the transition from blue collar to white collar, because the underlying pay systems are not well harmonised. Line management is concerned as well, and also considers the absence of merit increases as a weakness and think that variable pay is more about semi-fixed pay. Line management as well as unions complain about career planning and about the lack of a clear-cut procedure to promote people. In their opinion, the pay system is also a disincentive to job rotation.

The third dimension which was assessed, are the *links* of the pay system with performance, competencies, the external market, etc. Line management as well as unions are asking for the inclusion of skills into the system. HR also admits that the wrong variables are used and that degrees of freedom to reward the individual are too narrowly limited.

Interestingly, HR and the unions are radically opposed with respect to external equity, *i.e.* market positioning. HR focuses on the pay levels in comparison with the sector, whereas the unions also take the other sectors into account. This worsens the feeling of external equity.

The pay-performance link is a rather difficult issue for the unions as they consider it as both a strength and a weakness. Indeed, the system remains objective because it relates increases in fixed pay to age/seniority. On the other hand, they are aware of the fact that this might have a negative impact on the motivation of high performers.

France

Contrary to Belgium, the French subsidiary of the multinational organisation is not a production site. It is only a distributor. In France, its market share is rather limited. There are 26 distribution centres. In general, there are 1,500 employees working for the organisation's subsidiary in France, among which the majority (1,200 employees) are operational employees.

Pay Context

Concerning the *external environment*, it is noteworthy that in France profit sharing is a legal requirement for organisations with more than fifty employees. Socially speaking, the local representatives of the unions can make decisions without asking for the approval of their headquarters.

Regarding the *strategy*, this organisation ensures that its position is secured against its competitors. The organisation's market share in France is rather low, in comparison with Belgium. On the other hand, the organisation is also working on innovation. At the business unit level, an evolution is noticeable. The organisation started with operational excellence, but it is now interested in the customer intimacy[4]. At the functional level, HR looks like an administrative department and has to evolve into a more strategic way. The most important aspects of the HR vision are changes in the mindset from production towards brand/service, integration of the HR into the organisation, acquisition of competencies. One of the problems is that line management is not aware of its HR duties.

The company culture holds in it characteristics from both a clan-based and a market culture. The culture is characterised by close relationships, paternalistic, effective, emotional, sensitive, and sensible.

---

[4]   Some characteristics of customer intimacy include partnerships with customers, segmentation, empowerment, delegation, adaptability, service-orientedness, change-orientedness, measuring customer satisfaction.

Pay Vision and Strategy

The main characteristics of the pay strategy are: pay at market level based on total rewards, local degrees of freedom, cafeteria plans, strong link between rewarding and competencies/performance both at the individual and group level, and an important employee's involvement. In France as well, a huge gap separates intended from realised pay strategy, because in practice, there is not any explicit positioning; the limited risk sharing, the centralisation, the non-existent choices, the job and individual performance are the main characteristics.

Pay Systems

The main components of the pay system the operational employees are entitled to, are fixed pay, overtime pay, bonus, profit sharing, stock, shift work supplement.

As far as *fixed pay* is concerned, there is a framework (grading system) at the sectoral level, which implies minimum guarantees. The system is linked with the activities that have to be performed on the job. In theory, there are six grades at the company level. In practice, there are not any grades, and pay is strongly dependent on individual negotiations. Collective bargaining sets the minima. There is already a point factor job evaluation scheme in use, but it is not linked with rewarding. The purpose of it is to establish this link and to use one system from operational employees to management. More generally, supply and demand play an important role with regard to the underlying structure.

Increases in fixed pay are also part of a process of collective bargaining and are linked with the cost of living. At the individual level, increases in fixed pay depend on the evaluation made by the manager, within budgetary constraints. Salary increases are granted on a yearly basis.

There are two systems of *variable pay*. First, there is a team bonus, which is paid out yearly in cash. It is not subject to collective bargaining. Line management decides, which criteria are applied (3-5 criteria). In theory, the amount of the bonus lies between € 0 and € 500. In practice, however, most of the employees receive € 400, and everybody receives something.

The second system of variable pay rewards corporate performance and is subject to some legal constraints in order to get a tax-friendly treatment. It is based on market share and return on sales. 60% of this bonus is equally distributed among the employees and 40% is proportional with the salary. The amount of the bonus is limited to 7% of the annual gross salary. It is paid out in cash on a yearly basis. However, the amount of the bonus can also be put on a saving account, which is then invested in order to get a return. The system and specifically the general principles are subject to a collective labour agreement at the company level.

Pay Processes and Procedures

Employees' involvement is rather limited. HR makes pay decisions together with general and/or line management. HR initiates decisions and works out the more technical issues. The decision-making on the performance management of individual employees and the determination of the amount of variable pay per employee lie in the hands of line management. Furthermore, collective bargaining plays a key role in determining compensable factors, linking jobs with grades, linking salaries with grades, and determining criteria for shifts within or between grades.

As it happened in Belgium, employee satisfaction is assessed on a regular basis.

Evaluation

As far as *pay processes and procedures* are concerned, the lack of transparency is seen as a major drawback. As mentioned above, there is not any real pay structure or framework. Consequently, people do not have any idea of their positioning in the structure. From this approach also results that individual bargaining is fundamental with regard to the determination of pay levels and increases. In fact, there is a lot of flexibility, but not the right one. Employees also think they are not well paid (which contrasts with the reality). As far as the performance management process is concerned, stakeholder opinions are wide ranging. HR is rather positive, because there is some practice, without a formal process. Line management argues that goals and budgets are not realistic. They also point out the difficulty of setting goals for administrative employees and consider that HR would play an important role in coaching the performance management process. The employees ask for a more regular communication on the state of affairs concerning the objectives of the team in charge of determining the team bonus.

The opinions about the *functioning* of the pay system are rather negative. According to HR, there is a lack of rules and structure with regard to the settlement of fixed pay, pay increases, variable pay, and promotions. Line managers list the following drawbacks: absence of a link between fixed pay and job classification, size of the budget for pay increases, lack of clarity with regard to variable pay (more specifically, because some line managers use the team bonus in order to reward individual performance), and the credibility of job posting/lack of space for internal promotion. In their view, what is positive is that line management is independent with regard to increases in fixed pay once the budget has been decided. According to employees, the budget for granting pay increases is too limited. Moreover, flattening increases leads to disincentives. As far as variable pay is concerned, employees put the finger on sight-problems, *i.e.* external influences beyond the employees' control that have an impact on the team bonus. Finally, the employees also complain about the internal promotion as well as the credibility of job posting.

Germany

Nowadays, the German subsidiary employs more than 2,000 employees. In Belgium alike, there are production activities in Germany.

Pay Context

In the German subsidiary's sector, there are four geographically different areas of collective bargaining. Whereas the structure of the collective agreements at sector level is similar, differences about the agreements on pay appear. Although the collective labour agreements are narrowly drafted, opportunities for innovations are used, *e.g.* working on Saturdays without paying extra shift supplements, sales division bonus system.

The German branch of this multinational company results from a merger with a traditional and well renowned company in Germany. It was still an ongoing process, and many project teams were working on integration. The organisation's corporate *strategy* of targeted acquisitions as well as internal growth could also be found in the German situation. Furthermore, the portfolio contains highly recognised brands known for their high standard.

If we focus more on the *work organisation*, production processes are complex and need skilled personnel work. Work organisation is based on teams. Line management aims at moving towards self-regulated teams, which use the full potential of employees and relieve foremen. However, the idea of teamwork does not work as well as expected, more specifically in the case of teamwork across shifts in the field of maintenance tasks.

At an international scale, this multinational organisation provides a framework for the *HRM* that the German branch has to abide by while taking into account national differences. International guidelines have been set up over the implementation of the bonus system (variable pay for instance), although the German branch still has important degrees of freedom.

The German subsidiary has been intensively working on employee skills. From 1985 onwards, the improvement of employee skills in the production sites has become a major issue. Skilled personnel, as a result, are expected to show a higher commitment. Today, 50-60% of all the employees are skilled workers. The skills and the evolution of employees are among the responsibilities of the supervisor; but the HRM launches special training programs as well (*e.g.* special training for white-collar workers). There is not any general schedule or auditing for qualification and training. Most of the activities are individually negotiated and dependent on the employee, his level of education, and open vacancies. According to the wishes of the works council, this system designed for white collars should be extended to the blue-collar workers.

Recent developments about the *pay* issue deal with a new jointly agreed working time model from which Saturday stands as a normal working day; consequently, it is said that extra payments have not to be given. Another landmark development is the invention of a new service group that recruits personnel for easy tasks, which is not insured by the CLAs of this sector. These employees receive a lower pay than others working in the same sector, but it still fits the market. Other outsourcing activities have been prevented by these activities.

Pay Vision and Strategy

The company's actual market position is its leadership on the market with regard to fixed pay. However, it is noteworthy that among higher income groups, competitors from the same sector pay more. Trade unions strongly influence all the facilities in Germany. There are no further explicit characteristics of the pay strategy.

Pay Systems

As far as *fixed* pay is concerned, HR follows corporate guidelines and takes the general situation of CLAs in Germany into account. Grading follows summaric job descriptions and grading examples mentioned in the *Bundesrahmentarifvertrag*. Job descriptions supplied by the *Bundesrahmentarifvertrag* are used, but seem to be outdated. Besides job requirements, experience seems to be used as an additional criterion which determines fixed pay. Extra payments above the collectively agreed pay are a legacy from the past. Placement starts at lower grades. Until grade 6, there is only a fixed pay without being followed by further steps. From the grade 7 onwards, there are 1-3 steps at each grade. Theoretically, there are 11 grades plus one for apprentices, but in practice two of them are empty; another one only has one employee. Promotion within grades is gained after three and six years of work, respectively. The highest grade regularly accessed by blue-collar workers is grade 6. Exceptional blue-collar employees can reach grade 7. Apprentices are recruited after performing their training at grade 3. After half a year they move up to grade 4. Higher management and HR express their wish for more flexibility, so that they can make downward placements, especially.

The criteria for assessment are job-specific abilities and skills, attitude and code of conduct, training and general assessment (*e.g.* commitment). In most of the cases, promotion between grades is individually determined. In practice, grading decisions are frequently made while using the rule of thumb. Advancement to higher grades seems to depend on the employee's skills with respect to job requirements and open vacancies. Twice a year, the grading of all the white collars ought to be checked, if they apply for a promotion to another grade. Blue collars are not subject to this procedure, although there are plans for introducing this procedure very soon.

Variable pay does not exist due to the general high level of pay of the operational employees. Only management and sales division employees are eligible for bonus schemes. The maximum amount of the sales division bonus is 11.5% of fixed pay. Calculation of the bonus is based on market share and performance. We will not go further into the details of the management's bonus scheme because this falls beyond the scope of this book.

Pay Processes and Procedures

Grading decisions are based on assessments made by the supervisor and the plant manager. HR follows their recommendations in 80% to 90% of the cases.

Employee representatives participate in decision-making, although they have no say and no explicit power when decisions are made.

Evaluation

The main comment on the pay *processes and procedures* is a lack of flexibility. However, this seems to be solved by the grading system, because its outdated job descriptions allow a more flexible use and interpretation. Consequently, the system is widely accepted and causes a few conflicts. Still, there are discrepancies due to the outdated grading criteria, the lack of strategic and work organisation alignment, which might gradually build up pressure for change.

The work council is quite conservative with regard to the *functioning* of the pay system. They are not interested in the introduction of pay-for-performance, because in their view performance cannot be objectively measured and there are too many other factors which matter. The work council asks for changes regarding the fixed pay's underlying framework, more specifically for the introduction of job profiles, *i.e.* new descriptions of job characteristics.

We have already mentioned the work council's rather conservative attitude with regard to performance links. Here, we find huge differences in stakeholders' feelings and opinions. Contrary to the work council, line management hopes for the introduction of pay-for-performance, although fluctuation between teams, ongoing changes and a resisting work council raise difficulties, because currently 'performance does not pay'. Line management expects an increase in performance of up to 5% by a pay-for-performance system. However, HR does not want a pay-for-performance system at the top of fixed pay, as fixed pay levels together with shift work supplements and overtime pay add-ons are already very high. There are a few chances that pay-for-performance will be implemented because it would require changes in the collective bargaining agreement at sectoral level.

Line management expects that market developments will hopefully lead to growing demands and new chances for the introduction of performance-related pay. Changes deal with the development towards a multinational company, finding new measures for calculating performance and a stronger orientation towards cost control. To avoid difficulties in measuring individual performance, performance-related pay could be based on team performance.

To conclude, no real general alignment seems to exist between pay, work organisation, and strategy.

The Netherlands

The Dutch subsidiary of the multinational organisation consists of two production plants, which have been acquired, and a number of distribution centres spread over the country. The number of employees, 85% operating core, 15% management and sales, is slightly above 1,000.

Pay Context

At the time of the data collection, which took place in the first months of 2004, the Dutch economy, which belongs to the Euro-region, suffered from low levels of economic growth. In this context, the firm aims at standing out as a strong, modern, and innovating firm. This ambition was translated into a growth *strategy* that focused on product leadership, including an HRM-strategy that focused on employee development, team spirit, performance management, and – especially focused on excellent employees – retention efforts including the offer of attractive labour conditions. However, this HRM strategy, as far as the pay practices are concerned, was only poorly enacted in the case of the operational employees. From time to time, we will also briefly refer to managerial employees' pay systems in order to give the reader the opportunity to make some comparisons.

Pay Vision and Strategy

When the research was done, the subsidiary still had important degrees of freedom with regard to its pay strategy. In the description of this strategy, two key features stand out: transparency, linking pay and performance. Transparency and openness are achieved with high levels of formalisation of pay-related decision-making procedures. Moreover, all kinds of documentation about these procedures are made available to the employees through intranet, brochures, meetings, personal letters, and trainings.

As far as *market positioning* is concerned, it is worth mentioning that the firm appears to pay its operational employees slightly above the market level. However, this is not the outcome of any explicit positioning strategy. At best, it is a manifestation of an implicit strategy. Benchmarking also seems to exist within the fixed pay's underlying framework: job qualifications and grading systems tend to be shaped on systems developed by expert firms for the whole sector.

The second feature, *linking pay with performance*, is less clearly fulfilled, at least as far as the operational employees are concerned. Here, a huge gap can be found between intended and realised pay strategy. At the organisation's level, there is a strong tendency and attitude in favour of linking pay with performance. However, in the case of operational employees, national unions play a significant role and are, as such, a very important contextual factor. These unions have a rather conservative opinion towards linking pay with performance. Although the operational employees' pay system allows the granting of bonuses to those performing well, the degree to which it is done and the importance of the bonuses provided have nothing to do with the firm's overall performance. The bonus system is only incidentally applied and in a way, far from being systematic, which also implies that risk sharing is almost non-existent. We, thus, have identified an important gap between operational employees' pay system *as it is*, and *how it is used*. Most notoriously, the gap applies to team-based pay, which, on the one hand, is explicitly promoted by the firm's HR strategy, while being on the other hand practically non-existent in the daily pay practice for operational employees.

Pay Systems

Fixed pay's underlying framework for evaluating jobs is based on standard job attributes. The Dutch employers' association provides the system. Differentiation in fixed pay is rather limited and it is a matter of many, but minor steps. There are generally mechanical rules for taking those steps so that they are out of control of employees' initiatives.

As far as the grading structure is concerned, both the within-grades and the between-grades differences are small. The criterion for determining the entry level in the grade is the background and/or experience. Nine different grades represent nine different job families (in comparison with only four in the case of management and sales personnel). In addition to that, the number of steps within grades may amount to eleven (in comparison with six in the other case). Consequently, the employees are scattered over 75 grade-step combinations. The assignment of grades to employees is entirely the outcome of a procedure for weighting the responsibilities associated with jobs (however they are performed), a procedure, that moreover is copied from some outside source. The subsequent positioning within a grade is hardly less mechanical, while being only based on seniority (number of years in the job) or something comparable (experience that counts as an equivalent of a certain number of years in the job). However, there is one interesting element in the system which reduces its mechanical nature: the operating core employee him/herself may positively influence the speed of within-grade-step-taking by performing in a more or less excellent way. Once again, a huge gap seems to stand between operational employees' pay system and managerial employees' pay system, the latter being much more performance-oriented. For example, increases in managerial employees' fixed pay are entirely dependent on the individual's performance.

As mentioned above, variable pay is limited. There is not any formalised system, and variable pay is only incidentally applied. Theoretically, variable pay can amount up to 6% relative to fixed pay. In practice, variable pay is almost non-existent.

To conclude, we obtain the following main characteristics of the operational employees' pay system: It is largely, *but not entirely*, a fixed pay system; the fixed pay differentiation is simultaneously low and fine-grained; the system is based on a set of largely, *but not entirely*, mechanical set of rules.

Pay Processes and Procedures

As far as pay processes and procedures are concerned and more specifically negotiability and involvement, national unions play an important role. As such, the role of collective bargaining as regards linking pay with grades, is fundamental. In the case of management and sales, that role is played by the own workers' council of the firm.

As far as increases in fixed pay are concerned, line management decides and HR is in charge of the procedural control. The same holds for variable pay.

The firm conducts an employee satisfaction survey twice a year.

Evaluation

The survey – just mentioned above – includes pay-related issues such as the pay system's transparency, the performance assessment procedures that are related to pay, promotion perspectives and pay satisfaction. Apart from this form of data collection, which generally yields positive evaluations, there is not any systematic evaluation of the pay systems in use which tends to be performed. Objective facts about the way systems are used and their subsequent outcomes, according to what is expected, are missing.

Regarding the pay system for the operating core, the stakeholders agree with each other on two issues, one related to a positive aspect of the system and another one showing the negative aspect of it. Firstly, to echo the positive attitudes that tend to emerge from the employee surveys, all the employees are fairly well satisfied with the system's transparency, especially because its outcomes are always formalised in the Collective Labour Agreement; they are satisfied as well with the way employees are involved in the decision making processes that eventually result in the CLAs; finally they acknowledge the amount of fairness (everybody is receiving what he/she deserves) that tends to derive from the employees' involvement in the decision making process. Secondly, they all agree on an element of unfairness because distinctions are made regarding bonuses between the system for the operating core and the system for management and sales employees: in comparison with management and sales employees, the operational employees are far less rewarded for doing an excellent job. As a result, they have got a common plea while affirming that the bonus system should be upgraded for the operating core.

Paradoxically a contentious point is linked with the last mentioned point of agreement. For HR management and line management, the bonus system for the operating core is just a first step towards a strengthening of the pay-performance relationship, whereas the employees, and especially their representatives in the unions, are rather reluctant to even think about such a trend.

We can conclude that the firm's situation has, in many respects, an in-between nature. The pay strategy for the operational employees is reasonably well achieved in terms of transparency and involvement. It is not achieved in terms of risk sharing, team-based pay for performance, and individual pay-for-performance.

Conclusions

The purpose of this chapter was fourfold. Firstly, it has illustrated the way of conducting a pay audit and what dimensions should be taken into account in order to make the process successful. Secondly, it has put into practice the framework ('pay tree') that was developed and presented earlier in this book. As such, it has evidenced the practical usefulness of the concept. Thirdly, it has very clearly showed the added value of a stakeholder-driven approach, which was achieved as a result of an assessment of the pay systems by means of in-depth interviews with the main stakeholders, *i.e.* HR, line management, and employees' representatives. Finally, it has made international comparisons easier by focusing on a single case selected from various countries.

The tables on the following pages give an overview on the most important findings. They clearly show that legislation and collective bargaining limit the strategic space of this international company in shaping pay at the level of operational employees in all the subsidiaries.

Table 4.4a. Findings of the international case study

	Belgium	France	Germany	Netherlands
Pay context	• Strategy: product leadership • HR: active partnership, linking rewarding and performance, communication	• Profit sharing is legally obliged • Strategy: defender, movement towards customer intimacy • Low HR-maturity: HR=administration	• Strategy: targeted acquisitions, internal growth • HR: need for qualified personnel, self-regulated teams, skills	• Strategy: product leadership • HR: employee development, team spirit, performance management, retention
Pay vision and strategy	• Slightly above market • High risk-sharing • Non-financial rewards • Centralisation • Cafeteria • Democratic	• Market level • Strong link rewarding-competencies-performance • Local degrees of freedom • Cafeteria • Employee involvement	• No clear-cut choices/visions	• Transparency • Linking pay and performance • Team-based pay • Risk sharing almost non-existent
Pay systems – fixed pay	• BC: point factor evaluation, 10 grades, seniority-based • WC: point factor evaluation, 8 grades, based on age • Sector agreements only provide a minimum	• Grading on sectoral level=minimum • Point factor evaluation, not linked to pay • Company level: 6 grades in theory; in practice: no grades, individual negotiations	• Basis: job requirements and experience • Sector agreements only provide a minimum • 12 grades; from grade 7, 3 steps per grade, based on seniority • Promotion within grade: dependent on qualifications and vacancies	• Basis: job evaluation • 9 grades, between 6 and 11 steps per grade • Increases: once a year, adaptable according to performance assessment
Pay systems – variable pay	• BC: gain sharing • WC: gain sharing, ad hoc bonus, seniority premium	• Team bonus based on 3-5 criteria determined by line management • Profit sharing	• Does not exist	• Incidental bonus of about 6% • Performance-related • Poorly elaborated

Table 4.4b. Findings of the international case study

	Belgium	France	Germany	Netherlands
Pay processes and procedures	• Limited stakeholder input • Collective bargaining plays a major role in fixed and variable pay • Local degrees of freedom	• Collective bargaining plays a major role in fixed and variable pay • Limited employee involvement • Line management has an important role in performance assessment and variable pay	• 4 geographically different areas of collective bargaining with different pay CLAs • Trade unions: strong • Important local degrees of freedom • Supervisor responsible for placement and assessment, HR supports • Employees participate in decision-making, but have no formal power	• Important local degrees of freedom • Trade unions: strong • Increases in fixed pay and variable pay: line management decides, HR takes care of procedures
Evaluation	• Transparency and objectivity are strengths • Inflexibility of bargaining structure • Do the right criteria drive base pay? • Weak link between pay and performance: limited variable part, absence of merit increases • Lack of career planning • More integration of skills into the system • Difference: intended-realised pay strategy	• Lack of transparency • No real pay structure • Unrealistic objectives • HR should move from administration towards coaching the performance management process • Line of sight-problems	• Outdated grading criteria • Lack of strategic alignment • Lack of HR alignment (work organisation) • 'Performance does not pay' • Team-based pay as a solution?	• Important difference intended-realised pay strategy • Strong points: transparency, employee involvement, fairness • Operational employees are less rewarded for doing a good job

References

Kerr, J. & Slocum Jr., J.W. (1987), "Managing Corporate Culture through Reward Systems", *Academy of Management Executive*, 1, p. 99-108.

Treacy, M. & Wiersema, F. (1993), "Customer Intimacy and Other Value Disciplines", *Harvard Business Review*, 71, p. 84-93.

CHAPTER 4.3.3

Pay Systems in Europe, Their Strategic Alignment, and Outcomes: A Summary

Conny H. ANTONI

This chapter mainly aimed at analysing the relationships between pay, working conditions, managerial strategy, and organisational performance identifying indicators accordingly. Its outcomes support by and large our theoretical assumption that companies, which design work organisation and pay systems according to their strategy, achieve positive effects both on performance and quality of working life. We assume that in this case implicit, explicit goals and steering mechanisms fit together and cause these positive effects, while goal conflicts and conflicts of leadership are avoided or reduced.

Regarding the prevalence of pay systems, the ESWC 2000 survey shows that base or fixed pay is still by far the most dominant pay system (Paoli & Merllié, 2001). Modern forms of variable pay (pay-for-performance) that focus on the overall performance and also reward the effects of working more cleverly, such as team bonus and/or profit sharing and/or income from shares, are exceptions, as only six out of hundred respondents say that they get it (Antoni *et al.*, 2005). In contrast, about every third workplace in the EPOC study (EPOC Research Group, 1997) reports the use of modern forms of variable pay for the largest occupational group. Some more recent national studies even report higher figures, by putting forward a considerable gap between countries. The highest rates have been reported in the management surveys from the UK and Finland, whereas the lowest rates are found in The Netherlands and Germany (*cf.* chapter 4.2). Although the use of modern forms of variable pay has increased in the recent years, they still play a minor role regarding the amount of pay.

The research focusing on *demographic factors* still shows *gender* discrimination, *i.e.* lower pay levels for women in comparison with men doing the same jobs. *Age* is studied almost exclusively around the topic of seniority, which is related to higher pay. Concerning the relationships between pay systems and *employment conditions* there are a few results, indicating that modern forms of variable pay seem more popular with full-time workers than those working under temporary or part-time contracts (*e.g.* Baeten & Van den Berghe, 2002). Furthermore, modern forms of variable pay prevail more than others, if flexible working time is given. *Organisational or institutional factors* and their relation to pay systems have been scarcely studied yet. One of the few consistent findings is that modern forms of variable pay are more often found in the private than in the public sector, and in larger companies, whereas the results concerning union density seem to be inconsistent (*cf.* Godard, 2004; Pendleton *et al.*, 2001). Despite the varying prevalence of different pay systems between European nations, the relationships between pay system prevalence or pay levels and employment conditions, organisational, institutional or personal factors seem to be quite similar in Europe.

The current research on *work organisation and pay systems* lacks consistent definitions and measures of variables such as HPWO or high performance work systems (Godard, 2004). One more or less common result of the existing studies and our secondary analyses of the ESWC 2000 and EPOC survey is that aspects of HPWO are found more often with modern forms of variable pay, although correlations are rather low (*e.g.* Lay & Rainfurth, 1999; Pendleton *et al.*, 2001; Poutsma, 2001). However, the strength of the relationship between work organisation and pay systems considerably increases for companies with innovation strategies. This indicates the important role of strategy in the design of pay systems and work organisation.

The *relationships between pay systems, work organisation, and managerial strategies* have merely been studied so far. Results do not show consistent bivariate relationships. This might be due, in part, to the fact, that there is often a kind of "time lag" between changes in strategy and congruent changes in pay systems. Another reason might be the restrictions of collective bargaining, which might not only delay, but also restrict the alignment of pay system. Our analysis of the EPOC data showed that modern forms of variable pay are more often found in companies with an innovation strategy. For the British companies, this link is far beyond the average. This might be due to the fact that they operate in a very liberal market economy, in comparison with The Netherlands.

The results concerning the bivariate *relationships between pay systems, work organisation, and organisational performance* are very different between European countries as well as between different studies from one country (*e.g.* Nilsson, 1990, or Eriksson, 2002). The same holds for the relation between pay systems and work satisfaction (*e.g.* Holman, 2002, or Eriksson & Leander, 1995). In the EPOC survey modern forms of variable pay, high intensity of group delegation, and innovation strategy show positive bivariate links to two or three out of eight outcome variables, such as output increases due to group delegation. Regarding employee-related outcomes, the ESWC 2000 data shows that HPWO has much stronger positive relationships with indicators of quality of working life – such as job satisfaction – than pay systems.

Furthermore, our findings concerning the EPOC data show that alignment effects exist and that analyses should not be restricted to the links between two variables: interaction effects between group delegation and modern forms of variable pay resulted at least for three out of eight analysed outcomes. This means that more companies with modern systems of variable pay report reduction in costs, throughput times, and management personnel as a result of group delegation, if they rather have high intensity of group delegation. As other studies on high performance work systems show inconsistent results at best (Godard, 2004), the analysis of moderating variables could help to explain these inconsistencies.

Company strategy seems to be one important moderator of the relationship between *pay systems, work organisation, and organisational performance*. Our results of the EPOC data show that the effects of pay systems depend on strategy:

- If a company has an innovation strategy and high intensity of group delegation the type of pay system does not matter for group delegation effects.

- It is only when an innovation strategy is combined with low intensity of group delegation that outcomes depend on the modern forms of variable pay: these companies less often report management and employee reductions and more decreases in absenteeism. However, no differences were reported regarding throughput time, sickness and reductions in cost or output and quality increases.

- If a company has not any innovation strategy, the effects of high group delegation differ from the effects of low group delegation, if modern forms of variable pay exist:

  - Companies having low group delegation report less group delegation effects, *i.e.* less throughput time and employee reductions, less increases in output and quality, and less decreases in absenteeism; there is not any difference regarding management, sickness, and cost reductions.

  - Companies with high group delegation report more group delegation effects regarding cost, throughput time and management reductions, as well as output increases; whereas no differences seem to exist regarding employee absenteeism, sickness, and cost reductions or increases in quality.

The comparison between the effects of work organisation and pay systems indicates that characteristics of the work organisations have much stronger impact on the quality of working life, such as job satisfaction and stress. Regarding performance we do not have any data measuring directly performance outcomes. In the EPOC survey, only effects of direct participation were measured. Within these limits, our analyses indicate that the intensity of group delegation seems to be more important to achieve outcomes than pay systems. This supports the assumption that aspects of work organisation have stronger effects both on the quality of working life and on the performance outcomes than pay systems.

The data also support the alignment effects assumed in our theoretical model: interaction effects exist between strategy, work organisation, and pay system. This means that when these variables are brought together they do have stronger effects than considered on a side apart. Consequently, we should not only consider isolated variables to improve the quality of working life and performance outcomes, but we should rather align these variables on the basis of their explicit and/or implicit steering mechanisms for employee's behaviour, *e.g.* combining work organisations on the basis of the participation and self-regulation with modern forms of variable pay, which reward the goal attainment of the respective organisational unit. Otherwise, if strategy, work organisation, and pay systems imply different goals and directions for the employee's behaviour (*e.g.* combining innovation strategy, hierarchical control, and modern forms of variable pay) this might deteriorate performance and the quality of working life. These counteracting effects can be seen as one reason for the observed low bivariate correlations between work organisation and pay systems on the one hand, performance and quality of working life on the other hand. These relationships get much stronger, if one holds their counteracting effects under account and analyses the effects of work organisation with high degrees of direct participation and autonomy combined with modern forms of pay systems, such as team bonuses and/or profit sharing.

These results support the assumption that the alignment of company strategy, pay systems, and work organisation increases the company effectiveness. However, these data are only based on management assessments and both company and pay strategy are only rudimentarily measured. Therefore, we have studied in depth these relationships in our well detailed case studies, by applying a broader stakeholder perspective thereby the audit tool developed by the authors.

The retail banking case studies in three different banks located in Belgium, Finland, and Germany enabled us to give insights into the way national and company specific conditions influence pay, while controlling for sector influences by keeping the sector constant. Although these companies had specific strategies, work organisations and pay systems, management in all three case studies obviously tried to align strategy, work organisation, and pay policy. However, only the Finnish case illustrates an achievement of a full alignment; and the views of the different stakeholders regarding the effects of pay systems did correspond more or less to each other. In Belgium and Germany the different stakeholders differently assessed the effects of pay systems. Particularly in these two countries, but also in Finland, albeit to a lesser degree, national or sectoral collective bargaining seemed to hinder or at least slow down management efforts to align pay systems and to implement variable pay components, particularly at the expense of fixed elements. For this reason, it is easier to align pay systems for managerial employees, who are not subject to collective bargaining. Hence, managerial pay systems are already better aligned, or the first ones to be changed, as it was reported in the German case.

Our case study on the international company, with its Belgian, French, Dutch, and German subsidiaries even more pronouncedly points out the restrictive influence of institutional factors on the possibility of having the strategic alignment of pay policy. For example, whereas law stipulates the existence of profit sharing in France, it depends on the management's discretion in Germany. German management can decide whether it wants to introduce variable pay beyond the fixed pay subject to collective bargaining. Only the procedures have to be agreed on in the local bargaining. However, the case study also illustrates the interdependencies between pay system components. In the German subsidiary, the management refused variable pay components due to high fixed pay levels which stem from sectoral bargaining, even though – in principle – they were in favour of more performance-oriented pay systems. As collective bargaining strongly influences pay levels and pay increases at sectoral level, as a result, it limits the financial resources for further variable pay elements.

To sum up: we do have quite consistent evidence that the effects of pay systems on the company performance and quality of working life depend on the company strategy and characteristics of the work organisation, in particular. In order to improve efficiency, one should align pay systems and work organisations, such as combining participative work organisations and modern forms of variable pay, and take company strategy into account.

While interpreting these results, one should keep in mind that most of the studies reviewed are cross-sectional and causal relations cannot be identified. Furthermore, they rely on a single source and self-report data, which might bias results as only the subjective assessment of either employees or management is taken into account. The case study findings based on the audit tool show that the views of the different stakeholders on the effects of pay systems or other interventions can considerably vary. This raises doubt about the reliability of studies like the EPOC survey. Employee-related outcomes are the focus in the ESWC, but, conversely, indicators regarding organisational performance are missing. This highlights the importance of a stakeholder view for a thorough evaluation of pay systems, pay practice, and its outcomes, as we propose it in this book and applied it in the case studies.

The findings of case studies about the banks and the results of the different national subsidiaries of an international company show that the management tries to adopt a strategic approach by aligning strategy, work organisation, and pay systems. Management, in all the cases, expects better results from this alignment, but such factors as legislation and collective bargaining at the sectoral or local levels prevent or at least delay the alignment of pay.

References

Antoni, C., Berger, A., Baeten, X., Emans, B., Hulkko, K., Kessler, I., Neu, E., Vartiainen, M. & Verbruggen, A. (2005), *Wages and Working Conditions in the European Union*, Dublin: European Foundation for the Improvement of Living and Working Conditions.

Baeten, X. & Van den Berghe, L. (2002), "Participatie van medewerkers: houdingen en feiten op het vlak van financiële en organizatorische participatie", in L. Peeters, P. Mathyssens & L. Vereeck (eds.), *Stakeholder Synergie. Referatenboek, Vijfentwintigste Vlaams-Wetenschappelijk Economisch Congres* (Hasselt, 14.03.2002), Faculteit Toegepaste Economische Wetenschappen, Limburgs Universitair Centrum, Diepenbeek, Garant.

EPOC Research Group (1997), *New Forms of Work Organisation: Can Europe Realise Its Potential? Results of a Survey of Direct Employee Participation in Europe*, Luxembourg: Office for Official Publications of the European Communities.

Eriksson, M. (2002), "Lönesystem, produktivitet och kunskapsstimulans" [Pay system, productivity and knowledge encouragement], Chalmers Tekniska Högskola [Chalmers University of Technology].

Eriksson, G. & Leander, E. (1995), "Konsekvenser av individuell lönesättning – en enkätundersökning inom högskolan" [Consequences of individual pay – A survey within the university and college], Linköpings universitet [Linköping University].

Godard, J. (2004), "A Critical Assessment of the High-performance Paradigm", *British Journal of Industrial Relations*, 42, p. 349-378.

Holman, D. (2002), "Employee Wellbeing in Call Centres", *Human Resource Management Journal*, 12, p. 35-50.

Lay, G. & Rainfurth, C. (1999), "Königsweg Prämie?" [Bonus systems – A silver bullet?], Report from the Innovation in Production Survey, No. 13, Fraunhofer Institut für Systemtechnik und Innovationsforschung (ISI).

Nilsson, T. (1990), *Bonus för industritjänstemän – lönar det sig?* [Bonus for industry white-collar workers - Does it pay?], Stockholm: SIF [Swedish Union of Technical and Clerical Employees in Industry].

Paoli, P. & Merllié, D. (2001), *Third European Survey on Working Conditions 2000*, Luxembourg: Office for Official Publications of the European Communities.

Pendleton, A., Poutsma, E., Brewster, C. & van Ommeren, J. (2001), *Employee Share Ownership and Profit-sharing in the European Union*, Dublin: European Foundation for the Improvement of Living and Working Conditions.

Poutsma, E. (2001), *Recent Trends in Employee Financial Participation in the European Union*, Dublin: European Foundation for the Improvement of Living and Working Conditions.

CHAPTER 5

Conclusions and Discussion

Conny H. ANTONI, Xavier BAETEN,
Ben J.M. EMANS & Mari KIRA

In this final chapter, we aim at highlighting the major contribution of such a book in our opinion. There are two main dimensions in this book. The first dimension is a conceptual one; in chapters 1-3 we conceptualize pay issues and pay elements. We present the strategic rewards model and the pay tree as new concepts and tools. In the strategic rewards model, we integrate the factors into the business context that play a role in shaping pay and we describe these roles. We describe the pay tree as a tool, which can be used in auditing existing pay systems. Furthermore, we adopt a stakeholder approach, *i.e.* we summarize the major topics in the contemporary pay system development from the point of view of different stakeholders, *i.e.* from the employer's and employee's perspective as well as from the perspective of their respective representative organisations (*i.e.* employers' associations and trade unions).

The second dimension is an empirical one and built up on the secondary analyses of cross-national studies, a synthesis of research data from different countries as well as case studies. We carried out this empirical research with the purpose of identifying:

- both the converging and diverging development trends in the pay systems in different European countries as well as national specific conditions influencing pay systems in Europe;

- how national and multinational European companies deal with pay issues;

- what kind of pay systems are in use in European countries.

Based on these theoretical and empirical findings, we finally distinguish several areas in the empirical pay system research decisive for future, high quality studies on European pay systems.

As prior research has focused on executive or managerial pay at most, we focus on the pay systems of operational employees working under long-term or permanent contract, *i.e.* those long-term white- and blue-collar employees working in direct connection to the production or service processes of an organisation. This enabled us to analyse, the way legislative and collective bargaining regulations together with organisations' discretion shape pay systems of a major portion of the labour force. The emphasis only put on pay systems, base pay and variable pay elements, made the international comparison to a certain extent more straightforward, as other financial rewards are more dependent on national regulations, such as taxes and social security. Finally, we deal with private business enterprises, rather than also including the public sector.

Conceptual Findings

This book aims at discussing pay from a work organisational perspective, by considering pay settings as a HR practice in the context of other HR practices, such as the design of the work organisation. Therefore, the following questions are fundamental to be asked: does a pay system fit an organisation's other practices and its strategies? Which kind of factors does influence the degree of fit? Which consequences depend on that degree of fit? Consequently, we analyse drivers, structures, processes, and consequences of pay systems in contemporary work organisations. Furthermore, we address the interplay between pay and organisational environments – national, cultural, ideological, and political environments by introducing the strategic reward model.

We do not only describe, define, and exemplify European pay systems, but we also provide a theoretical and practical leverage for shaping pay – for adapting pay systems to the needs, values, and hopes of different stakeholders. This book is based on the idea that it is fruitful to consider pay settings within organisations as a social process, *i.e.* issues like pay levels, pay differentiation, pay equity, and pay administration have to be discussed and solved through dialogue between different actors within an organisation. Therefore, we adopt "a stakeholder approach". In other words, rather than looking at pay systems from the point of view of managers or employees, trade unions or employer associations, we have stepped in all these shoes and have experienced pay from the point of view of all the parties. We believe that our book makes a special contribution to the research on pay systems and practice with its comprehensive approach to the pay systems themselves and with the inclusion of different stakeholders. We are firmly convinced, that an issue as complex as pay systems, can only be fruitfully approached with the help of such an all-inclusive research approach.

Therefore, in chapter 2.1, the vast variety of financial and non-financial rewards that can be found as parts of the pay approach of modern organisations, has been defined within the systematising frame of the strategic reward model. Base and variable pay have been described in depth because the focus of this book is on financial rewards. Regarding base pay, an organisation has to select one or more pay structures, depending on its organisational structure, flexibility, and the number of hierarchical levels. Pay structures provide frameworks in which organisations can logically structure jobs or groups of jobs at various grades with varying bands and link them with a specific pay level. Pay systems can reward employees for their achievements, both at an input and output level, such as individual performance-based pay, team bonuses, profit sharing, competence-related pay, contribution-based pay, etc.

Chapter 2.2 presents an overview of the so-called essential pay characteristics. Starting from the premise that pay aims at optimising the employee-organisation relationship a model was developed consisting of the parameters that affect the way in which that role is fulfilled. We define characteristics as 'essential' when they affect the quality, *i.e.* the costs and/or benefits (inputs/outputs) of the employee-organisation relationship perceived by either the employees or the organisation. Therefore, the ultimate criterion for deciding on whether a pay characteristic should be called essential, is its *impact on the experienced employee-organisation relationship profitability.*

We distinguish four main categories of essential pay characteristics: 1) pay strategy and vision, 2) pay systems, 3) pay processes and procedures, and 4) workforce categorisation. *Pay vision and strategy*, which is the most fundamental and the least tangible one, represents the basic principles that underlie the pay approach, such as a firm's positioning relative to the labour market conditions or its tendency towards performance-based or job-based pay. The case studies confirm our assumption that pay strategy and vision can differ from the way pay is actually practiced. *Pay system* contains all the characteristics that together determine, firstly, which employee's contributions are compensated by which levels of pay and, secondly, the algorithms for making distinctions between jobs in terms of salaries linked with them (with respect to fixed or job-related pay) or for linking performance levels with compensation levels (with respect to variable or performance-related pay). *Pay processes and procedures* refer to the transparency, the (de)centralisation and the formalisation of two decision-making processes, one dealing with decisions about the monetary amount of individual employees' wages and the other one dealing with decisions about the design and maintenance of the pay system itself. *Workforce categorisation* describes whether companies apply different pay strategies, systems and procedures for different groups of employees, such as blue or white workers or core as opposed to flex employees.

These characteristics can be used for describing both the existing situation, as dealt with by an organisation, and the ideal situation, as contemplated by the different parties within the organisation, such as line management, HR management, and employees' representatives. The model can thus be used for many purposes, such as the comparison between an organisation's present state of affairs with some intended one, the comparison between views existing within the organisation, the description of trends within (categories of) organisations, the comparison between (categories of) organisations and, finally, the investigation on antecedents and consequences of pay systems that have actually been implemented. By using the model as a common vocabulary, discussions on such diverse issues become more focused. The group of authors of this book also developed an instrument addressing all the essential pay characteristics listed above and used it in the case studies described in chapter 4.

In chapter 3, we analyse pay from different stakeholder perspectives. Chapter 3.1 provides the employer's perspective on pay systems and provides the reader with a framework for strategic pay, clarifying the process steps and their sequence. First of all, it is argued that the role of pay systems has evolved from a more administrative tool in former times, into a more eminent and strategic role within HR Management nowadays. One could even speak of a new strategic management discipline. This strategic role is further stressed by the fact that job design is more flexible and that organisations have fewer hierarchical levels. In this context, pay systems need to be more flexible and have to be able to translate the organisations' characteristics and objectives into pay systems. This is exactly what strategic pay is about.

However, in practice, it gets much more complicated. The definition of strategic pay as linking pay systems with strategy is a too much narrow approach. First, there is a much broader set of contextual factors that should be taken into account and that can play a more or less important role depending on the situation, such as organisational and national cultures, shareholder structure, structure of collective bargaining or labour market characteristics. Secondly, a very important challenge is the development of pay as part of a *unique* total reward system, which is not only aligned with strategy, but also with the other HR processes, to get a competitive advantage.

Strategic pay management is about having a clear view on the contextual factors, being able to prioritise and make unambiguous choices leading to pay strategies. Technical insights and competencies will then enable the pay/reward manager to translate these strategies into concrete pay systems. To conclude, the combination of strategic insights with detailed technical knowledge on pay systems and the ability to use these technical tools is a huge challenge for the HR and Reward Management departments within many contemporary organisations.

In chapter 3.2, we analyse the employees' perspective. We draw the conclusion that a pay system – in order to induce the employees' pay satisfaction and job motivation – has to bring an appropriate amalgam of a well-chosen selection of equity parameters, such as performance or seniority, and need parameters, such as family or living conditions, together with carefully elaborated algorithms for dealing with these parameters, as a basis for inter- or intra-job differentiation. Furthermore, a pay system has to contain procedures that both respond to employees' needs for participation, recourse, accuracy and transparency and also respond to widely accepted workforce categorisations, such as the distinction between blue- and white-collar employees. 'Appropriate' does not only mean that the parameters, algorithms, procedures, and categorisations themselves are appreciated by the employees; it means too that they fit in with each other as well as with the existing culture and the power relations. For example, a substantial pay differentiation between high and average performers is more easily negotiated in the UK than in the continental Europe. Questions relating to culture, fair and transparent procedures as well as social and demographic categori-sations thus also have to be taken into account, if we want to understand the employee's perspective. Nevertheless, these entities do tend to be rather neglected by employee's representatives and employers in pay dialogues. The 'tree-like' representation of pay systems, as unfolded in chapter 2, shows that it is the Gestalt of those components together that shapes the nature of a company's pay system – rather than the separate components – and, consequently, determines the way it fits in with the perspective of the employees.

Chapter 3.3 analyses the attitudes of unions and employers' associa-tions to pay by examining the way collective bargaining typically con-fines and shapes pay arrangements in Europe. Whilst there are marked cross-national variations in union attitudes, there remain nonetheless common features. Unions have generally considered pay-for-performance or variable pay with suspicion. The concept is at odds with the predominant solidaristic emphasis inherent to unionism, with the fact that employers should bear the risk; moreover, it appears to threaten the institutionalisation of the employment relationship and thus the very existence of unionism itself. However, when they are under the pressure of employers or employees, unions generally accept pay-for-performance, if they give an opportunity to shape developments.

Unions expect to bargain over the design and operation of all the forms of reward, including pay-for-performance. They are often prone to make sure that none of the relevant groups are excluded from pay-for-performance and that employees have only few percent of their total pay which is truly at risk, thus confining variable pay to rarely more than 10% of the whole remuneration.

In addition to limit the members' exposure to risk, unions seek to guarantee transparent pay-for-performance arrangements and *ex-ante* specifications of objective criteria for the achievement of bonuses. They may also strongly support particular classes of pay-for-performance; group-based over individually based pay for example. In many respects, the evolving response of unions to variable pay shows the way collective bargaining is evolving to respond to the practical concerns of employers and employees.

Generally speaking, the employers' associations from different European countries adopt more similar approaches to pay arrangements than national unions do. Under the pressure of members, they have quite generally approved of a decentralisation of pay determination and a shift away from fixed pay to paying for performance, in particular. Furthermore, they generally promote variable pay because it allows greater flexibility at company level and potentially secures competitiveness along changing business cycles. Last but not least, they view variable pay to distribute corporate risk beneficially and motivate employees (Van het Kaar & Grünell, 2001). But employer associations are generally also keen that the processes of decentralisation and a greater local flexibility in pay are organised within the framework of multi-employer negotiations. This can be interpreted not only as a policy for self-preservation, but also as an acknowledgement of the dangers of unorganised decentralisation to individual employers. In particular, it may express concerns that without multi-employer negotiation such systems may otherwise spread only in addition to the complex array of payments to which employers are already committed.

Given these policies of unions and employers' associations, is there any 'strategic space' left to a company's internal decision-making and discretion on pay issues? We have shown that there is much flexibility in pay arrangements even when collective bargaining has a central influence on shaping pay. It is noteworthy that collective bargaining – even when it is put into practice at several different levels – does not preclude pay-for-performance. Multi-employer bargaining rarely precludes pay-for-performance and local employee representatives rarely refuse it as a matter of principle. However, where there is an established local union representation and/or a works council with statutory rights to negotiation (or indeed co-determination) over pay systems, local employee representatives will expect to bargain over the design and operation of variable pay and devote close attention to the criteria and procedures involved and the relative amount of pay tied to performance.

Generally, employers seeking to implement pay-for-performance in a thorough and professional manner will most likely find much room for discussion left by multi-employer agreements and local employee representatives.

Main Empirical Findings

In the empirical part of the book, the discussion is based on the existing survey material at the European level, both the ESWC 2000 (Paoli & Merllié, 2001) and the EPOC survey (EPOC Research Group, 1997); it is also based on national level surveys as well as on case studies. Regarding the prevalence of pay systems, our findings show that base or fixed pay is still by far the most dominant pay system for operational employees in Europe. Although the use of modern forms of variable performance-based pay (pay-for-performance) has increased in the recent years, they still play a minor role with respect to the amount of pay. The prevalence of modern forms of variable pay varies between nations; the highest rates have been found in the UK and Finland; the lowest rates concern The Netherlands and Germany (*cf.* the chapters on the different European countries). Concerning employment conditions, the few available results indicate that modern forms of variable pay seem more popular with full-time than with temporary or part-time workers (*e.g.* Baeten & Van den Berghe, 2002). Furthermore, the use of flexible working time also seems to correlate with the use of variable pay. Regarding organisational or institutional factors, modern forms of variable pay are found more often in the private than in the public sector and in larger companies. Research which focuses on demographic factors, such as gender and age, still indicate lower pay levels for women (when compared with men in equivalent jobs). Age, in turn, is related to higher pay. Despite the varying prevalence of different types of pay systems in European nations, the relationships between pay system prevalence or pay levels on the one hand and employment conditions, organisational, institutional or demographic factors, on the other, seem to be quite similar in Europe.

The main objective of the empirical analyses was to study, whether companies designing work organisation and pay systems according to their strategy achieve positive effects both on performance and quality of working life. Our research findings do indeed find some support for the assumption that such a contingency relationship might exist (Antoni *et al.*, 2005).

Both existing studies (*e.g.* Lay & Rainfurth, 1999; Pendleton *et al.*, 2001; Poutsma, 2001) and our secondary analyses of the ESWC 2000 and EPOC survey find correlations between work organisation and pay systems, although the correlations are rather low. However, the strength of the relationship between work organisation and pay systems considerably increases for companies with innovation strategies. This indicates the important role of strategy for the design of pay systems and work organisation.

Our analysis of the EPOC data shows that modern forms of variable pay are found more often in companies with an innovation strategy. For UK companies this link is far above the average. This might be due to the fact that they operate in a very liberal market economy, in comparison with *e.g.* The Netherlands. Only very few previous studies have analysed the impact of managerial strategies on pay systems and work organisation and they finally do not report any consistent relationships. This might be due, in part, to the fact, that there is often a kind of 'time lag' between changes in strategy and congruent changes in pay systems. Another reason might be the restrictions of collective bargaining, which might not only delay, but also limit the alignment of pay system.

The results concerning the relationship between pay systems, work organisation, and organisational performance are very different between European countries as well as between different studies from one country (*e.g.* Nilsson, 1990; Eriksson, 2002). The same holds for the relation between pay systems and work satisfaction (*e.g.* Holman, 2002; Eriksson & Leander, 1995). In the EPOC survey modern forms of variable pay, high intensity of group delegation and innovation strategy show positive links to two or three out of eight outcome variables, such as output increase due to group delegation. Regarding employee-related outcomes, the ESWC 2000 data shows that high performance work organisation practices (see chapter 4) have much stronger positive relationships with indicators of the quality of working life, such as job satisfaction than pay systems.

Furthermore, our findings concerning the EPOC data show that alignment effects exist and that analyses should not be restricted to links between two variables: interaction effects between group delegation and modern forms of variable pay resulted at least for three out of eight analysed outcomes. This means that more companies with modern systems of variable pay report reduction in costs, throughput times, and management personnel as a result of group delegation, if they have high intensity of group delegation rather than low. As other studies regarding high performance work systems show inconsistent results at best (Godard, 2004), the analysis of moderating variables could help to explain these inconsistencies.

Our results from the EPOC data show that the effects of pay systems depend on strategy. Company strategy seems to be one important moderator of the relationship between pay systems, work organisation, and organisational performance. If a company has an innovation strategy and high intensity of group delegation, the type of pay system does not matter for group delegation effects. Only if an innovation strategy is combined with low intensity of group delegation, the outcomes of group delegation (such as reductions in management, employee levels, and absenteeism), apparently depend on having modern forms of variable pay. If a company has not any innovation strategy, effects of group delegation differ for both low and high intensity of group delegation. If modern forms of variable pay exist, companies with low group delegation report less group delegation effects, contrary to companies with high group delegation.

The comparison between the effects of work organisation and pay systems enable us to show that the characteristics of work organisations have a much stronger impact on the indicators of quality of working life, such as job satisfaction and stress. We do not have any data measuring directly performance outcome. In the EPOC survey, only effects of direct participation were measured. Within these limits, our analyses indicate that the intensity of group delegation seems to have a more decisive impact on performance and quality of working life than pay systems do. This supports the assumption that the characteristics of work organisation have stronger effects both on quality of working life and on performance outcomes than pay systems do.

The data also support the alignment effects assumed in our theoretical model; interaction effects exist between strategy, work organisation, and pay system. This means that if these variables are aligned, they do have stronger effects in contrast with the case when they are independently considered. Consequently, one should not only consider isolated variables to improve quality of working life and performance outcomes, one should rather align these variables on the basis of their explicit and/or implicit steering mechanisms for employee behaviour. For instance, team participation and self-regulation should be combined with modern forms of variable pay which reward team goal attainment at the level of organisational unit. Performance and quality of working life may deteriorate, if strategy, work organisation, and pay systems imply different goals and directions for employee behaviour (*e.g.* if innovation strategy, hierarchical control, and modern forms of variable pay are combined). These counteracting effects can be viewed as one reason for the observed low bivariate correlations between work organisation and pay systems on the one hand and on performance and quality of working life on the other hand. These relationships get much stronger, if one controls for counteracting effects and analyses the effects of work organisation with high degrees of direct participation and autonomy combined with modern forms of pay systems, such as team bonuses and/or profit sharing.

These results from the secondary analyses suggest, as a result, that company effectiveness might be affected by the alignment of company strategy, pay systems, and work organisation. However, the surveys analysed are only based on management perspectives and have a very narrow view on a company and pay strategy. Therefore, we have further studied these relationships in our case studies applying a broader stakeholder perspective and having a closer look on company strategy and pay policy.

In the retail banking case studies, the audit tool developed by the authors was applied in three different banks in Belgium, Finland, and Germany. This enabled us to give insights into how national and company specific conditions influence pay, by controlling for sector influences, as the sector was kept constant. Although these three different banks in Belgium, Finland and Germany had company specific strategies, work organisations and pay systems, they also had much in common.

The management in all the three case studies obviously tried to align strategy, work organisation and pay policy, but full alignment had only been achieved in the Finnish case. Different stakeholders differently assessed the effects of pay systems, which is particularly apparent in the case studies of Belgium and Germany, whereas the views did correspond more in Finland. Collective bargaining at national or sectoral levels seemed to hinder or at least slow down the alignment of strategy, work organisation, and pay policy in all the cases: collective bargaining prefers collective pay settings and makes it difficult to include regulations which allow companies to tailor their pay systems and to implement variable pay components, particularly at the expense of fixed elements. The same is somewhat true, albeit to a lesser degree, at the company level, where company specific issues can be taken into account. That is why it is easier to align pay systems for managerial employees. Consequently, pay systems for managerial employees are either already better aligned or pay systems are changed first as the German case illustrates it. As collective bargaining at sectoral level determines pay levels and pay increases, this limits the financial resources for further variable pay elements beyond collectively agreed pay and, thus, limits the ability to align strategically variable pay components or systems.

The results of our case study in the Belgian, French, Dutch, and German subsidiaries of an international company showed even more precisely the restrictive influence of institutional factors on the possibility of the strategic alignment of pay policy. For example, whereas law stipulates profit sharing in France, it depends on the management's discretion in Germany. The management decides whether it is intro-

282

duced beyond the pay subject to collective bargaining. Only the procedures have to be agreed on in the local bargaining. However, the case study also illustrates the interdependencies between pay system components. In the German subsidiary, the management refused variable pay components due to the high fixed pay levels which stem from the sectoral bargaining, even though – in principle – they were in favour of more performance-oriented pay systems.

After comparing the findings of both case studies, *i.e.* comparing the pay policy of three different banks in Belgium, Finland, and Germany and of different national subsidiaries of an international company, it can be concluded that the management would like to adopt a strategic approach. The management tries to align strategy, work organisation, and pay systems, as it expects better results from this alignment, but factors as legislation and collective bargaining at the sectoral or local levels prevent or at least delay the alignment of pay.

To sum up, we do have quite consistent evidence both from our analyses of survey data and the case studies that the effects of pay systems on company performance and quality of working life depend on company strategy and the characteristics of the work organisation. In order to improve efficiency, pay systems and work organisations, such as combining participative work organisations and modern forms of variable pay, should be aligned and the company strategy taken into account. However, quite many inconsistencies still remain in the theoretical literature and the empirical findings, which have to be solved. Particularly, research lacks consistent definitions and measures of variables such as indicators of high performance work systems (Godard, 2004).

While interpreting these results, it should be kept in mind that most of the studies reviewed are cross-sectional and causal relations cannot be identified. Furthermore, they rely on single source and self-report data, which might be biased as only the subjective assessment of either employees or management is taken into account. The case study findings show that the views of the different stakeholders on the effects of pay systems or other interventions can considerably vary. This raises doubt about the reliability of studies like the EPOC or ESWC survey. While effects of direct participation on company performance are in the focus of the EPOC survey, employee-related outcomes are the focus in the ESWC, but – conversely – indicators regarding organisational performance are missing.

Consequences for Future Empirical Pay System Research

As a group, we have had an unusual opportunity to strive to carry out a co-ordinated and comprehensive case study and statistical research on the pay systems in different European countries. However, along our cooperation, it has become increasingly obvious to us that – in order to carry out relevant research on European pay systems – even more rigorous approaches are needed. For this reason we want to outline an agenda for future European pay systems research while hoping that our experiences will encourage both further research and support from the European Union.

The existing research outcomes appear too full of inconsistencies, *e.g.* regarding the spread of pay systems and their effects as well as gaps such as the integration of strategic management. This is due to many methodological problems, such as very divergent operationalisations that are used and questionable validity of sources (mono-method and single-source biases) that are used. If we want to make progress in the field, an unequivocal multi-source methodology, which focuses on a limited number of essential pay characteristics, is compulsory. Our case studies can be seen as pilots for that.

Our case studies clearly point out that it is not only worthwhile to focus on specific pay system characteristics on side apart (*e.g.* bonus schemes, stock options), but as well to study pay systems as a whole, *e.g.* including grade structures, criteria, decision-making, fixed and variable pay etc.

As far as pay drivers (*e.g.* strategy, culture) are concerned, we should not only study the influence of one specific driver. Instead, we should take a look at how the different reward drivers coincide with each other and which ones are more and less important dependent on situational factors. Even more importantly, pay research should find measures to identify these elements.

It is getting clearer that the concept 'strategy' is not well understood. For some people, strategy equals HR objectives, for others it means mission. There is a clear need for a much more concrete understanding of this concept, if we want to put into practice strategic rewards.

Finally, we call for a pan-European investigation on the presence of pay systems as well as their outcomes, in addition to in-depth case studies, using a multi-method and multi-source design, based on the stakeholder approach described in this book. The pay tree and the audit tool, developed by the authors of this book, offer a conceptual basis and an empirical method that could be used to elaborate an accumulative stream of research on pay system research.

References

Antoni, C., Berger, A., Baeten, X., Emans, B., Hulkko, K., Kessler, I., Neu, E., Vartiainen, M. & Verbruggen, A. (2005), *Wages and Working Conditions in the European Union*, Dublin: European Foundation for the Improvement of Living and Working Conditions.

Baeten, X. & Van den Berghe, L. (2002), "Participatie van medewerkers: houdingen en feiten op het vlak van financiële en organizatorische participatie", in L. Peeters, P. Mathyssens & L. Vereeck (eds.), *Stakeholder Synergie. Referatenboek, Vijfentwintigste Vlaams-Wetenschappelijk Economisch Congres* (Hasselt, 14.03.2002), Faculteit Toegepaste Economische Wetenschappen, Limburgs Universitair Centrum, Diepenbeek, Garant.

EPOC Research Group (1997), *New Forms of Work Organisation: Can Europe Realise its Potential? Results of a Survey of Direct Employee Participation in Europe*, Luxembourg: Office for Official Publications of the European Communities.

Eriksson, M. (2002), "Lönesystem, produktivitet och kunskapsstimulans" [Pay system, productivity and knowledge encouragement], Chalmers Tekniska Högskola [Chalmers University of Technology].

Eriksson, G. & Leander, E. (1995), "Konsekvenser av individuell lönesättning – en enkätundersökning inom högskolan" [Consequences of individual pay – A survey within the university and college], Linköpings universitet [Linköping University].

Godard, J. (2004), "A Critical Assessment of the High-Performance Paradigm", *British Journal of Industrial Relations*, 42, p. 349-378.

Holman, D. (2002), "Employee Wellbeing in Call Centres", *Human Resource Management Journal*, 12, p. 35-50.

Lay, G. & Rainfurth, C. (1999), "Königsweg Prämie?" [Bonus systems – A silver bullet?], Report from the Innovation in Production Survey, No. 13, Fraunhofer Institut für Systemtechnik und Innovationsforschung (ISI).

Nilsson, T. (1990), *Bonus för industritjänstemän – lönar det sig?* [Bonus for industry white-collar workers – Does it pay?], Stockholm: SIF [Swedish Union of Technical and Clerical Employees in Industry].

Paoli, P. & Merllié, D. (2001), *Third European Survey on Working Conditions 2000*, Luxembourg: Office for Official Publications of the European Communities.

Pendleton, A., Poutsma, E., Brewster, C. & van Ommeren, J. (2001), *Employee Share Ownership and Profit-sharing in the European Union*, Dublin: European Foundation for the Improvement of Living and Working Conditions.

Poutsma, E. (2001), *Recent Trends in Employee Financial Participation in the European Union*, Dublin: European Foundation for the Improvement of Living and Working Conditions.

Van het Kaar, R. & Grünell, M. (2001), *Comparative Study on Variable Pay in Europe*, Dublin: European Foundation for the Improvement of Living and Working Conditions.

http://www.eiro.eurofound.eu.int/2001/Study/TN0104201S.html.

"Work & Society"

The series "Work & Society" analyses the development of employment and social policies, as well as the strategies of the different social actors, both at national and European levels. It puts forward a multi-disciplinary approach – political, sociological, economic, legal and historical – in a bid for dialogue and complementarity.
The series is not confined to the social field *stricto sensu*, but also aims to illustrate the indirect social impacts of economic and monetary policies. It endeavours to clarify social developments, from a comparative and a historical perspective, thus portraying the process of convergence and divergence in the diverse national societal contexts. The manner in which European integration impacts on employment and social policies constitutes the backbone of the analyses.

Series Editor: Philippe POCHET, Director of the Observatoire
Social Européen (Brussels) and Digest Editor
of the Journal of European Social Policy.

Recent Titles

No.55 – *The European Sectoral Social Dialogue. Actors, Developments and Challenges*, Anne DUFRESNE, Christophe DEGRYSE and Philippe POCHET (eds.), SALTSA/Observatoire social européen, 2006, 342 p., ISBN 978-90-5201-052-6.

No.54 – *Reshaping Welfare States and Activation Regimes in Europe*, Amparo SERRANO PASCUAL, Lars MAGNUSSON (eds.), SALTSA, 2007, 319 p., ISBN 978-90-5201-048-9.

No.53 – *Shaping Pay in Europe. A Stakeholder Approach*, Conny Herbert ANTONI, Xavier BAETEN, Ben J.M. EMANS, Mari KIRA (eds.), SALTSA, 2007, 285 p., ISBN 978-90-5201-037-3.

No.52 – *Les relations sociales dans les petites entreprises. Une comparaison France, Suède, Allemagne*, Christian DUFOUR, Adelheid HEGE, Sofia MURHEM, Wolfgang RUDOLPH & Wolfram WASSERMANN, 2006, 243 p., ISBN 978-90-5201-323-7.

No.51 – *Politiques sociales. Enjeux méthodologiques et épistémologiques des comparaisons internationales / Social Policies. Epistemological and Methodological Issues in Cross-National Comparison*, Jean-Claude BARBIER & Marie-Thérèse LETABLIER (eds.), 2005, 2nd printing 2006, 295 p., ISBN 978-90-5201-294-0.

No.50 – *The Ethics of Workplace Privacy*, Sven Ove HANSSON & Elin PALM (eds.), SALTSA, 2005, 186 p., ISBN 978-90-5201-293-3.

No.49 – *The Open Method of Co-ordination in Action. The European Employment and Social Inclusion Strategies*, Jonathan ZEITLIN & Philippe POCHET (eds.), with Lars MAGNUSSON, SALTSA/Observatoire social européen, 2005, 2nd printing 2005, 511 p., ISBN 978-90-5201-280-3.

N° 48 – *Le Moment Delors. Les syndicats au cœur de l'Europe sociale*, Claude DIDRY & Arnaud MIAS, 2005, 2nd printing 2005, 349 p., ISBN 978-90-5201-274-?.

No.47 – *A European Social Citizenship? Preconditions for Future Policies from a Historical Perspective*, Lars MAGNUSSON & Bo STRÅTH (eds.), SALTSA, 2004, 361 p., ISBN 978-90-5201-269-8.

No.46 – *Restructuring Representation. The Merger Process and Trade Union Structural Development in Ten Countries*, Jeremy WADDINGTON (ed.), 2004, 414 p., ISBN 978-90-5201-253-7.

No.45 – *Labour and Employment Regulation in Europe*, Jens LIND, Herman KNUDSEN & Henning JØRGENSEN (eds.), SALTSA, 2004, 408 p., ISBN 978-90-5201-246-9.

N° 44 – *L'État social actif. Vers un changement de paradigme ?*, Pascale VIELLE, Philippe POCHET & Isabelle CASSIERS (dir.), 2005, 2e tirage 2006, ISBN 978-90-5201-227-8.

No.43 – *Wage and Welfare. New Perspectives on Employment and Social Rights in Europe*, Bernadette CLASQUIN, Nathalie MONCEL, Mark HARVEY & Bernard FRIOT (eds.), 2004, 2e tirage 2005/2nd printing 2005, 206 p., ISBN 978-90-5201-214-8.

No.42 – *Job Insecurity and Union Membership. European Unions in the Wake of Flexible Production*, M. SVERKE, J. HELLGREN, K. NÄSWELL, A. CHIRUMBOLO, H. DE WITTE & S. GOSLINGA (eds.), SALTSA, 2004, 202 p., ISBN 978-90-5201-202-5.

N° 41 – *L'aide au conditionnel. La contrepartie dans les mesures envers les personnes sans emploi en Europe et en Amérique du Nord*, Pascale DUFOUR, Gérard BOISMENU & Alain NOËL, 2003, en coéd. avec les PUM, 248 p., ISBN 978-90-5201-198-1.

N° 40 – *Protection sociale et fédéralisme*, Bruno THÉRET, 2002, 495 p., ISBN 978-90-5201-107-3.

No.39 – *The Impact of EU Law on Health Care Systems*, Martin MCKEE, Elias MOSSIALOS & Rita BAETEN (eds.), 2002, 314 p., ISBN 978-90-5201-106-3.

P.I.E. Peter Lang – The website

Discover the general website of the Peter Lang publishing group:

www.peterlang.com